From Studen

From Student to Scholar guides graduate students through the "hidden" developmental transition required in writing a dissertation and moving beyond, to become a successful scholar. Identifying common rhetorical challenges across disciplines, author Hjortshoj explains how to accommodate evolving audiences, motivations, standards, writing processes, and timelines. One full chapter is devoted to "writing blocks," and another offers advice to international students who are non-native speakers of English. The text also offers advice for managing relations with advisors and preparing for the diverse careers that PhDs, trained primarily as research specialists, actually enter. On the basis of more than 30 years of consultations with graduate students, this volume is an important addition to graduate thesis seminars and composition courses, as well as an invaluable reference for writing centers, workshops, and learning support centers.

Keith Hjortshoj is the emeritus Director of Writing in the Majors and Senior Lecturer in the Knight Institute for Writing in the Disciplines at Cornell University, USA.

From Student to Scholar

A Guide to Writing Through the Dissertation Stage

Keith Hjortshoj

NEW YORK AND LONDON

First published 2019
by Routledge
711 Third Avenue, New York, NY 10017

and by Routledge
2 Park Square, Milton Park, Abingdon, Oxon, OX14 4RN

Routledge is an imprint of the Taylor & Francis Group, an informa business

Library of Congress Cataloging in Publication Data
A catalog record for this book has been requested

ISBN: 978-1-138-56942-3 (hbk)
ISBN: 978-1-138-56944-7 (pbk)
ISBN: 978-0-203-70426-4 (ebk)

Typeset in Sabon
by Swales & Willis Ltd, Exeter, Devon, UK

Table of Contents

List of Figures

Preface

The experiences that led me to write this book began long ago, around 1980, when I was teaching in an experimental tutorial course, open to anyone who wanted help with writing for any reason, in the Writing Workshop at Cornell University. Unlike conventional writing courses, based on preconceptions of what a particular class of students needed to learn, ours was entirely individualized and "student centered," before the term became fashionable. There were no standardized readings or assignments, we didn't grade student essays, and final grades for the course were S/U (satisfactory/unsatisfactory). Because Writing 137 was numbered at the bottom of the curriculum and satisfied first-year writing requirements, most of our students were freshmen who felt they were weak writers for various reasons, but more advanced undergraduates enrolled as well, along with occasional graduate students who were working on master's theses or dissertations. One semester I was given a special, confidential assignment to tutor the dean of one of the university colleges who was trying to develop a more informal, engaging style for writing a memoir. We worked on his drafts behind the closed door of his large office, late in the day, and his assistant brought us coffee in a silver carafe.

These meetings were confidential because a college dean wasn't supposed to have trouble with writing. At that time, at a prominent research university, nor were faculty members, capable graduate students, or advanced undergraduates. Even freshman writing courses retained some of the stigma of remediation: the need for "basic" instruction that everyone should have received back in elementary and secondary schools. Higher level writing courses for advanced undergraduates were scarce, and there were none, as far as I knew, for the hundreds of graduate students on campus who were tackling very difficult, unfamiliar writing projects. Through this early experience of teaching writing as inductive inquiry, to anyone who turned up, I was intrigued about all of those hidden problems that capable writers weren't supposed to have.

As an anthropologist teaching in one of the first writing programs to distribute instruction across disciplines, I didn't associate this inquiry with the field of English but thought of it, I suppose, as a kind of ethnography. This large research university was a peculiar, complex culture run by a small population of natives: established scholars and administrators. All the rest were migrants from other places who were passing through, preparing to live somewhere else or settling down, all trying to adapt to this unfamiliar environment: trying to fit in. As a first-generation college student from a farming community in Iowa (who thought in high school that Cornell University and Cornell College were the same place), I had also faced these adjustments to a foreign academic culture, and I was particularly interested in writing because language, especially written language, is an essential medium of adaptation and transition in this environment. College freshmen and foreign students weren't the only ones who were going through these difficult transitions. Advanced undergraduates entering concentrations, graduate students in professional training, PhD candidates completing dissertations, and assistant professors trying to publish to avoid perishing in tenure reviews were all using writing to represent themselves to be the kinds of academic beings they hadn't yet become, without revealing the difficulties involved in the process.

In 1987, therefore, I began to offer another tutorial course of my own, at a higher level. I no longer remember what I called it or how I got it approved by the curriculum committee, but it was really just a course number that allowed me to consult with anyone who came to our office looking for help they couldn't find elsewhere. To the extent that I thought of the needs of these prospective students categorically, I called them "institutionally unacknowledged writing difficulties."

This turned out to be a very large and complex category. In following years, as awareness of the course expanded, some of my students were undergraduates who needed instruction they couldn't find in other courses. A few were university employees who wanted help with the kinds of writing required in their jobs, extramural students working on their own writing projects, or faculty members struggling to complete manuscripts for publication. But most of these writers, and nearly all of them in later years, were graduate students who were working on master's theses, research articles, proposals, or dissertations. Because my time was limited, I made no effort to recruit students, but through the grapevine their numbers grew, and my colleagues in the Knight Institute for Writing in the Disciplines, Joe Martin and Barbara Legendre, taught additional sections of the course. Meanwhile, in collaboration with Harry Shaw, the director of the Knight Institute, I developed an interdisciplinary program called Writing in the Majors that supported instruction in advanced undergraduate courses. My collaborations with faculty and graduate teaching assistants in this program, including faculty workshops and graduate seminars, revealed the diverse forms, functions, and practices of writing across disciplines. Many of these disciplinary perspectives were published in two collections of essays by Cornell faculty members—*Writing and*

Revising the Disciplines (2002) and *Local Knowledges, Local Practices* (2003)—edited by Jonathan Monroe.

When I began to work with graduate students in my obscure little course, Cornell and other research universities seemed oblivious to their unmet needs and difficulties as writers, especially in the dissertation stage of doctoral programs. Apart from the varying amounts of guidance individuals received from their advisors or friends and help with "personal" problems from counselors in the health clinic and graduate school, they were on their own. Peer tutoring services in campus writing centers were usually staffed by undergraduates who had no idea what to do with dissertation drafts, and self-help books for dissertation writers were scarce as well. At a writing conference, I heard that when someone advertised a workshop on dissertation writing in a seminar room at Stanford, I believe, more than 200 people filled the hall. In fields of individualized research, especially, PhD candidates experienced the dissertation stage as a solitary, personal journey into unknown territory, and for this reason I thought of myself as an equally solitary, hidden teacher they might encounter there: The Teacher in the Wilderness. My students sometimes referred to me as "the Writing Guru," as though they had found me in a remote cave. I didn't prefer this role, but I was left to my own devices as well. Early attempts to alert the graduate school to systemic problems I observed got no response.

Around the turn of the present century, however, these systemic problems in doctoral education became matters of growing concern. As academic job markets continued to falter, PhD completion rates worsened in some fields and average completion times lengthened, to about nine years in branches of the humanities. In response, the Mellon and Carnegie Foundations among others, along with the Council of Graduate Schools (CGS), launched research and reform projects to reverse trends that doctoral programs had previously accepted as means of natural selection. In following years, dozens of books and hundreds of research articles investigated causes and solutions for mounting "crises" in graduate education and academic professions. Within the walls of compartmentalized doctoral programs, faculty members seemed largely unaware of these alarm bells, but graduate schools, writing programs, teaching and learning centers, and other university programs began to respond. Graduate writing centers, dissertation workshops and "boot camps," professional development programs, and career planning services for graduate students are now common features of research universities. In response to rising enrollments of international graduate students, these schools have also expanded language courses and support services that include more general training for dissertation work. A growing, international community of teachers affiliated with the Consortium on Graduate Communication (www.gradconsortium.org) has coordinated these initiatives in what has become a dynamic movement in higher education, surveyed in the collection of essays *Supporting Graduate Student Writers* (2016). Instructional materials and other publications for graduate students have increased accordingly, and you can find a comprehensive list of these resources, including many designed for self-study, on the Consortium web page cited above. As a result of these developments, a former Teacher in the Wilderness has become a retiring member of a growing profession, with known locations and lots of colleagues.

My direct involvement with this movement began in 2004, when Cornell's Graduate School became a participant in the seven-year PhD Completion Project sponsored by the CGS. In collaboration with Alison Power, the Dean of the Graduate School, and Associate Dean Ellen Gainor, I developed week-long retreats for long-term PhD candidates in targeted fields, along with a variety of campus workshops for candidates at different stages of their programs. Since the end of the CGS project, Dean Barbara Knuth and Associate Dean Jan Allen have continued some of these initiatives and developed others, including diverse graduate workshops and guides for professional development and a graduate peer tutoring program in the Knight Institute staffed by PhD candidates trained by Tracy Hamler Carrick, the current Director of the Writing Workshop. Many of the observations and examples in this book are based on my ongoing involvement with these programs.

Among the hundreds of graduate students I've worked with over these 30 years, at Cornell and elsewhere, about half were enrolled in master's programs, either as terminal degrees or as stepping stones to further doctoral studies. In an early version of this book, I tried to include related challenges of completing master's theses but doing so added unmanageable layers of complexity to the patterns of difficulty and transition I was trying to keep in focus. For those of you who are completing research-based master's theses rather than dissertations, however, most of the advice I offer in following chapters will be directly relevant. Like dissertations, research-based theses, in the forms of monographs or research articles, are supposed to represent works of scholarship, and for most of you, completing them will be an unfamiliar process, requiring skills and strategies very different from the ones you developed as student writers. Chapters concerning the transition to graduate work, the structures and reference frames of academic discourse, and the processes of completing these projects apply to you as well. Comparable master's theses are typically shorter than dissertations, and standards for significance in one's field may be less rigorous, but these are closely related types of graduate writing. For those of you who will continue your studies in doctoral programs, a master's thesis serves as a kind of practice dissertation.

The variations and comparisons I couldn't address concern the differing structures, time frames, and career goals of master's programs, which are quite diverse. Like doctoral programs, or as components of them, American master's programs typically begin with the completion of course requirements that resemble undergraduate studies, followed by a transition from student work to research, writing, and other training for a profession. Even in academic master's programs leading to a work of scholarship, however, the main difference is that time frames for this transition are greatly compressed. Many of my students in these programs were struggling to complete independent research and writing projects while they were taking courses and working on job applications: juggling competing roles as students, amateur scholars, and aspiring professionals all at once. Their main problem was managing their time and attention.

An academic "thesis," furthermore, is no longer a standard requirement, especially in the broad range of master's programs that train students for non-academic careers in business, engineering, education, public policy and administration, planning, health care, design, art, creative writing, criminal justice, and dozens of other fields. As they complete their degree programs, a large proportion of master's students are preparing to leave academic environments and working on final "projects" in which writing (if it's involved at all) takes diverse forms. Specialized guides for writing in these professions and degree programs are widely available and too numerous to list here. In a book intended to be focused and concise, I couldn't begin to include their variations.

For similar reasons, I've primarily described American doctoral programs and research universities and haven't tried to explain the differing educational systems and expectations of PhD candidates in other countries. Most of what I have to say about the challenges of completing dissertations and becoming scholars (including relations with advisors, the rhetoric of academic discourse, and the writing process, for example) will be equally relevant to those of you who are completing PhDs in Canada, Europe, the UK, and other countries. One reason is that American doctoral programs derived from European and British models, and the more recent globalization of scholarship has strengthened these ties.

Nonetheless, American doctoral programs were superimposed upon systems of undergraduate education that differed radically from those in other countries, and what it means to be a *student*, and a *student writer*, in these systems varies accordingly. The undergraduate writing programs, requirements, and forms of instruction that became standard features of 20th-century American education did not develop elsewhere. Nor, for obvious reasons, did the American association of writing instruction with English departments. My accounts of the ways in which undergraduates are trained to write, the common features of "student writing," the effects of grading systems, and the tightly structured expectations of undergraduates won't apply directly to those of you who were students in other systems. Neither will some of the terms I've used, such as "graduate student," which captures one's ambiguous, transitional status in the early stages of American doctoral programs while completing course requirements. In European systems, for example, the distinction between "student" and PhD "candidate" (or "postgraduate") is more clearly marked, as the beginning of an apprenticeship with a master scholar and the commencement of an academic career. The transition to scholarship remains a similar problem, with unfamiliar and implicit expectations, but it's a transition from very different student experiences and habits of learning.

If you are pursuing a PhD outside the United States, therefore, I rely on your patience and analytical skills to parse out the guidance most relevant to you. To the extent that I understand this relevance, from experience almost entirely in American systems, I'm most grateful for several years of collaboration with Swantje Lahm, on the staff of the innovative writing center Das Schreiblabor, at Bielefeld University in Germany, along with her colleagues Stefanie Haacke and Nadja Sennewald, now at Goethe University in Frankfurt. As part of the European Association of Teaching Academic Writing (EATAW), Bielefeld's writing center offers support services for PhD candidates very similar to those developing in American universities, and in my conversations with several of these candidates, during a visit to Bielefeld, they raised questions nearly identical to those of their American counterparts.

Although this book addresses graduate students directly to make it useful for individuals, I also designed it as a text for graduate classes and workshops, where many of its concepts first developed and were refined in teaching practice. Explanations, diagrams, and questions in Chapters 2–5, especially, can be used directly to focus discussions, structure informal writing assignments, and measure progress in small groups or courses.

Because the Knight Institute for Writing in the Disciplines is primarily concerned with undergraduate instruction, I couldn't have devoted so much time to graduate students without the support of successive Knight Institute Directors Harry Shaw, Jonathan Monroe, and Paul Sawyer, along with the former Director of the Writing Workshop, Joe Martin. Years of collaboration with Katherine Gottschalk, Elliot Shapiro, Tracy Hamler Carrick, and many other Knight Institute colleagues clarified the perspectives I've presented in this book. Wendy Martin, our office manager, made the Writing Workshop a welcoming refuge for graduate students. My conceptions of writing as coordinated movement came into focus through studies with Martha Hjortshoj and other teachers of the Alexander Technique. Discussions with Alexandria Peary, at Salem State University, and her analyses of mindfulness in writing (2018) helped me to understand what writers are actually doing in the present moment and what my previous work on writing difficulties actually meant.

I'm grateful to Bryan Root for producing the diagrams in this book and to my editors at Routledge—Laura Briskman, Nicole Salazar, and copyeditor Melanie Marshall—for efficiently steering this project to publication and offering timely advice in the process. The knowledgeable reviewers they commissioned also made many valuable suggestions in its early stages.

I'm indebted most of all, however, to my indispensable teachers over these years: the graduate students who have generously shared their experiences, ideas, and concerns with me.

References

Monroe, J. (Ed.). (2002). *Writing and revising the disciplines*. Ithaca, NY: Cornell University Press.

Monroe, J. (Ed.). (2003). *Local knowledges, local practices: Writing in the disciplines at Cornell*. Pittsburgh, PA: University of Pittsburgh Press.

Peary, A. (2018). *Prolific moment: Theory and practice of mindfulness for writing*. New York, NY: Routledge.

Simpson, S., Caplan, N. A., Cox, M., & Phillips, T. (Eds.) (2016). *Supporting graduate student writers: Research, curriculum, and program design*. Ann Arbor, MI: University of Michigan Press.

1 The Hidden Transition

Convenient Myths

When I've been laboring for months over drafts of an academic article or book chapter (such as this one) I sometimes remember that as an advanced undergraduate, ages ago, I was able to complete a 20–30-page research paper over a weekend, in essentially one draft, on a typewriter. I often wish I could still write with that speed and reckless stamina, and the memory is now an invitation to kick myself for my plodding indecision until I also recall those desperate feelings of urgency and pressure in the middle of the night under looming deadlines, the metabolic clash of exhaustion and manic delirium fueled by caffeine.

I can no longer write that way and can barely imagine how I did, but I do know why. Because my courses were in the social sciences and humanities, the last weeks of a semester were consumed by these intense, marathon efforts to finish "term papers," and from research on my students' writing methods I know that many of them still complete writing assignments with comparable speed, under comparable duress, now with the benefits of search engines and word processors.

When I reread a couple of those old undergraduate research papers I saved, I find that they're surprisingly coherent, imaginative, but fragile *simulations* of real scholarship, in need of reconstruction and a good scrubbing. But those research papers and shorter essays, along with their high grades, helped to get me admitted to a doctoral program, where courses in the first two years included similar assignments. I entered graduate school as an experienced, successful student writer and course-taker, as fully prepared as anyone to meet the challenges of writing in graduate seminars. By the end of my first year, however, those fast, fearless, nocturnal methods of undergraduate writing no longer worked. I didn't understand why, but cleverly constructed simulations of scholarly authority and conviction no longer sufficed. I couldn't ignore the second thoughts, the doubts and alternative approaches that threatened to derail a first draft, and I learned that I had to begin work on these assignments much earlier in the term if I hoped to finish them.

By the time I began to write my dissertation, after two years of research, those old ways of student writing were remote, almost surreal memories, like those of early childhood. Working several hours a day, I spent the first two or three months trying to draft an introduction that would sustain the development of my following dissertation chapters. With the feeling that I was creating an intellectual and rhetorical labyrinth from which I couldn't escape, I wrote and rewrote dozens of drafts, and as the alternative passages and impasses of the project multiplied, I often felt that I could never reach the end of it. My advisors seemed passively willing to help, but they were very busy; and as someone who thought he was a capable writer, I was too confused and embarrassed to explain the problems I faced. After a year of fretful, frustrating work on unfinished chapter drafts, I found a way through this maze with the help of three friends and fellow graduate students at the same stage who formed a writing group. In a spirit of generous, constructive candor, we read one another's draft chapters closely and thoughtfully, identifying dead ends and productive choices for moving forward. All of us finished our dissertations in the same term.

Now—when I've offered guidance to some hundreds of dissertation writers in almost every field of research, have studied the process of writing extensively, yet still find academic writing very difficult—I wonder what changed, exactly, in that critical period of my graduate studies when I was still a student, in some respects, but began to write in the role of an aspiring scholar? In this new role of authorship, why did those earlier, exigent strategies of student writing no longer work? Why does professional academic writing become so laborious and time consuming? And how do we learn to move successfully to the end of this complex, convoluted process? If we acknowledge that professional academic writing doesn't get much easier with cumulative knowledge, skill, and experience, what do experienced, productive scholars learn that can benefit novices—apprentice scholars—in the dissertation stage?

These are questions I hope to answer in this book, on behalf of new generations of graduate students who, as former student writers and in spite of many changes in graduate education, face the same challenges of adjustment to unfamiliar realms of professional academic discourse. All scholars, in all fields, have to contend with the changes involved in this transition from student writing to knowledge production, and this developmental transition doesn't always end with the completion of a PhD. Many faculty members, including graduate advisors, are still trying to figure out how to revise their writing strategies in ways that more effectively meet the critical demands of scholarship and publication.

The changes involved in this transition deserve focused inquiry and explanation because they remain largely unacknowledged in higher education—both mysterious and, it seems, institutionally mystified. Convenient myths encourage us to believe that the writing skills and strategies we develop in secondary schools and undergraduate studies should be a stable platform for writing at higher levels, without substantial change or explicit instruction. The writing abilities of the accomplished students admitted to graduate programs should continue to develop more or less naturally, as though by osmosis, in the loftier environs of doctoral programs. Like other complex skills, such as driving, writing should become both easier and more effective with knowledge and experience. We can therefore imagine that for the successful scholars we hope to become, brilliant writing flows almost effortlessly from brilliant minds.

For a variety of reasons, we all wish that these myths were true. Acknowledging the earlier developmental transition from high school to college, higher education concentrates writing instruction at the beginning of the undergraduate curriculum. A large industry (including elaborate writing programs, course requirements, and hundreds of textbooks) has developed around the effort to teach former high school students how to meet the unfamiliar expectations of college teachers. At higher levels of the curriculum, by the beginning of graduate studies, writing instruction rapidly diminishes, nearly to a vanishing point. Educators tend to assume that the small proportion of undergraduates admitted to selective PhD programs *should* be able to complete dissertations and publications without explicit training. The skills, strategies, and motivations that get these accomplished students *into* doctoral programs should continue to get the best of them *through* these programs and beyond, PhDs in hand, as accomplished scholars. Those who run into serious trouble in the process must lack the ability or motivation they need to contend with the rigors of academic professions, where "publish or perish" is not just a cliché.

While they often help to maintain these myths, most scholars know at some level, from their own experience, that they are false. While they assign undergraduate versions of professional writing (referenced essays, research papers, and scientific reports) with strict deadlines in the compressed time frames of course schedules—on the assumption that they are preparing students to think and write like real scholars in their fields—these professors inhabit an alternate reality of academic discourse unknown to most of their students, where writing is a fundamentally different kind of endeavor. Over periods of months or years, most of these teachers have been wrestling with their own writing projects—research articles, proposals, or books—through seemingly endless revisions. In this realm, the possibility of completing a significant writing project in a couple of days, in a single draft, is a childish fantasy. Even if they finish initial drafts fairly quickly, these scholars have just reached the beginning of long processes of revision, before and after submission to publishers. I once asked a large group of professors in diverse fields whether any of them had submitted manuscripts that were accepted without required revisions. The room was silent, until one person said he had heard of such a case but doubted it was true. Most of their submissions had been extensively revised over weeks or months before submission, and for research articles, the average duration of the process they reported was between one and two years. A psychology professor admitted that he had been trying to get one of his articles in print, through several versions, for seven years. While undergraduates usually complete papers on their own (unless an assignment is explicitly collaborative), scholars typically benefit from lots of feedback from colleagues in the process of writing and revision.

These complex realities of professional writing, along with the ways in which individuals adapt to them, are largely hidden from undergraduates, graduate students, and even colleagues in some disciplines. In fields of individual research and authorship, where the dissertation is typically a monograph, the writing process is highly privatized and occurs behind closed doors. In an outburst of frustration, a PhD candidate in political studies once complained to me that while she struggled with her dissertation, without much guidance, her advisor was mysteriously producing books and articles, as though by smoke and mirrors. "I want to see the writer behind the curtain!" she exclaimed. "I want to meet the Wizard of Oz!" And her choice of images indicated her suspicion that the ease with which her advisor seemed to produce all this writing was an illusion.

Whether her advisor actually wrote with ease or with anguish, the nagging question on this student's mind was "Why doesn't he teach me how to get these things written?" How do the hundreds of published articles and books you read in your graduate studies get finished? And why aren't the methods involved in this process a standard component of doctoral education? In her essay "Demystifying the Dissertation," Karen Cardozo (2006) characterized the dissertation stage in the humanities as a strange, dysfunctional factory in which apprentices are shown the complex finished products they are supposed to construct but aren't allowed to observe how they are made. "Because it is decentralized and largely privatized," she argues, "the process remains hidden to most graduate students, leaving them unprepared to negotiate the multifaceted challenges of the dissertation stage" (p. 138).

In most of the sciences and other fields where research and writing are more collaborative (and publications are typically co-authored), graduate students are more likely to observe the process and receive informal mentoring from "principle investigators" and other members of research groups. This collaborative research and writing process partly accounts for significantly higher rates of PhD completion and shorter completion times in the sciences than in fields of the humanities. Even in the sciences, however, the transition from student writing to scholarship—along with the need for explicit training in the unfamiliar, convoluted processes of knowledge production—is weakly acknowledged, and many graduate students have to develop these skills on their own, through trial and error.

In all fields of inquiry, experienced scholars have developed their own diverse methods for getting writing projects finished, but few of them know how to explain and teach these methods to novices, and writing strategies are rarely subjects of professional discussion.

If the great majority of entering students in doctoral programs completed their PhDs, one could argue that understanding why individuals succeed or fail was unnecessary. Since the 1960s and probably much earlier, however, average completion rates across American PhD programs have hovered around 50 percent, and in some fields, completion delays of two years or more are very common. For several decades, through significant changes in higher education and academic professions, nearly half of the students admitted to doctoral programs have continued to run into obstacles that prevent or postpone the completion of PhDs. Until the beginning of this century, research universities accepted this enormous waste of time and resources as the routine costs of maintaining rigorous standards in highly selective academic professions, with the unquestioned assumption that the most promising young scholars were the ones who survived. Although scholars at these universities have studied almost everything imaginable, very few of them critically examined the systems through which new members of their own professions are trained, selected, or rejected. When he was writing one of the first self-help books for PhD candidates (*How to Complete and Survive a Doctoral Dissertation*), the sociologist David Sternberg (1981) found so little reliable information about completion rates and times in doctoral programs that he had to compile his own estimates and termed this knowledge gap "something akin to a 'cover-up'" (p. 4)—a tacit, professionally antithetical agreement among scholars *not to know*. At the time, there were no national statistics even on the number of students enrolled in doctoral programs, and Sternberg concluded that "the dissertation doctorate is certainly the least understood institution in American higher education" (p. 5).

Over the past 20 years or so, the high rates, uneven patterns, and diverse causes of attrition in PhD programs have become matters of focused concern and extensive research, conducted by the American Council of Graduate Schools (CGS) in its elaborate PhD Completion Project, by several foundations, and by individual scholars. This recent attention to the individual and systemic problems that doctoral students encounter resulted from acknowledgement that graduate education is not just a test of individual abilities, to select for "talent," but also a complex process of socialization and training that some doctoral programs effectively support and others do not. On the basis of this awareness and information, most graduate schools in the United States (often in collaboration with campus teaching and learning centers) have begun to provide support systems, workshops, and services on professional development, dissertation writing, and other challenges that graduate students encounter, along with counseling services to address individual difficulties. Many universities now sponsor "boot camps" for PhD candidates and writing centers specifically for graduate students.

Recent research helps to illuminate common patterns of difficulty that were previously hidden in the shadows of specialized programs, where they were typically viewed as the individual struggles of weak candidates. But this expanding knowledge has also exposed its own limited potential to inform and improve graduate education within the central contexts that determine doctoral students' experiences: their own programs and relations with advisors. Like the self-help books and online forums that have emerged in recent years, the extracurricular services that graduate schools now provide partly compensate for the absence of professional development in many doctoral programs, but they haven't substantially altered the decentralized, unregulated systems in which these problems arise. The faculty members who administer graduate programs and advise their students are largely oblivious to current research and debate concerning problems in doctoral education at large. Most of them remain unaware of average PhD completion rates and times in their own programs; and because these programs function as nearly autonomous units that central administrations and graduate schools have little power to alter, occasions for faculty exchanges of information and strategies across disciplines are rare.

This fragmentation of knowledge and practices increases in the dissertation stage of doctoral work, when individual advisors, forming loosely structured committees, assume primary responsibility for guiding candidates through the remaining processes of research and writing. Because faculty advising has remained largely unregulated and individualized throughout the history of graduate education, there is no coherent, common body of knowledge, or even folklore, about best practices or shared experiences that advisors can pass on to successive generations of doctoral candidates in their programs. In focus groups with a total of 276 professors who had collectively supervised (as principle advisors) 3470 dissertation projects in 74 departments representing ten disciplines, Barbara Lovitts (2007) tried to elicit clear criteria for what these scholars considered to be "good dissertations" in their fields. The standards they initially offered were highly generalized and vague (on the order of "original, significant contributions" to knowledge), and a frequent comment was simply, "You know it when you see it." Subsequent prompted and highly structured questions gradually elicited more detailed criteria, critical assessments, and rubrics that Lovitts presented in her book *Making the Implicit Explicit* (2007). While the resulting agreements and variations she extracted from this research might be used to formulate standards for finished dissertations within or across disciplines, this study also revealed that in practice there were no common, *explicit* standards for good dissertations. The vast experience these scholars collectively brought to their focus groups was fragmented and unformulated—encrypted personal knowledge—of limited use to the novice scholars who faced the unfamiliar task of producing an acceptable dissertation. And because this ambitious study focused on the qualities of finished dissertations, it shed less light on the challenges that inexperienced scholars encounter in the complex processes of writing one.

From Lovitts' broader studies and other research, however, we know that successful completion of a PhD requires substantial changes in the ways of thinking, learning, and writing with which accomplished students enter doctoral programs. Admissions criteria and credentials do not reliably predict who will succeed or fail in these programs. Although faculty members continue to believe that the "smartest" and most "talented" candidates are the ones who survive, comparative research has found no significant differences in credentials and perceived potential between entering doctoral students who go on to complete PhDs and those who do not. Especially in the dissertation stage, the most capable and highly motivated PhD candidates often run into the most trouble. Success actually results from effective adjustments to the unfamiliar, changing demands of real scholarship. Because *being* a good graduate student is a process of *becoming* something else—a good scholar—individuals are most likely to succeed in program environments and advising systems that acknowledge the difficulties of this transition and provide the most support through the process. Varying levels and qualities of support largely account for differences in completion rates of more than 30 percent among PhD programs in the same fields at different institutions (Denecke, 2005, p. 7).

In the midst of this new research on doctoral education, self-help books and online support sites for dissertation writers have proliferated because writing difficulties have remained largely absent from the acknowledged causes of struggle and failure in PhD programs. Addressing writing problems was not included among the areas of concern and intervention that the CGS listed in its report on findings of the PhD Completion Project (Sowell, 2008), and direct references to struggles in the writing process are scarce in other critical assessments of doctoral education as well. Because the process of getting a dissertation written is by definition the ultimate remaining challenge for "ABDs" and an obvious cause of anguish and failure in the dissertation stage, this blind spot seems mysterious. While educators have begun to recognize that systemic weaknesses in doctoral programs prevent many capable, motivated students from completing PhDs, they have remained reluctant to acknowledge that capable candidates encounter significant writing difficulties in the process.

An underlying reason for this reluctance is a persistently narrow view of "writing" itself, as a set of learned skills or innate abilities that all capable PhD candidates should have previously developed. A need for help with "writing," in this narrow sense of the term, therefore implies a *lack* of ability and a need for remediation that, if acknowledged, might suggest low admission standards. Because writing difficulties in dissertation work are actually entangled with problems of motivation, program environments, research, and individual circumstances, they may seem indistinguishable from these other, more specific causes of attrition and delay. Another potential reason is that graduate advisors in the disciplines aren't trained or expected to teach "writing skills," and campus writing specialists are rarely able to teach writing at this level of specialized discourse. The transitional, developmental difficulties with writing that graduate students commonly encounter therefore arise in a void of institutional expertise and responsibility. Very few university instructors possess the training or experience needed to assist PhD candidates with the diverse forms and subjects of dissertation projects across disciplines, and most of the workshops and other services that graduate schools now offer are extracurricular options. While specialized courses in professional communication are built into the curricula of graduate professional schools in fields such as law, business, and medicine, where professional writing and speaking are essential job descriptions for prospective employees, curricula in PhD programs rarely include such courses.

As training for academic professions, the great majority of graduate-level courses now available on oral and written communication, including teaching, are designed for international students who use English as a foreign language. Although the teachers who provide this instruction are trained primarily to address the linguistic challenges their students encounter, their courses include more general help with project development, the writing process, and adjustment to the demands of advanced studies of potential value to graduate students at large. This explicit attention to shared, transitional difficulties partly explains why PhD completion rates in American universities are substantially higher for international students in most fields than for their "domestic" counterparts: those presumed to be fluent in academic English, familiar with our educational systems, and fully prepared to meet the demands of doctoral work without comparable assistance.

This institutional acknowledgement of their writing difficulties, as normal problems of adjustment, can also explain why international students are most likely to take advantage of graduate writing centers, dissertation workshops, and other services open to graduate students at large. The most commonly accepted explanation is that international students need the most help with writing projects, but another, less openly acknowledged factor is that international students feel least stigmatized by revealing their needs for assistance—not just with questions of grammar and syntax, but also with problems of adjustment and difficulties in the writing process that any graduate student might encounter. Native English speakers more often feel that the need for such assistance represents weak ability. Although the professional academic writing they are trying to emulate is a social process that routinely involves collaboration, collegial advice, and peer review (as I'll explain in Chapters 3 and 4), PhD candidates often believe that capable writers should be able to complete dissertation projects entirely on their own, as though they were take-home exams, and that help in the process is remedial.

Those of us who work extensively with graduate students and faculty know that this reluctance to reveal writing difficulties isn't just an irrational fear, resulting from insecurity or vanity. There are good reasons for which our consultations with graduate students are typically confidential. When I tell faculty members that I help graduate students with dissertation writing, most of them falsely assume that I work with incompetent writers and marginal students, in need of remedial instruction in "basic" writing and thinking skills that more capable, talented candidates already possess. One of them said, "Yes, we do have some *problem students* in our department." And when I replied, with annoyance, "Some students in your department also have problem advisors," he looked bewildered and changed the subject. In casual conversations, two professors from another department had used the same term to describe a graduate student who had removed a notoriously negligent yet demanding, abusive chairperson from her dissertation committee—a necessity that cost her more than a year of additional work developing a new project in a different research group. They referred to her nonetheless as a "problem student," and in their view the problem was hers, not that of their department or her former advisor.

The best graduate students, from this perspective, are those who need the least attention and guidance. I've heard many faculty descriptions of those who have apparent difficulties and ask for lots of help with their dissertation work as "needy" or "troubled" students. They seemed troubled, in fact, because their experiences and circumstances were troubling, in ways that often led to confusion and emotional distress viewed as symptoms of underlying personal, "psychological" conditions. In the early years of my work with graduate students, the only institutionalized support for struggling dissertation writers was offered by psychological services, in the campus mental health clinic. Such assumptions about their writing difficulties explain why dissertation writers often seem embarrassed and apologetic—as though they were confessing abnormal personal problems—when they first come to me for help with extremely common writing difficulties.

What this book intends to remediate, therefore, are not the weak abilities of PhD candidates. From years of experience, I know that the overwhelming majority of you who have entered doctoral programs are fully capable of successfully completing dissertations. What I hope to remediate, instead, are common myths and misconceptions that make this inherently and normally difficult process *unnecessarily* difficult, in ways that undermine your ability. This book is meant to illuminate and solve common problems of adjustment in phases of a developmental transition that seems, in the fragmented contexts of specialized programs, to represent individual, personal struggles. My underlying goal, therefore, is to normalize developmental patterns of difficulty often experienced as abnormal, unique problems resulting from personal attributes or circumstances.

While the transformations involved in becoming a scholar are necessary for everyone who hopes to complete a PhD, individuals run into varying amounts of trouble in this process for reasons that have little to do with their potential for success in academic professions. Some of the most brilliant scholars and teachers in every field were among those "troubled" graduate students who struggled to complete their dissertations. Many doctoral candidates who failed to complete PhD requirements could have become brilliant scholars in their fields, and in an earlier book, *Leaving the Ivory Tower*, Barbara Lovitts (2001) closely examined the causes and effects of these failures. Regardless of their potential for success, individuals respond to the necessity of change with varying amounts of agility or resistance. Those who cling to research and writing strategies they used successfully as college students often encounter the most difficulty in the dissertation stage of doctoral work. Inexperienced or weak writers in their undergraduate studies are often most open to the development of new skills and strategies. Varying forms of dissertations, standards, educational traditions, research contexts, and conceptions of writing and authorship among disciplines can also determine the relative ease or difficulty with which individuals complete PhDs.

Most of all, however, these individual variations result from the amounts and qualities of guidance that graduate students receive from their programs and advisors. Because there are few general, institutional standards for this support, some doctoral programs offer no substantial training in dissertation work and professional development for academic careers, while others actively nurture this development. Both within and among these programs, some graduate advisors attentively guide candidates through all stages of dissertation work and help to solve problems that arise in the process. At the opposite extreme, others leave advisees entirely to their own devices, with the convenient assumption that the best PhD candidates will somehow get their dissertations done. I've known many faculty advisors who masterfully steer candidates through the dissertation stage, with extraordinary skill and commitment to their success. I've known several others who should be fired for their arrogance and negligence.

For these reasons, some of you will have little need for the explanation and advice this book offers, beyond reassurances that you are on the right track and encouragement to celebrate your good fortunes or wise decisions. For the rest of you, I've tried to compensate for uneven support through this transition, provide the kinds of guidance you do not receive in your programs, explain the most likely causes of your difficulties, and help you to solve these problems. Although graduate students have limited power to change the systems in which they pursue PhDs, I'll suggest initiatives you can take to use these systems to your advantage.

My critical assessments of graduate education are therefore intended to broaden and clarify your understanding of common problems and solutions in dissertation work, not to attribute blame for these problems. Factors that include enduring traditions of doctoral education, the priorities of specialized research, and the resulting fragmentation of knowledge and experience affect everyone involved. In their own doctoral programs, as I've noted, your faculty advisors were trained primarily as research specialists, not as advisors, administrators, or teachers even in their own fields, much less as writing teachers. When they completed their own dissertations, even less institutional support and collective knowledge about the process was available. Their own writing strategies, along with their approaches to advising and teaching, have developed largely through individual trial and error. Because the resulting practices are so diverse and the traditions of decentralized autonomy are so strong, graduate school administrators have little power to regulate or regularize doctoral program structures or individual advisors' methods. While all of these factors conspire to obscure common developmental patterns and to personalize resulting difficulties, there are no conspirators or conspiracies at work. In the bewildering variety of doctoral studies, general features of the "hidden" transition I've described are hard to see, but no one, as far as I can tell, is deliberately hiding them. The main value of a broad, critical understanding of inherent problems in graduate education is not to blame others for the difficulties you encounter but to lift from your shoulders the disabling conclusion that you are to blame.

In the beginning of my consultations with dissertation writers, 30 years ago, I couldn't see these patterns either. At the time, the prevailing assumption that writing difficulties in the dissertation stage were personal and often "psychological" problems put me in the awkward role of a writing therapist. Because I doubted such explanations and was a professional writing teacher and social scientist, not a clinical psychologist, this role felt wrong to me and dishonest—complicit in perpetuating institutionalized myths that undermined the confidence and abilities of the writers I was trying to help. In practice, however, I couldn't find alternative explanations for writing problems so diverse, unpredictable, and entangled with individual projects and circumstances that they seemed to defy generalization.

Because I couldn't yet identify common patterns across specialized fields—and because my students appreciated focused, confidential attention to their own projects—for several years I confined my assistance to individual consultations in the privacy of my office. In a single day, successive meetings with these students might concern the illumination of themes in a Victorian novel, mathematical models of the spread of an epidemic disease, the effects of differing plant communities on the survival of an amphibian species, the recognition of deception in online communication, or the detection of radiation from a distant galaxy. Because the forms of dissertations had also diversified, about half of these projects were traditional monographs; the rest were actually research articles for inclusion in increasingly common "paper options" (which I'll discuss further in Chapter 3). Some of these writers were in early stages of the process, struggling to formulate a viable research question or make sense of data analyses. Others were composing drafts of chapters, reorganizing drafts, or having difficulty with stylistic revisions. From one of these appointments to another, I was working on sentence-level revisions, the reorganization of passages or chapters, or the conceptual framework of an entire dissertation. And in some cases, when writers were blocked or mired in their projects, our discussions concerned motivations, time management, writing methods, or the particular circumstances that undermined their progress. The devil, as the saying goes, was always in these details, and solving the real problems that dissertation writers encounter appeared to eliminate the possibility of offering advice that would be useful to all of them. I therefore viewed each of these projects as a unique puzzle that the individual scholar needed to solve and that I could gradually understand most usefully in its own peculiar frame of reference.

Through hundreds of these consultations, however—with graduate students (and occasionally faculty members) in nearly every field of research—I gradually began to see some common patterns of difficulty, including patterns of variation across and within disciplines. With increasing frequency, the problems I observed seemed familiar, and the solutions I offered were ones I had learned from discussions with other writers, often in different fields of research. These observed patterns eventually provided the basis for interdisciplinary graduate workshops and seminars, along with summer writing retreats I led for ABD candidates who had become mired in their dissertation projects. Some of these endeavors developed in collaboration with the Cornell Graduate School, under its grant from the PhD Completion Project of the CGS. With clearer understanding of the rhetorical conditions and transitions from which most of these difficulties emerged, I wrote a small booklet for doctoral candidates at Cornell in which the broader themes of this book, for a general audience of PhD candidates, began to develop.

The End of Schooling

The changes involved in the transition from student writing to scholarship are broadly rhetorical ones, and because the term "rhetoric" has a confusing variety of meanings, I should explain that in this book the term refers not only to forms of the *products* of writing but also more broadly to the *circumstances* in which they're written and to the *processes* through which they come about—factors that include the author's motivations, audiences and standards, contexts, and time frames. This broadly rhetorical perspective acknowledges that writing occurs not just on paper, or on a keyboard, but also in the midst of our lives. When rhetorical conditions change, therefore, the nature and implications of writing change as well.

These rhetorical factors are also somewhat hidden—obscured by common generalizations about writing and writers.

> Writing is a set of basic skills, a craft, or an art.
> Writing is a window to the mind, a representation of thought or intellect.
> Jane is a good writer.
> John is a bad writer, because his skills are weak, or because he isn't very bright.

Such generalizations and judgments hold little power to explain why a piece of writing works or doesn't work for specific purposes, or why it works in one context but not in another, or why individuals write easily and well in one circumstance and less easily or successfully in others. Rhetorical analysis offers variables with which we can understand changes that otherwise seem mysterious.

With these analytical tools, for example, I can now understand why writing became increasingly difficult and time consuming for me even at the beginning of my graduate work, when I was still writing assigned papers for courses and teachers, similar to the ones I produced with such reckless speed as an undergraduate. The form of this writing didn't substantially change. Nor did the language skills or intellect I brought to these projects. What changed, instead, were the standards, motivations, and sense of audience with which I approached these projects. Without conscious awareness of these variables, I had begun to think of myself as an author and scholar, now writing for other scholars, and this shift in my persona altered the nature and meaning of writing itself. It also altered the process of writing and the time frames in which this process occurred. No longer just simulating scholarship to complete an assignment and get a decent grade, I cared more about—and more often questioned—the validity, clarity, and intellectual depth of what I was saying. Resulting doubts, deliberations, and revisions made the process increasingly convoluted and slow. The good writing I produced as an undergraduate was no longer good enough. Understanding why these changes occurred might have relieved my confusion, frustration, and the erosion of confidence in my ability.

In a seminar I taught for graduate students, on writing and teaching, a biologist named Ben offered a concise, metaphorical summary of these rhetorical changes. In an account of shifts in his writing strategies, Ben described the lab reports and essays he produced in his undergraduate work as "a series of one-night stands," performed with a sense of urgency for quick gratification, perhaps, but with limited commitment and significance in his life. In contrast, he described the dissertation research articles he was currently working on as "long-term relationships": serious commitments that required patience, persistence, thoughtful revision, and help from his friends. The *products* of these stages in his development—the assigned lab reports in his undergraduate courses and the research articles he now wrote over periods of months—looked similar in many ways. His *motivations* for writing, the *processes* of completing them, and their *implications* in his life were dramatically different. The belief that undergraduate assignments prepare students for these "long-term relationships" with writing projects is therefore rhetorically naive—comparable (if we extend Ben's metaphor) to an assumption that casual sex prepares people for successful, enduring partnerships.

When we compare the opposite ends of the long trajectory of higher education, from the beginning of undergraduate studies to the final stages of dissertation work, the contrasts that Ben described seem obvious. Somewhere along this path, everyone who completes a PhD must adapt to rhetorical conditions that alter the nature and implications of writing. But when do these changes occur, exactly, and how? This developmental transition would be more clearly acknowledged and marked, perhaps, if it began predictably at a certain stage in one's academic career; but gradually or suddenly, individual students reach this turning point at different stages, for a variety of reasons that are largely unpredictable. Describing the evolution of their own writing methods and experiences, all of Ben's classmates who had reached the dissertation stage were aware of the rhetorical contrasts he drew. For some of them, however, this transition began much earlier, even before they entered graduate programs, when they were writing undergraduate honors theses or collaborating with professors on co-authored research articles. For example, a PhD candidate in the social sciences recalled the shock she experienced when her senior thesis advisor told her to completely rewrite what she thought was a finished draft.

> Not only was I traumatized by having to start working in November for a 'paper' that was due in June, but the comments from my advising professor were painful. I distinctly remember turning in a chapter that was largely copied from a course paper I had written a year earlier that had received a very good grade. The comment from my advising professor: throw it away and start over. I thought she was crazy.

A few of the students in this seminar had begun to work on articles for publication, proposals, or conference papers in the early stages of their graduate programs, when they were still completing course requirements, and by the time they began dissertation work they had already developed new ways of approaching and completing writing projects:

> Writing as a graduate student is a totally different business. The goals are complex, the stakes are higher. As a graduate student I no more write for a particular professor who has to give me a passing grade. The audience I have in mind while writing consists of professionals in the field. My writing, therefore, has to be contentful, clear, and well structured. At this point, I cannot even conceive of beginning to write without an outline, I revise and make changes, sometimes obsessively. I have as many people as possible give me feedback. Don't I sound like I've just tamed writing? Well, I haven't. Writing projects are still very intimidating and I still procrastinate (as I am as I'm writing about it).

Others wrote much less in their graduate courses than in their undergraduate studies and viewed dissertation work as a looming, mysterious challenge for which they were unprepared. Some students in the first year or two of doctoral programs still used undergraduate writing methods to complete assignments in their graduate courses. They did not yet see reasons to change these strategies but were aware that dissertation work would pose entirely different problems. And many other students I've known shared my experience of drifting into and through this transition as an unaccountable cognitive shift. No one warned us that the way we wrote should change, or how, or why. It just did, for reasons we didn't understand.

Some of these variations occur across disciplines, but even within a single doctoral program, students in the same year are at different levels of development as scholars and writers. In your own PhD programs, some of you entered directly from undergraduate studies at small colleges or large universities, while others have completed master's degrees or worked in professions of varying relevance to your doctoral studies. While a few of you may have been authors of collaborative research articles, the process of getting something published remains a complete mystery and distant goal for some of your peers. Although you are members of the same class, moving through the same sequence of curricular stages and requirements in a projected, normative schedule of progress toward your PhDs, you may encounter very different challenges in the process at different times.

In the normal structure of American doctoral education, nonetheless, we can observe some common, incremental changes. In the first two years or more, graduate-level courses appear to be more specialized continuations of undergraduate studies in the same fields. Graduate students are often enrolled in classes with advanced undergraduates, completing the same assignments, much of their time and attention governed, as in undergraduate work, by course syllabi and term schedules. Familiar vestiges of student life therefore linger through the early stages of doctoral programs, gradually dissolving and mingling with more professional responsibilities of teaching and research assistantships, individual interests narrowing to particular lines of inquiry and concerns with research design pursued by particular kinds of scholars, until the "student" part of the term "graduate student" no longer holds much meaning in your experience. "Writing"—once a medium for completing assignments and course requirements—eventually becomes a much more significant, essential means of establishing your identity as one of these scholars, engaged in knowledge production within a professional community. Although this transformation can occur at different times, in diverse contexts, and in a bewildering variety of ways, we know that it *must* occur, through changes in most dimensions of your academic life.

In most doctoral programs, what is often called the "comprehensive exam" marks the official beginning of the dissertation stage of doctoral work, when PhD candidates have completed all requirements except dissertation research and writing. Although the rhetorical transition to knowledge production and professional writing actually began earlier for many of you, as a symbolic turning point, the comprehensive exam represents some institutional acknowledgement of a significant change in your identity and role: now not simply as a graduate "student" but as a PhD "candidate."

Because some form of the comprehensive exam is a feature of nearly every PhD program, the meaning of this event deserves more explicit acknowledgment than it typically receives. Graduate school is in many ways an example of what anthropologists call a "liminal" condition: a long process of transition from one social identity or status to another. In that liminal condition of becoming, one's identity remains somewhat ambiguous, as exemplified by the American term "graduate student" itself: someone who has graduated but remains a student of sorts, in the process of becoming, but not yet being, a certified scholar. Like adolescence, when one is no longer a child but not yet an adult, liminal conditions are typically bewildering and potentially hazardous. With rites of passage, therefore, traditional societies clearly mark stages in this disorienting process of transformation and guide individuals through it.

Apart from their elaborate graduation ceremonies, however, academics are pretty inept at orchestrating and signifying their own rites of passage, especially in doctoral education. In the first years, course requirements (and qualifying exams or master's stages in some programs) mark progress toward the ultimate destination of a PhD, marked by the dissertation defense and commencement ceremonies. Through the late, dissertation stage of becoming a scholar, however, individuals are often set adrift, responsible for their own transformation in the most liminal and potentially bewildering of all stages in higher education.

Because it is a common point of departure for this stage, the comprehensive exam can potentially clarify an important shift in one's status—from graduate *student* to PhD *candidate*—and to lay out a sensible path for completion of the process. Like other aspects of doctoral education, however, the comprehensive exam assumes a variety of forms and functions, both across and within programs, along with diverse names. The term "comprehensive" represents the traditional use of the exam to assess a candidate's general knowledge of a discipline, considered essential for pursuing more specialized research. Many years ago, a senior professor of anthropology told me that when he took his exam at Berkeley in the 1950s, Alfred Kroeber asked him to name (from memory, north to south) the Native American tribes on the coast of California. Some programs still use the exam to assess "comprehensive" knowledge of a somewhat narrower subfield or the candidate's ability to produce and defend referenced discussions of central issues in that field. Although the meaning is rarely made explicit, these are essentially final exams of your accomplishments and credentials as a student—a learner—to determine whether you are ready to move on to the next stage in your career as a real scholar. In many programs, potential candidates receive specific questions they must respond to in writing (in time frames that vary from a couple of days to an entire term), followed by an oral exam in which they defend their responses and answer other questions from their advisors. Cornell's term for the exam, "Admission to Candidacy," is refreshingly explicit, and its Graduate School website states that passing the "A Exam" means that the student is "ready to present a dissertation." (Cornell University Graduate School, n.d.).

In order to present a dissertation, however, you still need to produce one, and while the traditional comprehensive exam was retrospective, increasing numbers of programs now use this occasion for the more directive, forward-looking purpose of evaluating and revising the candidate's dissertation proposal. The written portion of the exam, then, is a draft of the proposal itself, and the oral exam is often termed a "proposal defense," with the potential value of ensuring realistic goals and viable methods for research and writing in following months.

If I had the power to institute a common form of the exam in all programs and disciplines, this is the form I would choose, with the additional requirements that advisors must provide prior guidance in development of the proposal, thoughtful advice for revisions, and regular consultations through the research and writing process. The proposal itself would also be a fully developed, reasoned explanation of the project—with an introduction, literature review, detailed methods, and projected findings—not just a chapter outline. In some cases, advisors approve ostensibly well-organized outlines of dissertation contents and send candidates off into unforeseen quagmires of conceptual and methodological problems. In their most constructive, collaborative forms, these discussions can prevent months of confusion and struggle with unwieldy, misbegotten projects that, in many cases, were never thoroughly vetted by experienced scholars.

At the end of this rite of passage, when you've passed it, I would add an explicit celebration of its meaning as the end of a long era in your life. Finally—after some 20 years of formal education in which you spent large proportions of your waking lives attending classes and completing assignments, your time heavily structured by academic schedules and responsibilities—*you are done with school.* Unless you choose to do so for your own reasons, you will never be obliged to attend another class in the role of a student. Your work will never again be evaluated by school grading systems. All of those report cards, transcripts, and standardized test scores by which schools measured your worth will become irrelevant to your future.

Like the transition it signifies, this End of Schooling deserves more attention than it usually receives. The rather murky, liminal identity of a "graduate student" lingers beyond this moment and through the dissertation stage. In common usage in the United States, there are no terms that clearly distinguish PhD candidates from other graduate students. Many of you will still be supported by teaching assistantships, research grants, or fellowships and continue previous work in research groups. When you pass your exams, advisors and friends will congratulate you for clearing this hurdle on the continuing track of doctoral work, but you may not feel that your lives and identities have substantially changed.

But the End of Schooling is nonetheless a momentous event, worthy of a big celebration. Students at all levels celebrate the end of a term or a school year as a temporary relief from the constraints of schedules, classrooms, assignments, and grades. Now, as former students, you are free from these conditions forever! Whether you choose to celebrate with a wild party or with a quiet evening at home, you should pause to consider what this turning point means in relation to the past and future: the skills, strategies, and priorities you should now leave behind, as a former student, and the ones you will need to develop as a scholar.

This process of sorting and changing is complex. Habitual ways of thinking and writing, developed over some 20 years, can be elusively persistent and difficult to alter. Familiar ways of approaching tasks, organizing your time, and establishing priorities as a student become nearly automatic, to the point that you don't have to think about them. But when you reach the End of Schooling, whether incrementally or suddenly, many of these habitual ways of doing things will no longer work. Beyond this turning point, further progress will require deliberate, strategic changes based on awareness of what you are doing and why. For this reason, we'll begin with analysis of the rhetorical contexts and conditions from which you entered graduate programs and must move beyond.

References

Cardozo, K. (2006). Demystifying the dissertation. *MLA Profession*, 17, 138–154.

Cornell University Graduate School, (n.d.). http://gradschool.cornell.edu/requirements/exams/exams-phd.

Denecke, D. D. (2005). Ph.D. completion project: Preliminary results from baseline data. *Council of Graduate Schools Communicator*, 38 (9), 1–12.

Lovitts, B. E. (2001). *Leaving the Ivory Tower: The causes and consequences of departure from doctoral study*. Latham, MD: Rowman & Littlefield.

Lovitts, B. E. (2007). *Making the implicit explicit: Creating performance expectations for the dissertation*. Sterling, VA: Stylus Publishing.

Sowell, R. (2008). PhD completion and attrition: Analysis of baseline data. [Research Report] Retrieved from Council of Graduate Schools website: www.phdcompletion.org.

Sternberg, D. (1981). *How to complete and survive a doctoral dissertation*. New York, NY: St. Martin's Griffin.

2 The Rhetoric of Student Writing

Common Ground

What do all of you who are enrolled in doctoral programs have in common? Considering the broad range of your research interests, institutions, and backgrounds, not very much, except that you have all converged, for diverse reasons and from different paths, into a similar stage in the trajectory of higher education. And in that trajectory, you are all former undergraduates, previously enrolled in a great variety of colleges and universities in the United States or abroad.

This common feature of your backgrounds is so obvious that it may seem irrelevant to your current experience, no more meaningful than the fact that we were all once children. For apprentice scholars and writers, however, this banal observation is packed with meanings that we can benefit from unpacking, to examine their implications.

I'm not suggesting that your experiences as student writers, or those of undergraduates at large, are uniform. Although productive writing becomes equally, inescapably important across fields of advanced graduate work and academic professions, its importance varies considerably across branches of the undergraduate curriculum. Writing assignments are the basis for communicating and evaluating learning in fields of the humanities and some of the social sciences, whereas demonstrations of quantitative skills or scientific and technical knowledge, on problem sets and exams, tend to define performance in other concentrations. Some of you therefore entered doctoral programs as highly experienced and accomplished student writers; others entered with very limited writing experience and instruction in your chosen fields. I'm arguing instead that regardless of these variations, some very general conditions, with complex implications and effects, characterize student writing itself, along with the ways in which students think about and approach writing tasks.

Some of these factors are so inseparable from the condition of *being* a student that they seem given: unquestioned and unquestionable bases for all academic writing. These include *courses*, as contexts for writing; *assignments*, as occasions for writing; *teachers*, as primary audiences for writing; *grades*, as measures of writing quality; and *course schedules* and *due dates*, as time frames in which writing occurs. Whether writing assignments were central to your coursework or marginal, took the forms of essays or technical reports, were graded for literary quality or for delivery of factual content, your approaches to completing them probably began with these given conditions and assumptions.

The teachers who assigned these writing tasks probably assumed, in turn, that they were preparing you to write and think like scholars in their fields, through the replication of professional forms of communication. But college teachers can be remarkably naive (or, in more positive terms, idealistic) about what they are actually teaching and what their students are actually learning. To complete these tasks successfully, college students primarily learn to contend with the rhetorical conditions and constraints of *student* writing: to simulate the products of real scholarship in contexts very different from the ones in which real scholars write. Whether the skills they develop for this purpose actually prepare them to *become* scholars is a question we'll consider further, but these two ways and experiences of writing are, in any case, fundamentally different. Conflating them, as we'll see, can lead to confusion, resistance to change, and illusions of preparedness.

In many respects, student writing can be best understood as a category unto itself. If we ignore the diverse forms and styles of its products and consider processes and time frames, student writing most closely resembles some types of journalism. One Saturday morning, for example, I found a journalist friend working on an investigative article for a major news magazine. On his desk was a pile of source material he had previously assembled for the writing stage, which he was just beginning, and he told me with calm confidence that he would have the article on his editor's desk by Monday morning. His writing strategies and looming deadlines, as a professional journalist, weren't substantially different from mine when I produced research papers for my undergraduate courses, except that he was writing in the morning, with professional composure and authority. When I asked a recent PhD in biology why she was abandoning academics for a career in science journalism, she said with a wry smile, "Because six years is too long to wait for the results to something." Following months of writing and revision based on years of doctoral research, she had finally begun to get the long-delayed gratification of publishing her own findings. In her new career as a journalist, an article based on the research of other scholars would be finished and published in a week or two. For this quick turnaround, the approaches to writing she developed as an undergraduate, meeting tight deadlines for papers based on secondary sources, were more useful than the ones she developed in her doctoral work.

When we approach any writing task that is more or less familiar, we begin with what I'll describe as certain rhetorical "settings." These influence every aspect of what follows, including specific qualities of voice and style, the speed and difficulty of the process, and the form of the product. Some of these settings are taught and learned through instruction; others develop through cultivated intuitions, trial and error, and imitation. Even when you begin to compose an informal email message, you aren't "just writing" in a rhetorical vacuum. You might assume, for example, that you'll be finished in five minutes or less, without making substantial changes. Other assumptions and predictions, such as your sense of audience, will determine the voice you use, the time you spend considering what you are about to say, and whether you proofread the message before you hit the SEND button. When students begin to work on writing assignments, they enter the process with awareness of the forms and reference frames in which they will write, to meet the implicit and explicit standards of their teachers in the time they have available for the task. These settings will affect how the process unfolds, and to the extent that they are experientially constant, these settings will seem to define writing—or at least academic writing—in general. Because these contexts structure their experience, it's extremely difficult for most undergraduates to imagine (or for anyone to teach them) how these rhetorical constants in their experience will change when they are no longer students. In following sections, as a basis for comparison with scholarly writing in Chapter 3, we'll examine these "constants" of student writing as potential variables.

Evolving Forms and Expectations

Both teachers and their students usually assume that current rhetorical features of student writing are also historical constants. We tend to assume, in other words, that college teachers 50 or 100 years ago and those in the present have assigned essentially the same kinds of writing, under similar conditions, for similar purposes. This assumption invites comparisons, in which student writers in almost every period have appeared to be worse writers, less prepared to meet current expectations, than those in previous eras. Throughout my long career as a writing teacher, I've heard hundreds of these complaints that students in the present "can't write" or "can't think" as well as those in the vaguely remembered or imagined past. We'll critically examine these beliefs because the detrimental effects of such comparisons with all of those imagined Good Writers don't end with college graduation.

In the history of student writing, however, the main constants are the complaints themselves. In American colleges, designated writing courses and requirements began with this perception of decline, when the great majority of entering freshmen at Harvard failed the first assessment of their writing skills in 1874 (Brereton, 1995, p. 45). These new concerns about student writing accompanied the beginnings of dramatic changes in higher education that would soon transform the traditional, classical curriculum, devoted to the cultivation of young gentlemen, to more specialized academic departments and curricula, meant to train broader populations of students for a variety of professions in which written communication skills were essential.

In following decades of rapidly expanding enrollments, writing courses became fixtures of undergraduate curricula at almost all colleges and universities with the lingering stigma of remediation, to compensate for perceived "preparation gaps." To explain the miserable performance of freshmen on that first writing assessment, the Harvard faculty primarily blamed teachers in secondary schools who remained targets of criticism in later periods, through successions of "literacy crises" attributed also to weak admissions standards, new student populations of immigrants and lower classes, bad parenting, television, and further developments in media. Regardless of the causes, in every period student writers appeared to be getting worse: less prepared than previous generations to meet the current standards of college teachers.

When we read the Harvard faculty's blistering criticism of freshman writing in 1874, however, there doesn't appear to have been much room for further decline, and there is no substantial evidence that this deterioration occurred. Andrea and Karen Lunsford (2008) published a test of such claims in a study titled "Mistakes are a Fact of Life." With an emphasis on error, the authors compared the results of analyses of student writing samples conducted in 1917, 1930, 1986, and 2006. This comparison revealed that although some definitions, types, and distributions of error varied over these 90 years, the adjusted frequency of errors in student writing remained remarkably consistent, at roughly 2.3 errors per 100 words. Through periods of dramatic social, cultural, and demographic change, college students have remained no more error-prone or careless than those in the past.

To account for *perceptions* of decline, however, the most interesting finding in this study is that writing assignments became significantly longer and more challenging. In 1917, for example, the average length of a student paper was only 162 words. In the three following studies, average length increased to 231 words in 1930, to 422 words in 1986, and more rapidly to 1038 words in 2006. The types of papers assigned changed as well. Although the authors did not describe typical assignments in the early studies, in 1986 the majority of papers were still personal narratives, and other evidence indicates that assignments in earlier decades were most often short personal reflections, evaluated for their literary style and correctness. By 2006, however, assignments most frequently called for a "researched argument or report," followed by "arguments with very few or no sources" and "close reading or analysis." Personal narrative had dropped to fifth in frequency, and most of the other genres, such as "proposal" or "process analysis," were also versions of professional academic forms (p. 793).

In other words, over the past 30 years or more, teachers have increasingly assigned the types of writing they produce as scholars in specific fields, and it's likely that much of their perception of decline in student writing ability results from the increasing difficulty and disciplinary variety of the tasks they assign. Personal essays or reflections are comparatively easy forms of writing to produce, because the author's own experiences and thoughts provide an authoritative frame of reference. Referenced arguments, proposals, scientific reports, and research papers require the construction of reference frames and forms of discourse situated in particular academic disciplines, in which the author is a novice and the audience/teacher holds authority. Undergraduates are therefore obliged to simulate knowledge and authority they do not possess; and they must adopt and abandon these academic personae and reference frames, in a variety of forms and disciplines, with mercurial speed and agility.

In 1985 when these changes were occurring rapidly, the composition theorist David Bartholomae (1985) described their implications most explicitly in his essay "Inventing the University":

> Every time a student sits down to write for us, he has to invent the university for the occasion—invent the university, that is, or a branch of it, like History or Anthropology or Economics or English. He has to learn to speak our language, to speak as we do, to try on the peculiar ways of knowing, selecting, evaluating, reporting, concluding, and arguing that define the discourse of our community. Or perhaps I should say the various discourses of our community, since it is in the nature of a liberal arts education that a student, after the first year or two, must learn to try on a variety of voices and interpretive schemes—to write, for example, as a literary critic one day and an experimental psychologist the next, to work within fields where the rules governing the presentation of examples or the development of an argument are both distinct and, even to a professional, mysterious.
>
> The students have to appropriate (or be appropriated by) a specialized discourse, and they have to do this as though they were easily and comfortably one with their audience, as though they were members of the academy, or historians or anthropologists or economists; they have to invent the university by assembling and mimicking its language, finding some compromise between idiosyncrasy, a personal history, and the requirements of convention, the history of a discipline. They must learn to speak our language. Or they must dare to speak it, or to carry off the bluff, since speaking and writing will most certainly be required long before the skill is "learned." And this, understandably, causes problems.
>
> (pp. 134–135)

"Inventing the University" was addressed primarily to an audience of writing teachers, and the "problems" Bartholomae described weren't confined to student writers. Increasingly diverse, disciplinary forms of student writing have also complicated what it means to teach writing to prospective and current undergraduates. *How can we prepare students "to try on the peculiar ways of knowing, selecting, evaluating, reporting, concluding, and arguing that define . . . the various discourses of our community"? Who is responsible for providing this instruction—the disciplinary specialists who assign these diverse forms of writing or composition specialists, who are usually trained in English or related fields of the humanities? If the essential features of academic writing differ from one discipline to another, what does it mean to teach writing in general, beyond the "basics" of grammar, sentence structure, or punctuation?* These questions became subjects of ongoing, unresolved arguments among writing teachers and program administrators who, collectively, still haven't made up their minds.

Meanwhile, student writers have had to contend with conflicting, changing expectations immediately, and the perception that they are continually "underprepared" for these challenges results in part from the dissonance between preparations and realities, when the "rules" for Good Writing in one context become false in another. The most successful students, who seem best prepared, are those who can adapt to shifting expectations in new contexts most swiftly and effectively. When they encounter unfamiliar demands, these students readily abandon strategies they previously learned and improvise new ones, more appropriate for the tasks at hand.

The rhetorical challenges involved in making these rapid changes of voice and personae do not characterize academic writing in general; they arise primarily in undergraduate writing. High school students receive general education, in which writing is largely confined to the category of "English." Even in courses meant to prepare students for college, writing instruction prepares students more directly for college admissions and performance on standardized tests, including the AP English exam, than for the realities of undergraduate work. On the other side of undergraduate studies, college professors and graduate students are writing specialists: actual members and aspiring members of those narrowly focused "discourse communities" that undergraduates must circumstantially imagine and "try on," like changes of costumes and roles in different plays. Unlike their teachers, undergraduates, especially in the first two years of college, are interdisciplinary beings who migrate among four or five academic disciplines in the course of a week, adopting somewhat different roles, as learners and performers, in each. The challenges and strategies required, which we'll examine more closely, are nearly unique to the condition of being an undergraduate. In each of their classes, students must pretend to be what their teachers actually are or, as graduate teaching assistants, have chosen to become.

As perceived "preparation gaps," problems of adjustment to these diverse, unpredictable expectations largely result from the fact that secondary education, especially in public school systems, is heavily standardized and undergraduate instruction is not. Most colleges and universities maintain principles of "academic freedom" that allow individual departments and faculty members to determine learning goals, standards, and forms of instruction independently, without much concern for coordination or conflict with those at lower levels or in other courses their students are taking. Each class is a distinct realm of discourse that undergraduates enter and leave, dispersing to other realms, as though they were stepping through mirrors. Even among related fields, college teachers know very little about instruction going on down the hall or in neighboring buildings through which their students migrate each day, with their heavy bags of assorted course materials, as academic nomads. Specialization, academic freedom, and the resulting fragmentation of knowledge and experience partly explain why teachers remain unaware of gradual, collective changes in the difficulty and variety of assignments across the curriculum. It also explains why test scores and other standardized credentials for college admissions (or, in the case of the GRE, for graduate admissions) can't reliably predict individual success or failure in fundamentally different, unstandardized environments. In their efforts to prepare students for this *transition* to college, the best high schools take such factors into account, essentially by simulating the varied challenges of simulation their student will encounter. But this kind of instruction is labor intensive and requires knowledge of current expectations and forms of assignments in undergraduate courses—luxuries that most high schools and their teachers can't afford.

Since the 1960s, therefore, the most common renditions of academic writing taught in secondary schools have been highly generalized, all-purpose models for structuring essays. The most popular models are versions of the "five-paragraph theme" taught initially in lower grades and expanded, in various ways, for more advanced assignments in high school.

Most of these templates for academic writing derive from the "keyhole essay" presented in Sheridan Baker's influential textbook *The Practical Stylist*, first published in 1962. The "keyhole" shape results from Baker's observation that academic essays typically begin with an *introduction* in the form of a funnel, narrowing from general background on the topic to a "thesis statement": a central argument, hypothesis, or research question. *Body* paragraphs follow, each beginning with its own topic sentence, leading to a *conclusion* that moves, though an inverted funnel, from the specific back to the general. The term "five-paragraph theme" resulted from common injunctions that the introductory paragraph and thesis should introduce three subtopics or "points," discussed in three body paragraphs and summarized in the inverted funnel of the conclusion (see Figure 2.1).

As preparations for meeting the diverse, nuanced expectations of undergraduates that Bartholomae described, such formulas seem absurdly simplistic recipes for redundancy or opportunities to avoid real thought about a subject. "Say what you're going to say. Say it. Say you've said it," is the homily many college freshmen told me they had learned in high school. Legions of overworked secondary school teachers have continued to use these models, however, because they are almost irresistibly efficient and convenient. Nearly any topic can be divided into three subtopics, listed in the introduction and used as the topics of body paragraphs, and the template itself provides simple criteria for efficient, comparative grading. When my son was in middle school, he showed me one of these formulaic essays he had written, on types of fire engines, just returned by his English teacher. In one handwritten page,

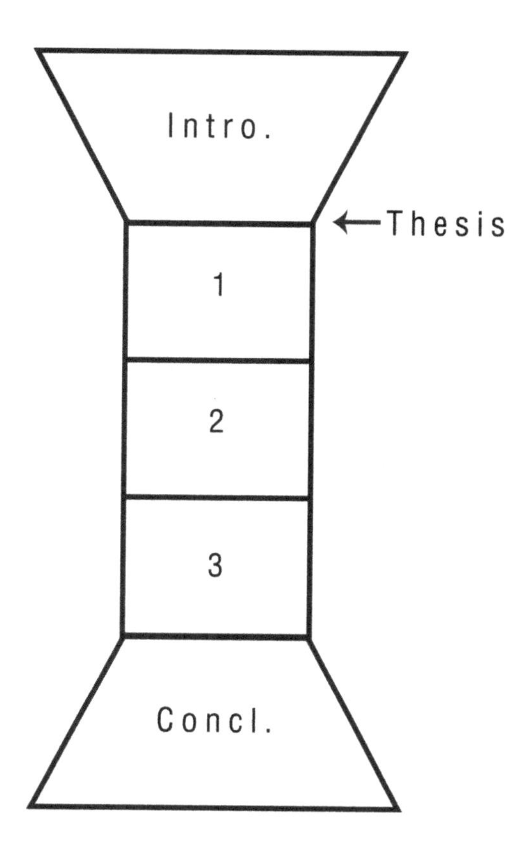

Figure 2.1 The Five-Paragraph Essay

he began with a generalization about fire being a benefit and threat to mankind, moved quickly to three types of fire engines, described each of them in a paragraph, and concluded with generalizations about their value in controlling the age-old danger of fire. At the top, his teacher had written: "Very Good! A."

> "Pretty good, huh?" my son said with a smirk, hoping for outrage. Refusing to take the bait, I asked, "How long did you spend on it?" "About 20 minutes," he replied, and I told him that sounded about right.

Teachers who use these models often argue that they provide reliable foundations for developing more complex essay structures, and more sophisticated students often revert to such templates for quickly organizing timed essays for in-class exams or standardized tests. In Chapter 3 I'll explain the ways in which the underlying logic of this model, according to Baker's intentions, becomes useful in much higher realms of graduate and professional work.

In practice, however, following generations of secondary school teachers more often used versions of this model as recipes for conformity and to facilitate comparative grading, in ways that often replaced the kinds of reasoning and intellectual development Baker hoped to encourage. Rigid, habitual use of such templates reduced the diverse realms of academic discourse that college freshmen encounter—all analysis, argument, and explanation—to the trisection of topics.

As a consequence, most college writing teachers have viewed these "preparations" for college writing as obstacles to the development of writing ability in real undergraduate courses. In these contexts, students who continue to use simple formulas can't contend with the increasing variety and complexity of assignments until they stop doing what they were taught to do. For example, a college freshman once came to me for help with an assignment she had failed to complete, in a literature course. To demonstrate that she was a capable writer, she showed me three papers she had written, with grades in the B range, for a political history course the previous semester. All of these papers began with a more or less apt quotation from someone famous, used to introduce a topic divided into three points, discussed in three sections and briefly summarized in the conclusion. This, she explained, was how she was taught in high school to write all essays, and until now it had worked pretty well.

The assignment in her literature class, however, asked her to discuss related themes in six short stories, and she had no idea how to begin. She was essentially blocked—incapable of writing anything—until I convinced her, with difficulty, to abandon her habitual approach and actually think about the stories she had read, as the basis for analysis and organization. The underlying problem wasn't the three-part form she had learned. It was her use of this form to avoid the kinds of observation and thought that college assignments required.

Like other writing teachers, I've often taught against these all-purpose models in courses for undergraduates. I'm therefore aware of the irony when I use adapted versions of the "five-paragraph theme" diagram in my consultations with advanced graduate students who are working on highly specialized research articles and dissertations. And there are other ironies as well. The formula that this freshman learned in her high school English course, for example, ran aground in a college English course but worked fairly well in political studies, where similar formats and explicit "road maps" are common features of professional articles. In some respects, with small modifications, the "five-paragraph theme" diagram applies best to writing in science labs (at the opposite end of the curriculum from English) where the research question or hypothesis in an experimental report typically lands at the bottom of that funnel-shaped introduction, framing narrower sections for methods and results, leading to the inverted funnel of the conclusion. Versions of these templates, described in undergraduate lab manuals, are derived from the structures of professional research articles.

As writers move from secondary schools through undergraduate studies and graduate programs, therefore, required forms of writing alone can't account for the continuities and discontinuities through which strategies work, no longer work, and must change. To understand what it means to write successfully in these contexts, and then in others, we have to consider other factors as well. Following generalizations will correspond with your own experience to varying degrees, but they're meant to stimulate reflection on what you learned as student writers and may need to unlearn, or at least revise, in your work as scholars.

Simulation and Frames of Reference

Whether student writers try to use a standard format for all assignments or approach each assignment as a new challenge, the fundamental rhetorical problem that David Bartholomae described remains. To the extent that teachers expect students to think and write like scholars in their disciplines, student writers must "try on" the personae of knowledgeable authors they do not happen to be. They must replicate conventional forms of communication in professional communities they have not yet entered, with the semblance of authority and conviction they do not yet possess. They must write as though their arguments and explanations emerged from broad familiarity with realms of knowledge and debate they know relatively little about. And in matters of hours or days they must simulate types of writing that result from years of scholarship.

For the purpose of learning, there's nothing inherently wrong with such exercises in simulation. The imitation of voices and personae is essential to all language acquisition and explains why young children, most receptive and unformed, learn languages so quickly. When student writers must quickly adopt a variety of academic roles and voices during a term, the flexibility of youth is on their side.

I expect that you recall this imitative frame of mind when you began to work on writing assignments in school: the necessity of pretending to be someone you were not, adopting voices that weren't entirely your own, for audiences and purposes you had to imagine—writing as though you were deeply invested in ideas that first occurred to you an hour earlier, perhaps to "answer" the arguments of experts you didn't know and who would never read what you had to say. Such tasks seem easier, and certainly more enjoyable, when assignments make their imitative, playful functions explicit: *Imagine that you are a science advisor for a sci-fi film about an alien invasion* or *Imagine that you are a social psychologist designing an experiment to measure high school students' abilities to detect online deception*. Otherwise, writing becomes a kind of routine, obligatory fraudulence, a continual task of posturing in a tone of sober sincerity. There's some poetic justice, at least, that in student responses to their assignments teachers usually get some version of what they really asked for, and therefore deserve. When they complain that student papers read like inept parodies of professional writing, it's because they assigned imitations of the kinds of professional writing they ask students to read. Because they've become specific kinds of academic beings and writers, college teachers can be remarkably unaware of the variety of literary forms, voices, types of evidence and reasoning, sources, or systems of reference—ways of knowing and representing knowledge—to which their students must adapt.

For example, a history professor once complained to me that his students didn't know how to use quotations and references, because their papers were loaded with quotations from "secondary sources" (i.e., historical research literature) rather than "primary sources" (original documents). On the same day, an astrophysicist also complained to me that his students didn't know how to use references, because they included lots of quotations from research articles (which his field termed "primary sources") rather than simple numerical citations. He didn't want them to use *any* quotations. Yet in a sociology course, teachers would probably expect them to use quotations from theory and research literature to build convincing, referenced arguments. The correct way to write in one course becomes wrong in another.

Some of the ways in which students adapt to these differing expectations are more constructive than others. Cynical students view them as a game of strategically "giving teachers what they want" while concealing the deception and sounding sincere. Those who are too sincere, honestly revealing their ignorance and doubt in their own voices, often sound naive or even stupid. Wiser students, those most likely to enter graduate programs, view these rhetorical role changes as learning exercises: opportunities to try on various academic identities, ways of thinking and writing, for the purpose of choosing one they might really pursue and eventually embody in advanced studies and careers. Wise teachers, in turn, are aware that they are asking students to produce versions of specific, unfamiliar kinds of writing and provide relevant instruction.

For all of these students and teachers, however, the basic rhetorical conditions of student writing—its contexts, audiences, purposes, and time frames—promote certain ways of writing and discourage or even eliminate others. Whether an assignment acknowledges or conceals role-playing, and whether students are fascinated with the subject or just anxious to get the assignment done, all successful student writers must remain aware that they are completing a course requirement, assigned by a teacher who is their primary audience, in the limited time they have available for this work, with the end result of a grade. If undergraduates tend to view assigned papers and reports as "one-night stands," as Ben recalled, the main reasons are the time limitations attached to these assignments and the fact that the product of this effort typically has no future or consequence beyond the moment when it's graded and returned. The learning involved in the process may endure, and the grade a paper receives may have consequences, but the student paper itself, as a piece of written communication, is unlikely ever to be read again by anyone, including the author.

Even for the most capable, highly motivated students, ignoring these rhetorical conditions can be perilous. Teachers say that they want undergraduates to think and write like real scholars in their fields, with "original" ideas based on critical reading and established lines of reasoning. They frequently complain that students are just summarizing readings, pulling facile arguments out of thin air, or failing to rethink and revise their work. But *actually* thinking and writing like a scholar—or like a graduate student—can get undergraduates into deep trouble. In my senior year of college, I became far too invested in a couple of research paper projects and engaged in real inquiry that required extensive reading, analysis, and revision. I fell behind in my other classes, submitted the papers late, and was penalized on one of them for an argument that was "too ambitious." Among undergraduates, writing blocks sometimes result from the kinds of deep, exploratory engagement that teachers hope to encourage, when a precocious student tries to simulate the process of scholarship, not just the product. Asked to choose a poem to discuss within a volume of the poet's work, one of these students spent most of the time available considering poets she admired and still hadn't decided between two when she came to me for help. After I forced the decision by asking to see one of the volumes and locking it in my desk drawer, she developed three equally interesting and complex ways of understanding the poem she finally chose. As a sophomore major in an entirely different field, she was basically trying to reinvent, for a paper in one course, whole traditions in literary theory—an approach to the task more appropriate for a doctoral candidate over a period of months. Although she eventually finished the paper (and her teacher loved it), the time and attention involved carried high costs in her other work, and she failed to complete other assignments.

For her English professor and other scholars in literary studies, the conceptual framework that this sophomore was trying to assemble for her paper represents what I'll call an *implicit frame of reference*: a broad knowledge of theoretical trends and professional literature in this field, assembled through years of reading, writing, and other professional activity. For scholars, this familiarity with established knowledge, current research trends, and unresolved issues is a necessary condition for knowledge production: *a point of departure for writing*. Within this implicit reference frame (and in ways we'll explore further in the following chapter), scholars take theoretical positions, focus on particular lines of inquiry, and identify knowledge gaps and significant research questions from which research and writing projects begin. In the books, dissertations, or research articles they produce, they build a much narrower *explicit frame of reference*—represented in literature reviews and works cited—around these focused questions or arguments.

Student writers can only simulate the products of real scholarship because they don't have the background knowledge necessary to identify significant questions and viable positions or to build an explicit reference frame that rationalizes their significance within a discipline. Nor can they simulate the processes through which these products come about, because they don't have time. The sophomore mentioned earlier got into trouble because she was trying to do what was circumstantially impossible: to construct, essentially from scratch and in a period of about three weeks, an authoritative reference frame necessary for a real work of scholarship. In a group of professors and graduate students from various fields that we assembled to discuss their expectations of student writers, several of the professors agreed that they were looking for "original thought" and wanted students to "discover new ideas." A doctoral candidate in the group, closer to the experience of being an undergraduate, argued that this bar was set too high. "Perhaps," he said, "we should just expect them to discover ideas that are new and original to *them*." As learners, in other words, they can produce new knowledge for themselves, but they aren't likely to produce knowledge of original significance to the world at large.

One could argue that there are exceptions and qualifications to these generalizations about student writers, especially in advanced undergraduate work. As I've noted, senior theses and ambitious term papers sometimes engage undergraduates in versions of real disciplinary research over longer time frames, and undergraduates sometimes participate in faculty research and writing projects within established lines of inquiry. To some extent, courses, assignments, and required readings construct disciplinary reference frames within which students can identify significant questions and choose viable positions for writing. Courses allow students to visit, like participants in a factory tour, the complex and highly specialized realms in which disciplinary knowledge is made. Teachers become guides through these environs, and writing assignments, like the structured "experiments" in a science class, offer them simplified hands-on experience in making something that resembles the real work of this discipline.

If we envision the implicit and explicit reference frames of academic writing as concentric circles, however, we can see the differences between real works of scholarship and the typical student renditions of this work, along with some of the rhetorical problems involved. For experienced scholars, the boundaries of the explicit scope of a research article are defined within a much broader arena of background knowledge. A study of the evolution of a particular plant species in a particular ecosystem, for example, acquires focus and significance in an established area of research within the broad disciplines of evolutionary biology and ecology. Against this implicit background, however, the article will begin more narrowly with a review of previous research

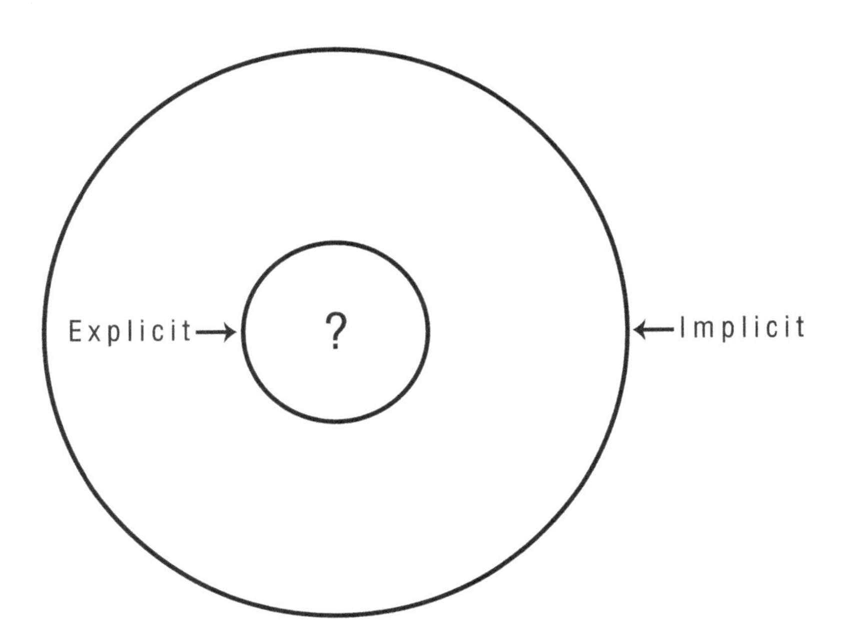

Figure 2.2 Scholar Reference Frames

on this type of plant, ecosystem, or evolutionary question, narrowing further to the identification of a knowledge gap and the specific question this study attempts to answer. The dimensions of this explicit reference frame are therefore much smaller than the knowledge base that makes this focus possible.

These implicit and explicit dimensions of the work are interdependent. Without broader knowledge of established theory and research in their fields, scholars can't identify significant, focused questions or build frames of reference to other research that demonstrates this significance. Knowing what they are doing as writers, where the article should begin, and the other writing they should cite requires awareness of what they are *not* doing and the broader areas of research they will *not* mention. *Focus and definition result from informed, implicit exclusion.*

Student writers are rarely in a position to make such decisions. For each of their writing assignments, undergraduates must construct a new reference frame from materials they can assemble (or were given) for the task at hand. In typical student papers, what the writers tell us represents most of what they know about the subject or perhaps (when they imply knowledge they don't possess or make assertions they can't support) even more than they know. In other words, the boundaries of the implicit and explicit reference frames nearly coincide:

Obliged to produce research papers, for example, undergraduates often begin by choosing a topic and then gathering potential source material that seems relevant and sufficient for the scale of the project. Before they begin to write, they read (or at least scan though) this material and take notes, looking for information, arguments, or potential quotations that could be useful. If the assignment requires a position or focused question

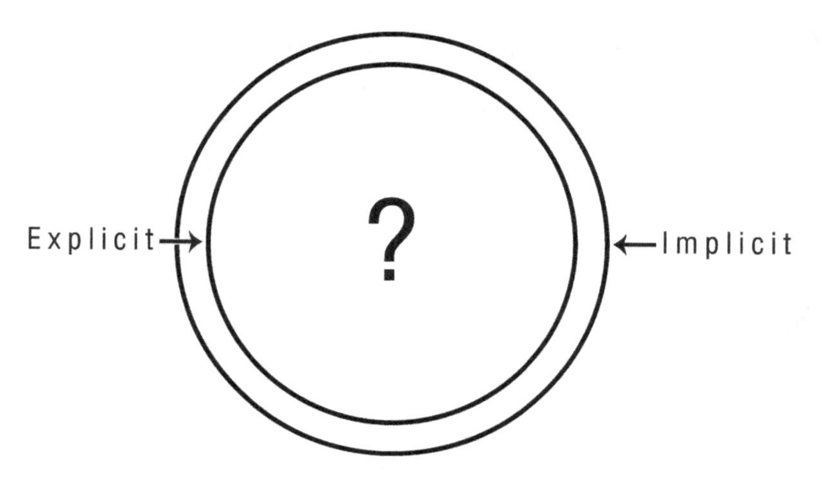

Figure 2.3 Student Reference Frames

they should answer, they will try to develop one from these readings and notes. If they already have a position on the subject, they may look for source material that supports it. Other students might begin to plan and write the paper before they have gathered sufficient references and look for the material they need in the process. In either case, they will typically use most of the sources they assemble for the project, and research questions or arguments will be focused within these limited reference frames, not within the broader realms of research in an academic discipline.

As a consequence, the great majority of the explanations, questions, or arguments these papers present in the guise of "original" contributions to fields of research are, within those fields, common knowledge, previously falsified, insufficiently supported, or of marginal significance. Although this characterization of student writing may sound critical and dismissive, it isn't. Like all writers, undergraduates can only do some version of what is possible, given the conditions in which they are writing. In the enormous volume of student writing produced each term, sufficient to fill container ships, there are no doubt some brilliant, original ideas that could be tested, substantiated, and become persuasive in arenas of scholarly research and debate. Unconstrained by disciplinary conventions, undergraduates sometimes have startlingly fresh, interesting ideas. I once asked a professor of entomology whether college freshmen could ever come up with original, significant questions about the beehives they observed in his class. To my surprise, he said, "Oh, of course they do. Every semester." In themselves, however, good questions or bright ideas aren't contributions to a field of inquiry, and without lots of help from him, his students could not identify, frame, attempt to answer, and communicate these questions as forms of written knowledge in his field. Occasionally, undergraduates pursue such ideas in collaboration with their teachers or go on to pursue them in graduate programs. In the normal contexts of undergraduate studies, however, students don't have the time, skills, or resources for real knowledge production, and these rough gems remain undiscovered.

Performance and Process

Although teachers frequently complain about the quality of student responses to their assignments, when I read these assignments, I'm more often impressed that undergraduates can get them done in the time available. Asked to simulate unfamiliar forms of writing and take authoritative positions in fields of research they know little about, in a small fraction of the time scholars would spend, the great majority of students manage to produce *something* worth reading and grading by the deadline. How do they do it? And how did we do it when we were undergraduates? With awareness of the rhetorical factors involved, we can return to questions I raised at the beginning of this book about my own writing experiences. How did I manage to complete long, complex research papers in a couple of intense, marathon sessions of writing? And why did these methods no longer work for my graduate courses and dissertation?

These questions are harder to answer than you might expect. A teacher gives students an assignment, and at the end of the class they disperse. When the due date arrives, a week or two later, their papers materialize, in hard copy or as electronic documents. What happened in between? How did the students get this writing done? As a rule, teachers have no idea. In their evaluations of the products of this writing activity, as graded performances, they often make inferential statements about the process: "I can tell you spent a lot of time on this essay," or "You obviously wrote this in a rush, without taking time to revise and proofread." But these inferences are often wrong.

Although most of the challenges, learning experiences, and potential "teaching moments" of writing occur in this hidden process, teachers focus on its products for three related reasons:

- Comparative grading attaches primary value to products as measurable performances.
- Teaching and evaluating writing as a process, to the extent that we can, is extremely time consuming.
- The products of writing are observable, as tangible objects, but most dimensions of the process are not.

Consider, first of all, what writing is: *the use of shared symbolic systems to communicate across time and space.* This is one of the most complicated things that humans do. Writers themselves can't fully explain what they are doing or how they do it, and in the expanse of our existence as a species it's something people learned to do very recently, only about 5000 years ago. Even now, the uniquely human ability to write and read, unlike the ability to speak, doesn't come naturally. Individuals must learn these skills, and until the past century the vast majority of people in the world remained illiterate.

The peculiarity and power of writing, as a medium of communication, lie in the disconnection between the moment of utterance, when writing occurs, and the moment of communication, when an audience reads what we wrote. While we're writing, the audience isn't there. When an audience receives this communication, in a different time and place, the writer isn't there. Only this slender, tangible thread of mutually intelligible symbols, of words and sentences, connects the writer and reader. And across those spatial and temporal divides, most of what happens remains a mystery.

Although our educational systems emphasize the forms and qualities of products, teachers have tried to prescribe and regulate the writing process, most often as a sequence of stages. *Consider what you want to say. Make an outline. Use the outline to compose a draft. Read over the draft and revise.* Even when they assign outlines and drafts in stages, however, teachers can't accurately observe or regulate what writers actually do, because they aren't there when it happens and because most of what is going on is unobservable. On one level, writing is an embodied, physical activity, and although it's most often solitary, we can sometimes observe writers at work in classrooms, libraries, and other public places. Because writing is also mental activity—linguistic, cognitive, intellectual, and sometimes emotional, partly conscious and partly unconscious—observation reveals very little of what they are doing or why. Even in the midst of others, writers at work appear to be alone or in their own worlds of imagination, because cognitively they are trying to bridge that gap between themselves, in the moment, and imagined readers elsewhere, at other moments. Even when we are close enough to observe what they are writing, we can't determine what they are thinking, the decisions that lead to a sentence, or why they are writing so quickly or slowly. We don't know what this activity represents in the larger process of the project, over previous hours, days, or weeks. And even in brief periods when they interrupt composing, stare at the screen or look away, delete a sentence, pause, and type a new one, we don't know why. The production of a simple text involves thousands of these decisions and activity shifts that writers themselves can't fully recall or explain; yet most of what we know about what they are doing is what they can, and choose to, tell us, in retrospect. What they tell us collectively, furthermore, is that they are using a bewildering variety of methods, often resulting from individual preferences, personalities, circumstances, schooling, or enduring habits. Terms most often used to describe stages or dimensions of the process—such as *prewriting*, *composing*, or *revising*—don't begin to describe its real complexity and variety.

In the 1970s, therefore, when composition specialists began to advocate teaching writing as a process and to investigate what student writers were doing, they discovered what linguists and cognitive psychologists already knew: that the use of written language is unfathomably complex and extremely difficult to study. Most of what these writing specialists learned, in the end, was that their previous assumptions were false or, at best, simplistic. While most instructional accounts of the process described a linear sequence of stages, for example, they found that actual writing activities are highly recursive, or "loopy." Ostensibly in the "composing" stage, for example, student writers and others frequently pause to read over what they have written, revert to "prewriting" activity or planning, or go on to "revise" and "edit" the draft they are still composing. Progress therefore occurs not in a straight line but in overlapping spirals of writing, reading, rethinking, and rewriting. They also learned that students weren't necessarily using methods they were instructed to use and may have produced required outlines or rough drafts, for example, *after* they completed the finished papers they turned in.

In my following accounts of writing methods, therefore, I don't pretend that I fully understand what student writers or scholars (in Chapter 3) are actually doing. For that matter, I don't fully understand what I'm doing when I write. Before they largely abandoned efforts to understand the process in the 1990s, however, and reverted to the more familiar, tangible study of texts, composition scholars did illuminate some interesting dimensions of this complex activity. Most of what I have to add to this knowledge is based on what student writers, graduate students, and others have told me in consultations, classes, and more formal studies of their methods.

Our ability to write is rooted in our more natural ability to speak. In conversational speech, when audiences are immediately present, waiting to hear what we are about to say, those recursive loops of deliberation that slow writing down untangle into a continuous line of words and sentences. To varying degrees, speakers pause to think, interrupt the flow with "placeholders" (*Umm . . . well . . . you know*) to buy a little time, and rephrase statements that seem unclear (*What I really mean is . . .*). But the presence of a listener greatly reduces those delays and engages our ability to put language and thought together quickly and continuously, like skillful musicians improvising on stage. When we're writing, on the other hand, the absence of the audience offers nearly endless opportunities to pause, reflect, and reconsider the construction of a single sentence, which can take a few seconds, several minutes, or more than an hour.

To write quickly, therefore, we need to reduce these deliberations and release language at a pace closer to that of speech, with a stronger sense that we are communicating directly with an imagined audience. With analogies to music that we'll pursue further, writing then resembles improvised performance more than deliberate composition or rehearsal for future performance. Along with the simulation of products, this improvisational approach to composition distinguishes the processes of most student writing from those of experienced scholars.

In comparative research on "Revision Strategies of Student Writers and Experienced Adult Writers," Nancy Sommers (1980) argued that the college freshmen in her study avoided real revision because they conflated certain aspects of writing and speech. Citing Roland Barthes's (1977) observation that speech, unlike writing, is "irreversible," Sommers suggested that this confusion resulted, ironically, from instructional efforts to include revision in the process. For students who were taught to complete papers in a sequence of stages—*first write a draft, and* then *revise it*—revision become an "afterthought": a chance to cosmetically "fix up" or polish what you've already said. As one student explained, "I don't use the word rewriting because I only write one draft and the changes that I make are on top of the draft. The changes that I make are usually just marking out words and putting different ones in." (p. 381).

Expedient optimism, under time constraints, further encourages student writers to think of the first draft, while they're writing it, as the finished product and to avoid substantial revisions. One of my own students candidly explained these underlying motivations:

> Right from the beginning I knew that my first draft was going to be my last. The only revisions that I made to the first draft of my paper were typos, and occasionally I would fix awkward sentences. There were absolutely no changes in the ideas, theme, and organization of the paper because they were already determined before I started writing. Part of the reason I did this was time constraints, but most of the time I just didn't feel like it: the sense of completion was so great that I just couldn't bring myself to go back and correct the paper.

In contrast, the "experienced adult writers" Sommers quoted viewed writing as a recursive, exploratory process in which composing and revising were overlapping, ongoing efforts to discover what they would eventually say to their readers:

> I rewrite as I write. It is hard to tell what is a first draft because it is not determined by time. In one draft, I might cross out three pages, write two, cross out a fourth, rewrite it, and call it a draft. I am constantly writing and rewriting.
>
> (p. 383–384)

When they began to write, these authors didn't imagine that what they were saying was what their audiences would receive, as in speech. The delay between utterance and communication that distinguishes writing from speech offered them the opportunity to reconsider, reconstruct, and polish what would eventually become communication and performance.

Although they reveal significant patterns, such generalizations about the practices of whole categories of writers have many exceptions. As I've noted, student writers often revise extensively while they compose, and those instructed to produce outlines or rough drafts in "stages" don't always follow these instructions. While some experienced authors use exploratory drafts to discover and revise what they want to say, many others begin with detailed plans and try, at least, to avoid messy revisions. Although it's true that scholars typically revise their work extensively and recursively, they often begin with predetermined forms governed by disciplinary conventions and submission guidelines, along with central arguments, research claims, and results that remain unaltered. As models of "professional" writing methods, comparative studies in this period often used examples of novelists and other "creative" writers who described writing as an exploratory "journey into the unknown," but these are unreliable models for academic writers. Like novelists in some respects, scholars are telling stories about their research, but they know in advance how these stories are told and, in most cases, what they are about. Many novelists, in turn, follow detailed plots they worked out in advance. John Steinbeck claimed that he knew the whole story of *The Grapes of Wrath* (1939) while he was composing this 600-page novel, over a period of about six months, in one essentially finished, handwritten draft. In his writing journals, however, he described this self-imposed regimen as a "prison sentence" that undermined both his health and his marriage (Steinbeck, 1989).

Regardless of these variations, the notion that student writers can and should produce writing in the ways that professional writers do is naive. The generalization that holds true is that the conditions in which students write encourage them to think of what they are doing, from the beginning of the process, as *performance*. Along with other factors we'll examine, time constraints, above all, nourish the hope that what a student is writing at the moment will be essentially finished—the hope that it won't need to be substantially revised. And this performative sense of what we're doing at the moment is fundamentally different from the working assumption that we're still rehearsing, constructing and reconstructing versions of what audiences will read: still *preparing* to perform.

Because the actual process of writing is largely unobserved or unobservable, most college students are unaware of this distinction. They assume that their professors and other academic authors also *perform* writing, but more skillfully, as polished utterance, much in the way that some of these scholars can stand before a class and deliver what appear to be spontaneous yet clear, coherent lectures. Students often imagine that when one has become sufficiently knowledgeable, articulate, and experienced, authorship will become a simple matter of releasing those brilliant utterances onto the page and sending them off to the publisher, much in the way that students write and "turn in" their own amateur renditions of scholarship. This romantic notion of professional writing is false, of course, but teachers rarely disillusion them.

Writing teachers and others who assign projects in stages that include exploratory drafts and revisions will object to these generalizations, with some justification. Staged assignments with guidance for revision are certainly improvements over the traditional, and still prevalent, assignment and grading of finished products. In further analogy to music, the most common method of training undergraduate writers is comparable to asking novice musicians to compose and perform a difficult piece, with little time for rehearsal, then pointing out the ways in which they messed it up and asking them to compose and perform a different piece. Among their classes, furthermore, their teachers assign different genres, evaluated by differing standards. Some are looking for technical correctness. Others emphasize cohesion, adherence to form, clarity of expression, originality, depth of understanding, or all of the above. The correction of flaws in one performance will not reliably avert weaknesses in another, for a different audience. Experience therefore accumulates through a series of more or less inept performances, and the best students become adept at strategically anticipating shifting expectations on the first try.

In real music education, of course, students typically work on the same pieces through extensive practice and rehearsal, gradually revising and refining particular passages toward the possible goal of performance. This incremental process of reiteration and revision is much closer to that of professional academic writing. Like actors, dancers, and other performing artists, musicians are trained in the methods of rehearsal, and they are acutely aware of the distinction between rehearsal and performance—that playing a piece badly is a necessary stage in the process of learning to play it well. Experienced scholars know that the purpose of a first draft, as one chemist told me, "is to make you aware of your own confusion," and that successive revisions, like rehearsals, are "opportunities to recover from that confusion." The drafts eventually submitted for publication, as manuscripts, are like dress rehearsals, still subject to potential revision before the final performance.

Assigned "rough drafts" and revisions delay performance and give students limited, structured opportunities to reconsider what they have written. In the contexts of undergraduate courses and grading systems, however, it's nearly impossible to replicate the incremental, recursive processes through which real works of scholarship come about. I know because I've tried, through a variety of teaching strategies. I'm not sure what my students learned from these experiments, but I learned some important lessons. Among them is the extent to which rhetorical conditions determine our approaches to writing, even when we are trying to change our strategies or imagine that they have changed. In one of these classes, in which I accidentally became a student writer again, I also realized how deeply habitual performative approaches to writing can be.

In this writing course for advanced undergraduates, most of them in the social sciences, I delayed "performance" and the institutionally requisite grading of student papers to the end of the term, when students submitted portfolios of essays they considered more or less finished. During the term, we read some common published work, raised some central issues as occasions for writing, and students started a series of essays. For reasons I'll explain further in the next chapter, I was also trying to undermine the emphasis on individual performance in undergraduate studies and replicate the social dimensions of scholarly writing. In class, therefore, we spent most of our time discussing students' projects and working on their drafts in smaller groups. When my students thought a paper was nearing completion, the author read aloud the draft while the rest of us looked at copies. "Is it done?" the writer usually asked, and we then discussed what seemed finished or needed further revisions. Because I was essentially training my students to do most of the work in class, my role as the teacher was diminished. While they were absorbed in their group discussions, I felt left out, so I decided to write a couple of these essays as well, joined one of the groups, and submitted my drafts for feedback.

One of my essays, titled "A Taste for Mediocrity" and inspired by Eric Schlosser's book *Fast Food Nation* (1989), tried to explain the cultural logic that leads Americans to choose chain restaurants and prepared foods that are predictably unremarkable: not very good or good for them, but always unwaveringly the same. Because I was very busy (in part with my "real" writing projects) and had a fairly clear sense of what I wanted to say, I produced the first draft quickly, in a couple of hours. I recall thinking, with hubris, that I shouldn't spend a lot of time on the essay because I was much more experienced and skillful than my students and didn't want to discourage them or appear to be showing off. If I left the draft a bit unpolished, I thought, they could make helpful suggestions, but I didn't expect that they would recommend substantial changes.

Their responses, in my group review session, shattered these assumptions. The ideas about mediocrity and conformity in the two halves of the paper were interesting and potentially connected, they said, but they couldn't figure out how they fit together. I remembered being vaguely aware of this problem while I was writing but thought I had hidden it with clever phrasing or that my students would be too timid to point it out. In a teacherly voice, one of the students began in her written comments on the draft, "I think that you have *two* very good but also very different topics going on here. You start out very well with . . ." Following accurate summaries of my two arguments (and with a passing, deferential nod to my role as her teacher) she made the dreaded transition to the bad news:

> I understand the shaky relationship you are drawing between these two subjects, and I mean it in the nicest and most instructive possible way to say that as a reader, you don't carry me through—I feel pushed around and left wandering. I think this paper would be improved if you ruthlessly cut one subject or another.

"Good luck," she concluded (with a smiley face emoticon), and my heart sank. Rewriting the damned paper was inescapable, and my Inner Student Writer was kicking and screaming at the prospect. In this peculiar context I had created, our roles had flipped. As the teacher of a class meant to undermine the role of a student writer, I accidentally became one, in ways that were deeply familiar and nearly impossible to overcome. At the time, I was also working on an article for publication, spending many hours revising evolving versions toward one I would eventually show to colleagues. Then I would need to revise it further before I submitted it as a manuscript that would need more revision before it was published. In a course in which I was trying to give my students some comparable experiences, however, I reverted to performative writing and tried compulsively to make my first draft the last. When my "teachers" made revision unavoidable, I felt I had given them a bad performance, and rewriting a hastily composed draft felt like a burden or a punishment. Many years after the end of my own schooling, contextual factors revived these old ways of writing nearly intact.

This revival occurred even without the additional factor of grading, which motivates performative writing (and teaching) and was always on my students' minds. Although I had delayed this judgment to the end of the term, it remained a largely hidden but looming condition for my students' writing in the course. In class discussions of drafts or in response to my written comments, some of them timidly asked what that version of an essay "would get" if I graded it then, as a normal teacher would. After class or during office hours, individuals asked me to tell them "where they stood" in the class or to explain the grading criteria I would use. Accustomed to receiving grades throughout the term for every paper, quiz, or problem set, as American students usually do, they asked these questions as though I were keeping their real grades secret, in my mind or in a clandestine gradebook. In the context of schoolwork, the notion of writing in the absence of grading—just to communicate clearly, understand something, achieve recognition, or develop one's abilities—was nearly inconceivable.

This does not mean that student writers are oblivious to the strengths and weaknesses of their own work or that they rely entirely, for assessment, on the judgments of teachers. Even when they hope to avoid extensive revision (as I did), they usually recognize the limitations of the work they managed to produce. In more conventional courses, I always asked students to explain, on the back of a paper they were about to turn in, what they considered to be its strengths and weaknesses, and in most cases, they could tell me pretty accurately:

- I know the conclusion is different from what I said in the intro, but I didn't have time to go back and rework it.
- I didn't give enough evidence for the first point I was trying to make, but this was all I could find.
- Most of what I said came from X, but since I agree with everything he says I didn't know how to make the argument my own, and you didn't just want a summary, right? Or a bunch of long quotes?

These are the kinds of observations that motivate scholars to revise early drafts of their writing projects, before they show their work to other readers, and in response I often just returned these papers without reading them and gave the writers further time to act on their own perceptions. But teachers at large rarely elicit these student assessments of their own work as a basis for revision. They usually assume that the versions student writers submit represent the best they could do, given their abilities and circumstances. Whatever students turn in represents performance, and responsibility for assessing its quality lies with the teacher. When I had asked my students to write assessments of papers they were about to turn in and gave them a couple of days to follow their own advice, without collecting or reading what they wrote, one senior in the class was visibly angry and confused. "What's bothering you?" I asked, and she replied, "You aren't doing your job!"

This concentration of agency and authority in the role of the reader/teacher discourages the kinds of self-motivated assessments and revisions through which real works of scholarship develop, especially in the early stages. Even when they have time, students are reluctant to invest in revisions that might not improve the paper, or might even make it worse, in the eyes of their teacher, the ultimate authority over its quality.

Motivations and Standards

"A Taste for Mediocrity" would be a good name for the *process* of writing that paper for my class as well as for the subject—fast writing as well as fast food. Because it was just an ephemeral paper for a class, for an audience of undergraduates who knew even less about the subject than I did, I began with the intention of getting it done quickly and lowered my standards for the product accordingly.

"A Taste for the Extraordinary" would have been a better name for the process of writing the professional article I was working on at the time. To get that article published, for an audience of experts in my field, I needed to say something new and significant that I could convincingly substantiate. The product should sound knowledgeable and thought through, fully grounded in my field yet original and cleverly presented. To meet these high standards that I attributed to my readers, I was willing to spend a lot of time. Among the variable "settings" with which we approach writing projects in different circumstances, *motivations* and *standards* are especially useful for explaining the speed with which we write. The differential relations between these factors heavily determine whether we get a writing project done quickly and easily or more slowly and laboriously.

To visualize these settings, imagine that when you are writing, your motivations to get the work done and your standards for this work are two slide switches, like those on a sound mixing board (see Figure 2.4).

When we begin writing tasks, our rhetorical sense for what we're doing sets these switches in various positions, with effects I can describe with a pair of formulations:

- Writing becomes relatively quick and easy when our immediate motivations are high and our immediate standards are low.

- Writing becomes slow and difficult when our immediate motivations are low and our immediate standards are high.

I emphasize our "immediate" motivations and standards, in the present moment, because that's when all writing occurs. In that moment, our motivations to get a project (such as a dissertation) finished *eventually* may be quite high, but our motivations to work on it now, to get some of it done, can be very low. In turn, our standards for the finished product can be very high, but our immediate standards for what we're writing now, as in an exploratory draft, may be much lower.

These variable settings explain why an individual's writing on one task can occur almost without pause and then, on another project, slow to a

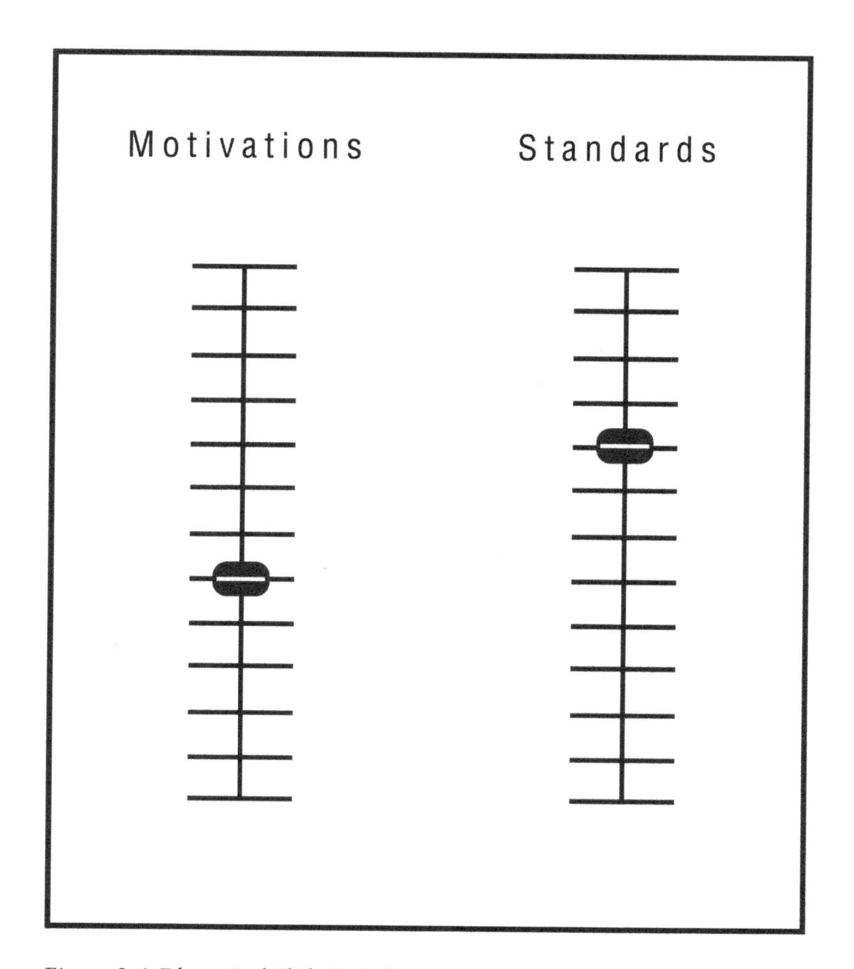

Figure 2.4 Rhetorical Slide Switches

hesitant, recursive crawl. Apart from brief text messages, the closest we can come to completely linear written utterance, comparable to spontaneous speech, is "freewriting," described by Peter Elbow in his book *Writing Without Teachers* (1973) as an exercise to reduce cognitive impediments to expression and develop our "writing muscles." The only rule for freewriting is that you shouldn't stop writing whatever you are thinking. Don't pause to think about what you are writing, to read what you've said, or to change anything. Under these conditions, anyone who is even marginally fluent in a written language can produce a page of handwriting in about five minutes because, in the moment, freewriting pushes the motivations setting to the top and the standards setting to the bottom. Writing continuously is the immediate motivation, and freewriting eliminates all standards for what we produce.

If, as your teacher, I added any conditions to this exercise—e.g., that all sentences should be correctly spelled and punctuated, or that I would ask you to read your work aloud to the class—the standards setting would rise and lower your motivation to write continuously. With additional conditions, you would write increasingly slowly and cautiously. At the opposite extreme, imagine that your motivation setting at the moment is extremely low but your standards for what you might produce are extremely high. Imagine, for example, that you have months to produce a dissertation, and little incentive to get something written today, but feel that everything you write should be dazzlingly profound. With those settings, getting something written now might seem pointless and, in any case, nearly impossible.

I should add that these settings do not reliably determine the quality of what we write. By inspiration or chance, quick, spontaneous expression is sometimes brilliant and fluent. Writing produced with slow, deliberative effort to meet high standards can be dreadful. On the other hand, to the extent that we can deliberately change these settings, greater speed and ease aren't necessarily our goals. Some kinds of writing require more time and labor than others, and individuals with different tendencies—to write too carelessly or too slowly and cautiously, need to move in different directions. As a consequence, good advice for some writers can be bad advice for others. Freewriting can be useful and interesting, but it isn't likely to produce even a first draft of a research paper, much less a dissertation. "Just write whatever comes to mind" isn't good advice to a student already inclined to do that: to get a paper finished as quickly as possible. For that reason, teachers more often encourage student writers to spend *more* time, to think more carefully *about* what they are saying, and to revise. But serious writers, willing to spend more time to meet higher standards, often need to move in the opposite direction. Already inclined to believe that more time, thought, and effort will produce better results, they're vulnerable to deepening entanglements in fussy, unproductive tinkering with sentences, especially if they're trying to make this version worthy of the high standards they've set for their work. Lowering their standards in the moment and raising their motivations to get some work done can help to release the natural flow of language and ideas. They need to acknowledge the possibility, at least, that *less time and effort will produce better results.*

The ideal, therefore, is not any particular setting of these variables but their deliberate, flexible adjustment to varying goals and contexts, which can change not only from one writing project to another but also through the writing process and in successive drafts. As complex projects move closer to completion and release to the audience, for example, standards for what we're currently writing normally rise, and this is the point when tinkering with sentence structure and phrasing is usually most appropriate. Writers who are always imagining, or hoping, that the first draft will be the last—that the audience is already reading and judging what they're saying—lose this flexibility.

The contexts in which undergraduates write typically raise motivations to get writing done with relatively low standards (compared with those of scholars) for the kinds of academic writing they produce. These settings explain why students can complete difficult assignments at more or less the speed in which I wrote that "Mediocrity" paper for my class: roughly one page per hour. They also explain why I became so invested in imagining that what I wrote was nearly done and dreaded the prospect of revision. The settings with which we produce something affect the perceived difficulty or necessity of changing it. When writers intend to make the first draft the last, the language they use sets up quickly, like plaster. Once it takes concrete form on the page or screen, substantially changing its form seems very difficult—like destroying it and starting over. Interviews that some of my students conducted, in a study of the writing methods of freshmen, revealed these effects of the interplay of motivations and standards. At the beginning of an interview, one of these freshmen described himself as a procrastinating slacker: "When you're writing it's late, you know, and you're tired. You just want to get it done, so you say whatever. It could be garbage . . . you don't know."

At the end of the same interview, when asked if he ever revised his papers, his view of what he wrote had shifted: "No. What's there is, you know, what I really wanted to say. It's just like building a wall. So, changing it, saying something different is . . . well . . . like tearing the wall down." His writing had become, like speech, "irreversible."

We can easily see the direction in which this writer might need to change his motivations and standards. With different settings influenced by other circumstances, however, the writing we produce can become *too* malleable—like clay or even liquid—and endlessly subject to change. When I accidentally slid into the role of a student writer in my class, I felt almost palpably that my first draft was setting up in a form that was very difficult to change. For the professional article I was working on, however, there was no assignment, no looming deadline or immediate time constraint, no waiting audience with structured expectations. I had chosen to write the article for my own reasons, to communicate to other writing teachers something I considered important to say, and although I began with a fairly clear sense for what this was, my initial draft revealed further complications, doubts, and new approaches that quickly drew me back into the large loops of reading further sources, forming alternative plans, and rewriting. The mess of drafted portions I had composed were continually exploratory, and the challenge I faced was that of fitting them together in a more cohesive version, closer to something I could imagine submitting to a journal as a nearly finished product. My problem, the opposite to that of most student writers, was that the substance of language remained too soft and malleable. The intended forms of sentences and passages still melted into other forms, raising further possibilities. The poet William Stafford (1978), whose views of writing I've long admired, said "all of these things are expendable, and the more expendable you keep feeling they are, the more likely you are to have things happen to you" (p. 116). For writers like me and for many dissertation writers, in this context of professional writing, the main question is *How do you* stop *more things from happening to you? When will these versions of the article become* less *expendable and approach being finished?*

I'll try to answer these questions more directly in following chapters. Here I'll just note that our lives as writers would be much easier if we could locate these rhetorical slide switches and directly control them. When I realize that I'm obsessively fiddling with sentences in a first draft, I tell myself that I should lower my standards and get on with it—that no one else will read this version and that tinkering will be more useful later, when I actually know what I want to say. Sometimes this reminder helps, but actually altering the settings is difficult.

It's probably more realistic to say that real rhetorical conditions, combined with our individual tendencies and habits, largely control these settings. When I've abandoned struggles with a difficult project and dash off an email message, the rhetorical shift suddenly, almost automatically, transforms a plodding, fussy writer into a speedy one. I didn't make that happen. It just did, for better or worse. Most of us have suffered the consequences of electronic messages we should have composed more slowly and thoughtfully, but once we've shifted into that familiar mode of quick writing, it takes deliberate, cognitive effort to slow ourselves down. In ways we'll examine further, writers most often get into trouble when they're mindlessly using habitual settings and resulting methods inappropriate for the immediate circumstances.

For the narrow purpose of getting writing done, therefore, undergraduates usually have time (i.e., the lack of it) on their sides. The conditions that teachers and institutions attach to writing assignments largely govern the motivation levels and standards that, combined with individual circumstances, seem appropriate for completing these assignments. Real time constraints, together with perceived standards attached to grading systems, heavily determine these settings. Successful students become adept at adjusting their strategies to the specific time frames, standards, and values of different projects. They allot more time for papers they consider difficult or important and deliberately limit the time they can spend on assignments of lower value to their grades or careers. Several students have told me they tend to procrastinate for the purpose of *narrowing* the time available, because under pressure they write faster, with higher motivations and lower standards. When this tendency becomes habitual and inappropriate for the task, however, it can get them into deep trouble.

This is one of the ways in which performative writing habits developed in undergraduate work can undermine effective adjustment to the unfamiliar process of completing dissertations and other important, long-term projects in graduate programs. When students become accustomed to writing under pressure, using looming deadlines to raise their immediate motivations to write productively, they often associate writing itself with that mental (and perhaps biochemical) condition of urgency. Used strategically, the pressure of impending performance can work well for course assignments, much in the way that actors rely on certain amounts of performance anxiety to sharpen their attention on stage. But what happens if a project requires lots of sustained, productive writing, to meet higher standards, when the deadline (the performance) is still months away? At the moment, on any particular day, you may not feel sufficiently motivated, "inspired," to meet those standards. You can spend weeks or months getting ready to write. And when the deadline does loom, with the requisite doses of pressure and adrenaline, it may be too late. Writers conditioned to working under pressure tend toward unrealistic optimism about the ease and speed with which they'll write when they feel "ready" to perform. Graduate students often convince themselves that the main difference between writing undergraduate research papers and dissertation chapters is the amount of preparation necessary to meet higher standards—a premise that is partly but not entirely true. They imagine that when they're finally ready to perform, under the familiar time constraints and pressures of the "writing stage," nearly finished chapters will flow forth from this compression at the speed of their undergraduate writing. But they rarely do.

For graduate students in the humanities, for whom knowledge resides primarily in texts, these preparations for writing usually involve lots of reading, note taking, and thinking about the project, to reach the point at which they feel sufficiently authoritative and lucid to produce real works of scholarship of their own. When they begin to write, however, and what they produce doesn't meet these high standards for performance, their immediate motivations to continue writing drop, and they often revert to further reading and thinking about writing. The comparable notion in the sciences is that the "write-up" stage, of packaging knowledge previously assembled, won't require much time or revision after all the results are in, the data is thoroughly analyzed, and knowledge claims are established. But scientists also have to introduce and substantiate these claims within disciplinary reference frames, in ways that will survive the scrutiny of experts. Meeting these standards, with accurate phrasing and references to previous research, takes more time and revision than novices might imagine, in processes that bear little resemblance to the "write-up" of an undergraduate lab report.

For graduate students who fall into these traps of postponement, the most common remedies offered by self-help books or friends are to set incremental, imaginary deadlines or follow regimens for time and output, as Steinbeck did. In terms of our rhetorical settings, the theory is that self-imposed rules will move those slide switches into more productive relations. Imagined deadlines should raise our immediate motivations to write by increasing the sense of urgency. Strict regimens for time or quantities of writing should lower our standards for whatever we're producing at the moment, to prevent critical assessment of its worth from undermining our motivation to continue.

Trying to meet a deadline or follow a regimen is certainly more productive than just waiting until you feel up to the task. On the other hand, if these strategies just feel like psychological tricks to make you more disciplined or competent than you would otherwise be, they aren't likely to work. The trouble with imagined, self-imposed deadlines is that we know they're imaginary. A large proportion of the graduate students who set these deadlines fail to meet them, and this failure can appear to confirm their suspicions that the real problem is that they're inept, undisciplined, or unprepared for such a daunting task. Just forcing yourself to produce requisite quantities of material each day can produce a lot of writing, but as I've observed in my own tendencies, these exploratory drafts won't necessarily make sense or fit together. I've known dissertation writers who've produced hundreds of pages in this fashion, but producing more of this "expendable" writing made the task of assembling a complete, cohesive draft around a central argument increasingly difficult, not less.

We can think of such strategies as attempts to make an unfamiliar process seem more familiar to former student writers, accustomed to writing in narrower time constraints, with higher motivations to get the task done and lower standards for the product. Sustained, productive writing is certainly a requirement for getting a dissertation done. Thinking about writing, reading, and preparing to write may be necessary; but in themselves these activities won't produce anything. Whether these strategies succeed or fail depends on other factors, and old ways of thinking about what we're doing have sneaky ways of undermining our efforts to break these habits. New, effective ways of writing develop most reliably from awareness of what we're actually doing: from familiarizing ourselves with the unfamiliar.

References

Baker, S. (1990 [1962]) *The practical stylist* (7th ed.). New York, NY: Harper & Row.

Barthes, R. (1977). Writers, intellectuals, teachers (S. Heath trans.). In *Music-image-text* (pp. 190–191). New York, NY: Hill and Wang.

Bartholomae, D. (1985). Inventing the university. In M. Rose (ed.), *When a writer can't write.* (pp. 134–165). New York, NY: Guilford Press.

Brereton, J. C. (ed.). (1995). *The origins of composition studies in American college, 1875–1925: A documentary history*. Pittsburgh, PA: University of Pittsburgh Press.

Elbow, P. (1973). *Writing without teachers.* New York, NY: Oxford University Press.

Lunsford, A. A. & Lunsford, K. J. (2008). Mistakes are a fact of life: A national comparative study. *College Composition and Communication, 59* (4), 781–806.

Schlosser, E. (1989). *Fast food nation.* New York, NY: Houghton Mifflin.

Sommers, N. (1980). Revision strategies of student writers and experienced adult writers. *College Composition and Communication*, 31 (4), 378–388.

Stafford, W. (1978). *Writing the Australian crawl: Views on the writer's vocation.* Ann Arbor, MI: University of Michigan Press.

Steinbeck, J. (1989). *Working days: The journals of* The Grapes of Wrath *1938–1941* (Robert DeMott ed.). New York, NY: Viking.

3 The Rhetoric of Graduate and Professional Writing

Turning Points

While all of you are former undergraduates, you also represent a very small subset—about 5 percent—of college graduates who chose and were chosen to pursue PhDs. Although most of you were subject to the general conditions for student writing I've described earlier, collectively you were not typical college students. Most of you attended excellent colleges or universities with strong undergraduate programs in your fields, and in those schools, you performed exceptionally well, with high grades and other strong credentials for advanced studies. In other words, you were unusually successful, accomplished undergraduates who adapted to academic work in ways that matched admissions criteria in your doctoral programs.

These common levels of accomplishment do not mean, however, that all of you wrote extensively or even very successfully in your undergraduate programs. As a rule, graduate admissions criteria reflect the priorities of undergraduate studies in their fields. Because fields of the humanities, for example, usually assume that knowledge resides in texts, which are also objects of research, undergraduates read and write extensively in these courses, and grades are based primarily on the qualities of their writing. Applicants' language skills and undergraduate performances as writers are therefore central criteria for graduate admissions as well. Because scholars in the sciences locate sources of knowledge in the world—its objective (or hypothetical) features and phenomena—they tend to view writing as the epiphenomenal "write-up" or packaging of this knowledge for purposes of communication. Beyond early completion of writing and breadth requirements, undergraduate majors in these fields may produce very little written work. Apart from lab reports, perhaps, their grades are based primarily on exams and problem sets, and graduate admissions criteria in these fields emphasize measures of applicants' scientific and technical knowledge and mathematical skills. Priorities of the social sciences, as usual, are distributed between these poles, from qualitative social and cultural studies to fields of highly quantitative and experimental research. Weak language skills are impenetrable barriers to graduate admission in some of these disciplines but not in others, and as a consequence, college graduates enter doctoral programs with radically different levels of training and experience in writing.

At advanced levels of every doctoral program or before, however, the production of acceptable written work—in the forms of dissertations, research articles, proposals, and conference papers—becomes essential to success: just as important and time consuming in physics or civil engineering as in history or comparative literature. Whether you wrote constantly or rarely in your undergraduate studies, all of you must become productive, effective writers in order to complete PhDs.

This fact is one basis for my argument that the skills and strategies that get you into doctoral programs differ from the ones that will get you through these programs and beyond. Taken alone, however, this observation would suggest that graduate students with the least training and experience in writing will have the most trouble completing PhDs, especially in later stages of their programs. On average, then, we might expect to find the lowest PhD completion rates and the longest completion times among candidates in STEM fields, in which international students still learning to use English as a foreign language are also most numerous.

Instead, the opposite is true. In fields that emphasize writing ability and experience in undergraduate work and graduate admissions, PhD completion rates are about 15 percent lower than those in the sciences, and completion times are considerably longer, by one to two years. Candidates in the humanities are also most likely to drop out of their programs in the dissertation stage, when writing is the main challenge remaining. International students, in turn, complete PhDs at a higher rate than "domestic" students.

Although many factors contribute to these patterns, they strongly suggest that undergraduate experiences and accomplishments in writing do not reliably reduce, much less prevent, writing difficulties in advanced graduate work; nor do limited experience or weak language skills necessarily prevent efficient completion of PhD requirements. We might conclude that the ability to get effective writing done isn't a significant factor in the success or failure of doctoral candidates after all; but we know this can't be true. Texts such as research proposals, dissertation monographs, constituent research articles, or conference papers are unavoidable requirements for all PhDs. And while standards for the quality of this work aren't always as high as those for publication, they are considerably higher than the standards for undergraduate writing in the same fields.

The rhetorical transition I've described in general terms helps to account for these peculiar patterns, and we'll now consider the changes involved more closely. If writing becomes a fundamentally different kind of endeavor in advanced graduate work, these changes can diminish, or even erase, the advantages of skills candidates developed in undergraduate programs. If writing in advanced studies poses new challenges to all doctoral candidates, in turn, those with limited writing experience are not necessarily disadvantaged, especially if awareness of their limitations makes them more open to the development of new skills and strategies.

In comparisons with their undergraduate writing, graduate students usually attribute the much greater time and effort they expend on their dissertations to the inherent difficulty and complexity of this work, along with the higher standards they must meet at this level. While these factors are obviously relevant, they can be used to rationalize all uses of time and effort in the process.

> *Why are you having so much trouble with this chapter?*
> *Because it's so complicated and hard to write.*
>
> *Why did you spend the past two weeks reading instead of writing?*
> *Because I didn't know enough to write this section.*
>
> *Why don't you show this draft to your advisors?*
> *Because it isn't yet good enough.*

The simple facts that dissertation projects are bigger, more complex, and subject to higher standards don't fully explain why completing them may take three years rather than three weeks or three months. Nor can they distinguish productive effort from wasted effort, or productive uses of time from counterproductive ones. They can't tell us, for example, whether further reading at a particular stage in the process is necessary for moving the project forward or a form of procrastination and avoidance that brings the work to a standstill. The long process of completing a dissertation involves innumerable decisions about what you do *now*, in the time available for this work. Collectively, these decisions determine how long the process will take, most of the difficulties you'll encounter along the way, and the qualities of the work you produce. I've known graduate students who spent weeks writing and revising chapters that undermined the cohesion of their dissertations, delayed its completion, and were eventually deleted from the finished versions. I've known many others who spent months reading and taking elaborate notes on references of little relevance to their projects, assembling masses of material they would never use, and then struggling to figure out how to fit this nearly random collection of pieces together into a single, coherent form. Through their ongoing decisions about uses of their time, they had created most of the difficulty, complexity, and delay they attributed to the inherent nature of the task at hand.

To make more thoughtful, productive decisions, we need to examine the rhetorical features of these tasks more closely. In the unfamiliar process of completing these long-term projects, past experiences and strategies set a variety of traps for graduate students to fall into. We'll begin, therefore, by revisiting the forms and reference frames of academic writing, to observe the specific changes involved in producing works of scholarship and the kinds of work necessary in the process.

Forms, Frames, and Movement: Where Do We Begin and, From There, Where Do We Go?

For several years, I taught a summer course for entering PhD students in chemistry who were appointed as teaching assistants in general chemistry lab sections the following term. My class, on writing chemistry, was part of a larger six-week TA training program, run by Stan Marcus, with several hours of classes each day. My class was ostensibly about teaching and evaluating scientific writing in student lab reports, but these reports were supposed to simulate forms of professional writing that the graduate students in my class would need to produce in coming years. Because they were preparing to become both teachers and writers, we spent most of our time reading and discussing examples of student reports and research articles from chemistry journals and analyzed the rhetorical similarities and differences between these kinds of scientific writing.

The lab manual for this general chemistry course, like most others, promised that experiments and reports would introduce students to scientific methods: experimental procedures, scientific reasoning, record keeping, replicability, and communication of findings. But what did these novice scientists hope to find out? In a course taught to several hundred students each year, in sections led by a battalion of TAs, the experiments were designed to teach what was already known: to introduce basic concepts and questions with predictable answers, through highly structured procedures that minimized risks of explosions and other mishaps. The lab manual prescribed a standard format for scientific reports, consisting of a brief *abstract*, followed by an *introduction* to the subject of the experiment and its question or hypothesis, sequential description of the *methods* and equipment used, an account of the *results*, and a brief *discussion/conclusion*, with error analysis. Other instructions included guidelines for presenting equations and figures. As I've noted, this standard format for scientific reports closely resembles the "five-paragraph theme" model for student essays, with narrower body paragraphs framed by the funnel-shaped introduction and conclusion:

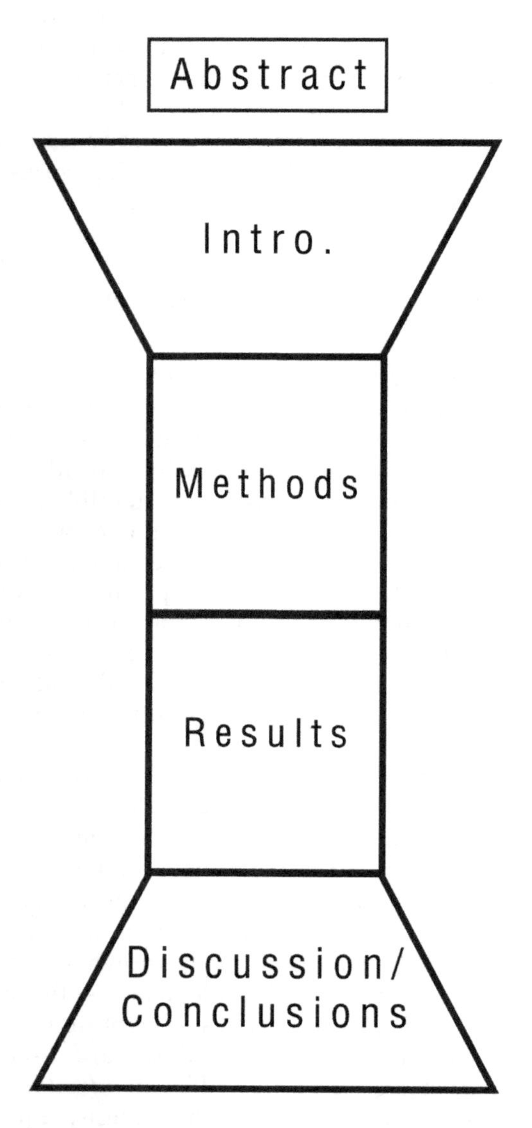

Figure 3.1 Experimental Report Template

The system for grading these reports allotted certain numbers of potential points for each section, awarded for essential, accurate information located in the correct section. Points awarded for each section were noted in the margin and added up as the overall numerical grade—as 19, for example, out of 25. This highly quantified system was meant to promote fairness within and across sections and to minimize complaints from competitive, grade-conscious students, most of whom hoped to get into medical schools.

The published research articles these graduate students chose for distribution to the class represented various subfields—organic, inorganic, physical, and analytical chemistry or chemical biology—with some structural differences governed by the nature of the studies and journal guidelines. As a rule, however, the structures of these research articles conformed to the sequence of five components prescribed as models for scientific reports in the undergraduate lab manual. Abstracts were followed by funnel-shaped introductions, narrower methods and results sections, and broader conclusions. Student writers also tried to simulate the conventional style of these professional articles: detached, objective reporting of facts, procedures, and reasoning. To this extent, it would seem that undergraduates were learning the basics of scientific research, reasoning, and communication, in forms comparable to the work of real chemists. When we moved beyond formal similarities to compare the rhetorical features of these student reports and professional articles, however, fundamental differences became obvious.

Although this kind of rhetorical analysis was unfamiliar to graduate students in chemistry, it wasn't difficult. All of them had written undergraduate lab reports at this level and had read many published research articles. Several had co-authored publications with their professors, either in undergraduate studies or in master's programs. Asked to compare student reports and professional articles, they responded quickly, and their answers to my questions were so consistent that I can reliably summarize them:

- Why is the writer writing?

  Student: To complete the assignment, demonstrate knowledge, and get a decent grade.

  Scholar: To communicate new, significant findings in the field; to enhance professional status; to bolster credentials for tenure or promotion to higher ranks.

- For what audience?

  Student: The teacher/TA.

  Scholar: Other experts in the field, journal editors, and potential peer reviewers of the manuscript.

- With what authority?

  Student: High school chemistry, understanding of relevant course material and of this experiment, and lab manual instructions.

  Scholar: General knowledge of chemistry and related fields; specialized expertise in this research area and of previous research of the subject; the author's unique design, experience, and "ownership" of this study.

- Through what process?

  Student: Usually one more or less corrected draft.
  Scholar: Multiple drafts and revisions, before and after peer reviews or resubmissions, sometimes to different journals.

- In what time frame?

  Student: Three to four hours or less.
  Scholar: Months.

Although the answers to these questions are fairly obvious, they focused attention on factors that formal similarities obscure, and they led to deeper questions about forms and reference frames in research-based writing. In this introductory lab course, for example, the manual instructions and grading system inadvertently encouraged students to think of the typical sections of a scientific report as containers for distinct categories of information. To get grading points, writers just needed to put correct information, findings, or equations somewhere in the right containers. To fill those prescribed, labeled containers, students could practice what they sometimes call a "memory dump." As a consequence, the sections of student reports we read were often incoherent jumbles of information, but the grading system offered teachers no means to evaluate and encourage factors such as cohesion or clarity of phrasing. When my students used this system in practice grading exercises, therefore, the grades they assigned to the same report were surprisingly inconsistent. Outlier grades sometimes differed by ten points out of 25. These results suggested that there were other hidden, qualitative factors involved, both in scientific writing and in grading.

When we discussed published articles, in turn, these graduate students were most impressed by the ones that were easiest to follow, even if the subject was complex or unfamiliar. Apart from the relative importance of their findings, the best articles, we observed, were the most clearly and directly "voiced." We could sense the writer writing, taking responsibility for directing the flow of information and guiding us through the constituent sections, pointing out what was important, anticipating confusion or skepticism, and orchestrating our attention, like a good tour guide. As George Gopen and Judith Swan (1990) explained in their detailed analysis of these qualities, "The Science of Scientific Writing," the framing, sequence, and flow of information is important at every level, from the structure of a sentence to that of the entire article. The same qualities characterized research articles that professors in several disciplines chose when I asked them to show me examples of "good writing" in their fields. Although the forms, subjects, and styles of these publications varied radically, all of them were beautifully voiced. The movement of the writing supported and directed the movement of reading, even through very unfamiliar territory. Recognition of these transdisciplinary qualities led me to attempt what had previously seemed impossible: a general definition of Good Academic Writing.

> Good writing establishes a clear point of departure, points the reader's attention in a certain direction, and sustains reading in that direction toward a destination.

This definition was reinforced by a conversation with the historian Bernard Lewis, following a lecture he delivered on the use and misuse of the term "fundamentalism" in reference to Islam. Lewis appeared to be speaking almost spontaneously and informally, rarely looking at notes on one slip of paper smaller than a postcard; but his talk was extremely clear, seamlessly organized, and reached its conclusion on schedule, nearly to the minute. In a meeting I requested, I asked Lewis how he prepared for this talk and what was on that slip of paper. Surprised and amused by the questions, he replied that when he had decided on a topic, he usually went for a walk and considered where the talk would begin, where it would end, and how he would get there. "That's what I write on the piece of paper," he said, "and it's the same for writing . . . even for books."

The apparent ease with which Lewis accomplished such feats relied on extensive knowledge and an extraordinary memory for names, dates, and passages of text—resources that seem to validate students' beliefs that accomplished publications and lectures represent brilliant utterance, emerging from a wealth of knowledge. For reasons we'll explore further, this ease is more often an illusion, and vast knowledge can make the task of writing more complex and difficult, not less. What I found most interesting at the time, however, was that Lewis described academic writing and speaking essentially as narration: storytelling.

This emphasis on narration isn't surprising in fields such as history, concerned directly with events and chronologies, but sections of research articles, books, and dissertations in most other fields also include histories and other chronological sequences. Introductions or literature review sections usually present histories of research leading to their central questions, and methods sections (or chapters) often describe temporal sequences of procedures. Writing itself is a linear sequence of words and sentences, from a beginning to an end, and reading, like listening, follows that journey over time.

In the stories that scholars tell, however, points of departure, destinations, and the journeys between are not necessarily historical or chronological. When we compared those chemistry research articles in our class, we observed that their sections represented a predictable way of telling a story of discovery. Following the preliminary abstract, which functions as a brief synopsis of the tale, the sections can be read as answers to a series of standardized questions:

- What were you doing and why?
- How did you do it?
- What did you find out?
- What do these results mean, and where should they lead us in the future?

As accounts of knowledge production, these research narratives typically lead us, in the introduction, from what was previously *known* to an *unknown* (the research question). The following methods section (or theoretical model, or interpretive framework) presents a *way of knowing*, followed by resulting *new knowledge*. The discussion/conclusion moves from the significance of these "findings" to *what remains unknown*, for future research. Presented as answers to the questions listed above, the resulting statements represent a narrative, epistemological outline for an entire article or dissertation:

- Here's what scholars have previously learned or come to believe about this subject.
- Here's a significant question that remains unanswered.
- Here's how I tried to answer this question.
- Here's what I learned.
- Here's what this finding means and what we (scholars in the field) don't yet understand.

The cast of this standard research narrative consists of research specialists and theorists who have collectively worked on assembling solutions to a complicated puzzle. They have succeeded up to a point, but you, the author, have identified a part of this puzzle that remains unsolved. The body of your work presents the research strategies and results it contributes to this collective endeavor, and the conclusion acknowledges remaining questions, as lines of inquiry that you and others should pursue further. Temporal movement through the work usually carries us from past to present to future.

This basic narrative structure is rooted in the earliest, broadly "scientific" communications in the 17th-century journal *Philosophical Transactions of the Royal Society*. With lots of variations it persists across the sciences and most of the social sciences, with more substantial variations in the humanities. Research questions or problems can be replaced by *hypotheses* that remain untested, *arguments* that contribute to debates, or *issues* that need attention. Rather than simply adding to existing knowledge, the author may intend to falsify previous claims or make a new argument, based on alternative methods, theoretical positions, or new interpretations of data or texts. "Methods" might consist of mathematical or theoretical models, interpretive perspectives, or ways of reading. Formal section headings in scientific articles might disappear in other fields or become chapter titles in books or dissertations. The information in this standard narrative sequence might get strategically moved around, for dramatic effect or by disciplinary convention. Work in literary studies, for example, might begin with the central question or with a specific passage the author intends to examine, and then broaden to literature review of previous studies, theoretical approaches, or related issues. But these are variations of fundamentally similar kinds of stories that scholars tell about their research, and the best writers among them are in this sense the best storytellers.

To tell a good story and figure out where to begin, of course, you have to know what it's about and what makes it potentially interesting to your intended readers. This is the main work of an introduction, which frames everything that follows. To understand why this introductory framing can become difficult for scholars, and much easier for students, we should look at the forms and functions of these "points of departure" more closely.

If you look back at those diagrams of student lab reports and five-paragraph themes, you'll notice that the funnel of the introduction descends from a line: a given point of departure and lid, of sorts, for the following content. For student writers, figuring out where to draw this line is relatively easy. Lab manual instructions usually provide the question this section will introduce, along with the central concepts, substances, and procedures involved in answering this question. The challenge of introducing this lab report on "Iron Ore Analysis by Titration of Dichromate," for example, was simply that of explaining the given topic of the experiment in a logical order. The student sensibly began with a textbook definition of titration and moved toward its specific use in the experiment:

> Titrations are a useful way of determining exactly how much of a specific substance is in an unknown sample. Potentiometric titrations work effectively when dealing with substances which can undergo oxidation reduction reactions. The standardized titrant solution is used to first titrate a known sample of the specific substance in order to determine the endpoint potential. The titrant solution is then used to titrate the unknown sample . . . In our lab the substance is iron and the titrant used is potassium dichromate.

The same pattern applies to essay assignments in the humanities or social sciences. In the explicit British phrasing, such assignments usually "set a question" the student should answer and indicate the frame of reference, such as relevant readings and issues, in which this question becomes significant. Writers can sometimes begin by simply rephrasing the assignment. When students have more freedom and responsibility to design an experiment or choose a topic, as in research papers, the task of framing and beginning is somewhat more complex, but for this purpose limited background knowledge and low standards for the significance of their work offer advantages. A paper can begin with explanation of the topic or issue one has chosen, with an "apt quotation," common knowledge, a sweeping generalization ("From time immemorial, fire has been both a benefit and a threat to mankind."). The following reference frame, leading to the "thesis" of the paper, can be constructed from the sources one has gathered in the "research stage" of this project. Once student writers have settled on specific topics, they can begin at almost any level of broader generalization that accommodates the knowledge and references they happen to possess. Beyond this teacher in the context of this course, the writer isn't really accountable to anyone, and drawing that line isn't difficult when you don't know much more than what the paper will say. The typical student paper is at once comparatively easy to construct and of little real significance because it is self-contained, imagined communication, like the argument of a speaker shouting from a soapbox in an empty park.

When you are actually writing *in* a discipline (not just about one) and are accountable for the validity and significance of what you say, the task of constructing a viable introduction becomes crucial to the quality and future of the project. Because you need to bring the significance of this study into focus within a much broader, implicit frame of reference, figuring out where to begin and how to frame this significance is an acquired skill for which the student strategy (including most of what you know) is an unreliable guide. What experienced scholars choose to tell us in a particular study represents a very small portion of the knowledge they have assembled over years of immersion in a discipline. Recalling those general chemistry lab reports at one end of a spectrum, imagine at the opposite extreme what writing a research article means for a scientist who is the principle investigator (PI) of a large, long-standing research group. For senior scholars in these fields, résumés of 200 or 300 co-authored publications are fairly common, and I knew one chemist who had published more than 1000 research articles and other communications. When we diagram the reference frames in which individual writing projects come into focus, we can see that any one of them represents a small area of explicitly relevant knowledge, overlapping with the reference frames of other publications in various stages of development. In and outside the sciences, productive scholars often have two or more research projects underway, each of which might yield a number of related publications:

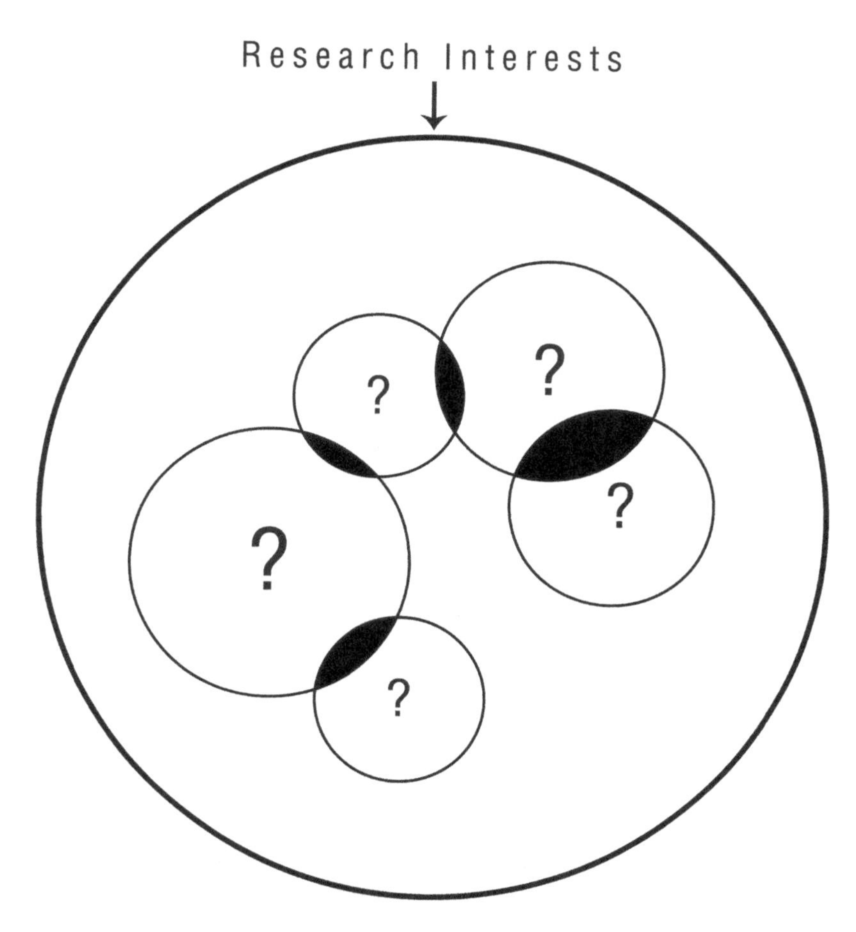

Figure 3.2 Multiple Projects in One Area

Each of these writing projects requires the identification of a distinct, focused research question the writer intends to answer, framed for a particular audience and purpose, often for a specific publication, and within a much broader body of knowledge in this and related fields. Prolific scholars become adept at recognizing, even in early stages of research, the focus and structure of potential publications in what might otherwise remain an entangled maze of inquiries, ideas, and findings.

I use this extreme example of multiple research and writing projects to emphasize that the same principles and strategies apply to PhD candidates, as novice scholars, who are working on one dissertation project. Whether this project is a monograph or a collection of related articles, it's especially important for you to realize that these focused questions and reference frames rarely identify themselves or emerge naturally from the process of expanding one's knowledge. In advanced graduate work and beyond, the process of writing no longer begins with "given" questions and reference frames, and the process of "discovery" in real research is therefore creative and constructive, not just receptive. A professor in experimental science once complained to me that undergraduate lab courses define an experiment, and therefore an experimental report, as "the shortest distance between a known problem and a known solution." The increasingly condensed, linear formats of research articles help to sustain that illusion that the research they describe began with known questions and efficient procedures that led to definitive answers. But these conventional stories about the research were usually *constructed* from a more complicated mess of educated guesswork and revision, even of the question one hoped to answer. This process is complicated further by equipment failures, miscalculations, unpredicted variables, and ambiguous results. When you start out with a hypothetical question at point A, you can only guess what and where point B (the answer) will be, and when it isn't what or where you predicted, you have to reformulate the question or choose a different route, with revised methods. In all writing in all fields of scholarship, the accomplished, constructed product conceals more than it reveals about the convoluted process through which it actually came about.

When we revisit those funnel-shaped introductions to student papers, therefore, the most misleading component for real scholarship is that horizontal line at the top that defines a given point of departure. For you as dissertation writers, as for all scholars, those narrowing lines on the sides of the funnel don't descend from a given lid. Rising and expanding from any specific research question, these vectors extend potentially to infinity, through intersecting realms of knowledge, inquiry, and reference of potential relevance to your study and with implications of increasing complexity. Understanding the goals of a particular labor movement at a specific time in a particular country, for example, becomes relevant in relation to the histories of labor movements before and after, within the broader economic, political, and social contexts of that place. This contextual significance invites comparisons with labor movements in other countries, in or outside its region, and these comparisons raise broader, theoretical issues in fields of labor history, economics, sociology, and political studies. Through ascending levels, a focused case study of one labor movement becomes increasingly entangled with widening realms of knowledge and debate that cross boundaries of time, space, and discipline.

In this maze of interrelated, potentially relevant lines of inquiry, where should your writing begin? Where should you draw the line between the implicit and explicit reference frames of this study? What areas of knowledge and reference should your introduction include and exclude? And how much do you need to know—to read or to reread—before you can answer these questions and begin to write?

To make these decisions efficiently, it helps to know how the introductions to works of scholarship are typically structured and the logical order in which they come about.

In the finished product, the conceptual structure of an introduction/literature review, which frames everything that follows, begins by defining the *area of research* in which its research question becomes significant. *Review* of published research or debate in this area leads to the identification of a *knowledge gap*: an unanswered question or an unresolved argument. The definition of this knowledge gap introduces the explicit research *question*, working *hypothesis*, or informed *argument* at the center of your study:

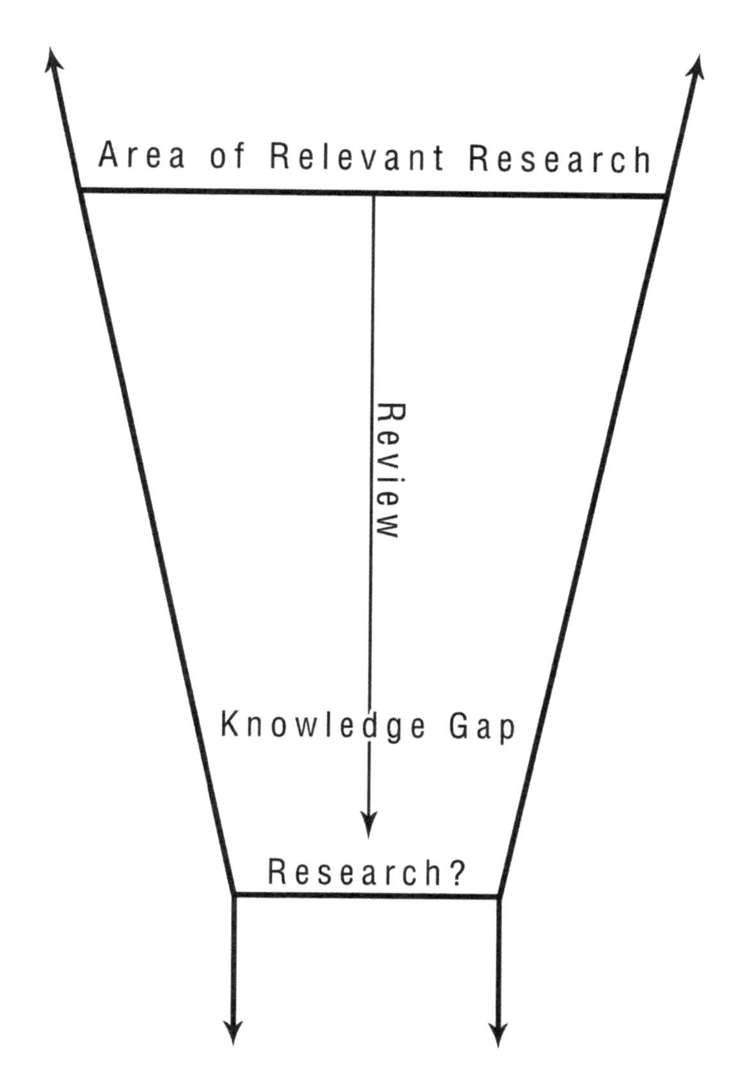

Figure 3.3 Conceptual Structure of an Introduction

Regardless of the way you present the components of this conceptual framework, they should be clear to your readers before they enter the more specific discussions of research methods, results, data analysis, or arguments in the body of your work. If they can't identify a focused research question or position, readers won't know what your study is about. Without a convincing rationale for its significance in your field and the identification of a knowledge gap or unresolved issue, a research question immediately raises another question: *So what?*

Experienced readers become very efficient at locating these components in predictable places, which vary from one discipline to another, and they become frustrated just as quickly when they can't find them. The reader's interest and patience for reading more detailed explanations in the body of the work depends on the strength and clarity of this introductory framework. In fields of the sciences and quantitative social sciences, most likely to present this structure in the order I've described, one can therefore "read" a research article or dissertation monograph—well enough to identify its central goals, significance, and knowledge claims—in a couple of minutes. I once tested this theory by teaching a class of entering freshmen how to find this information in physics research articles, asking them to write a one-paragraph summary of an article in a few minutes. They could do this fairly easily, without understanding much of what the article said.

For example, read this concise introduction to the article "The Empirical Basis of Color Perception," published in the journal *Consciousness and Cognition* (Beau Lotto and Purves, 2002):

> 1. Introduction
>
> Understanding the color percepts elicited by the light coming from some region of a scene has long been complicated by the fact that such perceptions are influenced, often significantly, by the spectral *context* of the target. Thus, when two spectrally identical target patches are surrounded by regions that return different distributions of spectral power to the eye, the sensation of color elicited by the two targets is no longer the same. This phenomenon is called *color contrast*. Conversely, two targets that return different spectra to the eye, can, depending on their contexts, look a good deal more similar than when they are both presented in the same neutral context. This phenomenon is called *color constancy*. The dilemma for vision science introduced by color contrast and constancy is that the color of visual targets are clearly influenced in a complex way by their surroundings. The significance of these facts and how they might be explained has been the subject of a long and ongoing debate.
>
> The purpose of the present article is to examine recent evidence that color percepts, including contrast and constancy, are determined empirically, in this case by past experience with spectral relationships. (pp. 609–610)

The first sentence of the introduction clearly defines the research area and general problem of contextual effects on color perception. The last two sentences of the paragraph define the knowledge gap as a problem of explaining these effects, and the final, one-sentence paragraph promises to fill this gap, in part, with empirical explanation.

In fields such as history or literary studies, where the objects of inquiry are usually texts rather than phenomena, the same elements may concern unresolved questions about these texts, alternative ways of reading and interpreting them, or new evidence. In this opening paragraph of her article "Truth and Artistry in the *Diary of Anaïs Nin*," Joan Bobbitt (1982) began with an account of the currently accepted way of reading Nin's *Diary* as spontaneous expression and announced her intention to reveal an underlying "calculated artistry at work on the basis of textual evidence":

> Beginning with the publication of Volume One in 1966, the *Diary of Anaïs Nin* has inspired both popular admiration and critical effusion. Nin offers the story of her life as a celebration of subjectivity and feeling, a self-proclaimed paean to unfettered emotion. From all indications, she has been accepted at her word. Critics have called the multi-volume work "a continuous moment of intimacy," as well as "an attempt to give visible shape and embodiment to human love." The author herself has been heralded as "the closest thing we have to Venus" and "a high priestess in the House of Erotica." Upon closer examination, however, the *Diary* reveals a determined self-consciousness of design and content, a calculated artistry which is in direct opposition to Nin's espoused ideal of naturalness and spontaneity.
>
> (p. 267)

For brevity, I've chosen examples in which the authors get down to business very quickly, but you can find the same structural elements spread more widely through longer introductions as well, including introductory chapters in dissertation monographs or books. Constructing this conceptual framework is much easier in some fields than in others, and introductions and literature reviews vary in length and complexity accordingly. Some experimental scientists, for example, are trying to solve specific problems that a small number of other scholars have worked on. When they get convincing, significant results, it's relatively easy to construct an introductory history of relevant studies: the progress scholars have made thus far, the remaining knowledge gap, and the ways in which their findings fill at least part of that gap. Introductions to research articles in these fields are often very brief—sometimes only a couple of paragraphs. At the opposite extreme, in cross-disciplinary fields of the social sciences and humanities, particular research questions may have implications in a wide range of previous studies, with long and complex histories in two or more disciplines. For these research projects, introductions and literature reviews can become very long, with categorical subheads, and figuring out what to include or exclude can becomes difficult.

Regardless of these variations, however, the construction of a coherent introduction—one that clearly frames the organization and significance of your entire work—*must occur from the bottom up: from your specific research question through expanding levels of implication and reference.* In other words, the logic of this construction develops in a direction opposite to that of reading its product, which usually begins with the general and narrows to a specific question or thesis.

For this reason, you can't effectively structure an introduction (or, for that matter, other sections of a study) without first knowing what your research question is and why it's important in your field. In workshops for dissertation writers, I usually begin by giving participants about five minutes to write (preferably in one sentence) versions of the research questions their dissertations will answer. Some can complete this little exercise very quickly. Others are obviously struggling to phrase a question, as though for the first time, or fail to produce one. In following months, the students who most easily and clearly stated the central questions for their projects usually make the most efficient progress. Those who continue to work without clearly defining the focal point of their projects run into the most trouble.

Beginning doctoral students often feel that identifying potential avenues for dissertation research is premature—that they are getting ahead of themselves before they're ready to make such important decisions. But early attempts to identify research questions turn your attention in a necessary direction: toward knowledge production and the development of the kinds of thinking that lead to professional communication. Some of the most brilliant, career-making dissertations I've read developed from ideas that occurred to graduate students toward the beginning of their studies. In following years, they deliberately assembled the methodological and conceptual tools necessary to refine and answer these questions. For example, in early stages of her doctoral work, one student recognized the potential for using statistical data from either side of a dramatic political upheaval as "natural experiments" for answering previously unanswerable questions in economics and related fields. When she went on to develop the skills necessary to analyze available data sets, the results of her early inspiration became the basis for her dissertation, several research articles, and an excellent professorial position.

In workshops for entering PhD students, therefore, I encourage them to keep a special notebook or electronic document where they record interesting ideas, questions, and critical perceptions that occur to them in their coursework, reading, and conversations. For this purpose, pay attention to your own thoughts and reactions:

- When you notice that you are skeptical of an argument, recognize an interesting, unanswered question, or imagine different ways of approaching a problem, register these responses and write them down—the more of them the better.
- Pay special attention to the conclusions of current articles and books, where authors suggest remaining knowledge gaps and directions for future research.
- Periodically review the ideas you've recorded, and as your studies advance, continue to evaluate their potential as future research projects, with an eye for the ones that seem most promising and interesting to you.
- If you identify a question or argument that seems particularly important, pursue it further with focused reading or discussion with your advisors and peers, and begin to consider research methods and reference frames.

Such early preparations for dissertation work seem to invert the normative trajectory of doctoral studies in which focused dissertation topics should emerge like fruit from a mature tree, when the time is ripe. Because students know scholars primarily as teachers or as authors, schooling suggests that the stature of these authorities results from what they know. The marked stages of doctoral programs reinforce this assumption that graduate students become authorized to pursue new questions when they have completed course requirements and comprehensive exams: when they know enough to do so.

While extensive knowledge is an important foundation for scholarship, knowledge production doesn't result directly from knowing a lot. Instead, *the careers of prominent scholars result from compelling interests in what they don't yet know*: the questions they can't yet answer, the problems still unsolved, the lingering mysteries, undefined factors, unresolved arguments, and misconceptions at the frontiers of every field. Real scholarship begins with something we *don't* know, and in this respect, scholars are continually thinking ahead and working on puzzles they can't yet solve. This process of knowledge production, like that of writing, is much messier and more convoluted than the product. Scholars often begin to frame and even write portions of intended publications in early stages of research, and when they have identified significant questions they intend to pursue, they often begin to consider the journals most likely to publish the findings they anticipate. These early formulations and drafts are in some ways institutional and professional requirements. If they need funding for their research (and perhaps for you, as their research assistants), they must submit proposals that clearly state their research questions or hypotheses, their proposed methods, predicted results, and conclusions, along with explanations of the potential significance of this research in their fields. These proposals are essentially educated guesswork: drafts of professional articles on research they haven't yet completed or, in some cases, even begun. Proposals to publishers, to secure book contracts, require similar early formulations of what the writers hope to accomplish. In this sense, the process of writing typically begins before and continues throughout the process of research. The most productive scholars are often planning their future writing projects long before they have completed their current ones. This messy, exploratory, inquisitive dimension of scholarship is what I'm encouraging you to emulate, as early as possible, before you feel "ready" to wade into it. Because this dimension is largely hidden from students, even in the early stages of doctoral programs, experiences of schooling set a number of traps for graduate students.

The traps I have in mind are ones I've previously introduced as features of student writing:

- Being assigned questions and reference frames.
- Simulating knowledge and authority you don't yet possess.
- Using writing and other measures of ability to demonstrate knowledge.
- Presenting most of what you know about a topic.

For many undergraduates, the imitative posturing involved in such performances is just a requirement for meeting teachers' expectations. For the minority who aspire to become scholars, however, these experiences can cultivate an underlying sense of fraudulence they hope to overcome in their graduate programs by expanding their knowledge and becoming real authorities in their chosen fields. To reach this level of authority, from which they can ask significant questions and begin to produce knowledge, they must first learn more.

But how much more? When do you know enough about a subject to ask and answer significant questions or make compelling arguments with authority? When are you ready to commit yourself to a specific line of inquiry, research problem, or position? Because those vectors of potential relevance extend from every line of inquiry to infinity, there is no end to what you could learn or feel that you should know. And because these realms of knowledge intersect in increasingly complicated ways, impossible to represent in the conceptual framework of a focused dissertation, pursuing them beyond a certain point carries you *away* from your goal, not toward it. When you feel that you don't quite know what you are doing and run into difficulty, the most obvious but misleading explanation is that you don't yet know enough.

Although new lines of inquiry emerge from more general knowledge of research in one's field, knowledge acquisition—learning—doesn't lead directly to knowledge production, any more than collecting lumber leads directly to building something from it. You can fill a warehouse with lumber that might become useful and imagine that more of it could be even more useful, but until you decide what you want to use it for, you'll just remain an accomplished collector of lumber. Productive scholars are not just accomplished collectors of knowledge. Knowledge production requires skills and intentions quite different from the ones students develop for learning more and demonstrating that they've learned enough of what others already know.

A large proportion of the graduate students who struggle to complete dissertations are caught in this trap of trying to find something new and significant to say by learning more, which can lead to a variety of avoidable detours and dead ends in the process. In retrospect, I can now recognize the misconception that led me to spend months drafting and discarding introductions: I imagined that I could find a central focus for my dissertation from the outside in, by producing an introduction that would logically lead to it. When a draft led instead to increasingly entangled and loosely connected implications of my research, I abandoned it and tried to construct a new one, even more complex, based on further reading and thinking. Because my anthropological research was on relations between Sunni and Shia Muslims in the history of a major Indian city, these potential implications extended along those expanding vectors through entangled cultural and social theories, comparative religion, British colonialism, urban studies, and the long histories of India and Islam. Because I assumed that I should be able to write and think my way through this maze to the central thesis of my dissertation, by introducing it from the right angle, I spent most of this time reading more, then writing, rethinking, and rewriting dozens of drafts that seemed, as my standards rose with the complexity of my ideas, increasingly inadequate. One of my main problems, which I'll discuss further in Chapter 4, was isolation. I couldn't escape from this trap until I found a group of readers who could tell me what was most interesting about my work and ways of conveying that focus to others.

I've known other PhD candidates who imagined that a focused dissertation would come about if they just kept writing, while continuing to read and think about the subject. A graduate student in literary studies came to me for help with 200 plus pages of material he had drafted for a study of a particular character in a Victorian novel. The chapter drafts he produced were endlessly exploratory and circular, and the obvious reason was that he hadn't yet decided what he wanted to say about this character. The reason he hadn't, he explained, was that this novel, other novels by its author, and related novels in the period had been studied extensively. As he didn't yet know enough about this research literature or about the trends in literary theory he might apply to his own analysis, he couldn't determine whether his own ideas were sufficiently original or interesting. More reading led to more writing around the edges of the subject, without bringing him any closer to the center. When I drew for him a version of that introductory funnel with the vectors extending to infinity, he acknowledged that his approach led him out into that expanding realm of conceptual entanglements that he called (while drawing knotted lines there on my diagram) "The Squiggles": where everything he read seemed vaguely relevant and interconnected in ways he couldn't reduce to the focused, linear explanation that writing requires.

When he sensed that he was heading in that direction, therefore, I encouraged him to return to the center of his study: to his own understanding of that novel's character, from which he could build a viable frame of reference to other research. Other authors and studies of related work couldn't tell him what he should say, in a dissertation that was supposed to offer an "original contribution" to knowledge in his field. Although he imagined that it was necessary work on his dissertation, most of this exhaustive (and exhausting) reading and literature review was actually reversion to student writing: for the purpose of demonstrating to real authorities (and perhaps to himself) that he had read and learned enough to meet their expectations.

In other cases, the same insecurity about one's knowledge and authority can continually interrupt and postpone writing, to the extent that candidates who have been "working" on their dissertations for months have little or nothing to show for their effort. Every attempt to write raises nagging questions and doubts that disrupt attention to what they are doing at the moment, reduce progress to a laborious crawl, or halt it altogether. In his thoughtful, engaging book *Writing for Social Scientists* (1986), the sociologist Howard Becker recalls getting derailed by these insecurities when he used words such as "culture" and "class" in the first draft of his dissertation—on race, professional culture, and class among Chicago schoolteachers—and imagined all of the alarming questions that expert readers might ask. "If I call it culture, I'm sure to get into trouble, and I'll deserve it, because I will be saying something I might not mean" (p. 49). Rephrasing the subject in terms of "class," however, raised other concerns: "Whose version would I mean? W. Lloyd Warner's? Karl Marx's? I might decide to go back over the literature on class again before using such an expression" (p. 50). The freedom of writing in these early stages then degenerates into the anxious avoidance of imagined risks: of potential criticism, misunderstanding, or exposure of ignorance. Further reading seems beguiling and safe because it's so familiar to good students, accustomed to emulating scholarly authority by learning more. Doing something with this material, in writing, creates visible evidence of your own judgment and ability, subject to potential criticism. When I asked one graduate student why she continually stopped writing to read more background material, she thought for a moment and replied, "Because reading doesn't leave tracks." As a consequence, Becker suggests,

> Most writers, even professionals, have trouble getting started. They start over and over again, destroying reams of paper, working over the first sentence or paragraph again and again as they find each successive try unsatisfactory in some new way. They start that way because they believe there is One Right Way. If they can only find

> the Right Way to begin, they think, everything will take care of itself, all the other problems that they fear are lurking ahead of them will disappear. They set themselves up to fail.
>
> (p. 49)

The examples thus far are from fields of the humanities and social sciences, in which candidates most often produce monographs based on their own research questions and designs. Candidates engaged in collaborative research most common in the sciences, with extensive guidance in identifying research problems and methods, are less likely to fall into the traps I've described, but insecurity about one's knowledge and authority can lead to other kinds of writing difficulties in these fields as well. Lee, a doctoral candidate in computer science, came to my office because his advisor, after reading his chapter drafts, had told him he was a terrible writer and should learn the "basics" of clear communication. When I read one of Lee's chapter drafts, in the field of robotics, the sentences and passages were extremely dense and difficult for me to understand, as I expected, but they seemed reasonably organized and correct. Because he told me that his advisor was known to be an exceptionally good writer, I asked him to show me examples of his advisor's published articles on the same type of research.

The contrasts were striking. In these articles, Lee's advisor had presented the relevant concepts and problems in artificial intelligence very simply and clearly, with a brief history of previous strategies for solving these problems. Sentences and paragraphs were much shorter than the ones Lee produced, transitions were clearly marked, and important factors and logical procedures were listed in bullet points. Although this field of research was unfamiliar to me, I could have summarized the substance of these articles without difficulty. When I read a page of one of these articles aloud to Lee and then read a page of his draft, he had a sudden revelation. "Now I get it," he said. "He's trying to make very complicated work easy to understand. I've been trying to show people how complicated and difficult my work is, to make it sound smarter."

As a possible solution to this problem, I encouraged Lee to rewrite one of his chapters in his advisor's voice and style. When he expressed concern that his advisor would recognize the imitation, I predicted that he wouldn't—that it would just sound to him like better writing. Lee rewrote a chapter within a week, and his advisor was amazed by the improvement. To make sure he was on the right track, Lee revised another chapter, with the same results, and dropped my class.

Related problems, resulting from the same insecurities, become most apparent in literature review sections or chapters, used less to rationalize the significance of one's own research than to demonstrate comprehensive knowledge of other research in the field. I've seen literature reviews that read like annotated bibliographies of vaguely related studies or long, entangled summaries of theoretical trends that seem tangential to the author's work. These writers explained to me that they feel obliged to acknowledge the work of prominent scholars in their fields, with deferential nods, to establish their own entitlement to contribute to these discussions. The effect, however, is just the opposite. To the extent that literature reviews shift the reader's attention *away* from the significance of your research, in deference to the authority of others, the clarity and importance of your work will diminish. We learn what you have read, but why you are writing and why we are reading become increasingly difficult to understand.

Once you've identified the central focus of *your* research and drawn that crucial line from which its story begins, references to other research and theory should lead us logically, without detours, to the particular knowledge gap you intend to fill, the hypothesis you will test, or the misconception you will dispel. For this purpose, indulge in egocentrism. Imagine that your literature review is a symposium on the significance of *your* contributions to the field. The other scholars you invite to address *your* audience, with introductory remarks, are those whose ideas are most directly relevant to the central questions and issues *you* will raise in your keynote address, as the star of the show. Whom should you invite to speak at your symposium, and in what order? This is the main question for structuring a literature review, and you can't answer it without knowing what you intend to say.

This author-centered advice isn't just a psychological remedy for faltering confidence. The insecurities that lure graduate students into these traps are often misconstrued as predispositions or personality traits, as though graduate admissions accidentally selected for anxious, insecure overachievers. Instead, these tendencies more often result from common, transitional misconceptions about one's authority as the author. It's probably true that within the professional communities you hope to enter, you are still a novice, an aspiring scholar. In your dissertation, however, you should become the foremost expert on the focus of your own research. In relation to your role as the author, even the most accomplished luminaries in your field will be reduced to the roles of potential guest speakers you decide to exclude or include in your work, perhaps even as objects of your critical scrutiny.

The Scope and Scale of a Dissertation

When you identify the central focus of your work—even if you revise this in the process—the perceived scale of the project should diminish. The task should seem smaller and less daunting. Further work on it, including background reading, should become more purposeful and efficient. When writers feel overwhelmed by the breadth and complexity of their projects, I tell them, "You should feel that your dissertation is much smaller than you are: something you spend part of your time constructing and set aside, then return to among other things you do, in the midst of your life."

I began to offer this advice following consultations with Ellen, a PhD candidate in sociology who talked about her dissertation project as a vast complex of entangled theories, cases, and implications she was only beginning to grasp. While trying to explain what she was still preparing write, Ellen looked up toward the ceiling or out the window and waved her arms, tracing broad constellations of ideas and events across time and space, as though she were describing the structure of the universe. I could understand very little of what she was saying, and when I asked her to compose a brief statement of the central focus of her dissertation, she couldn't produce one. To explain her difficulty, Ellen used the parable of the blind man trying to comprehend an elephant: "I want to write about the whole elephant, but when I start it's just the tail, or the trunk." To better understand her conception of the project, I asked her to diagram the relations between herself, her dissertation project, and her field of research. The concentric circles she drew illustrated the problem very clearly:

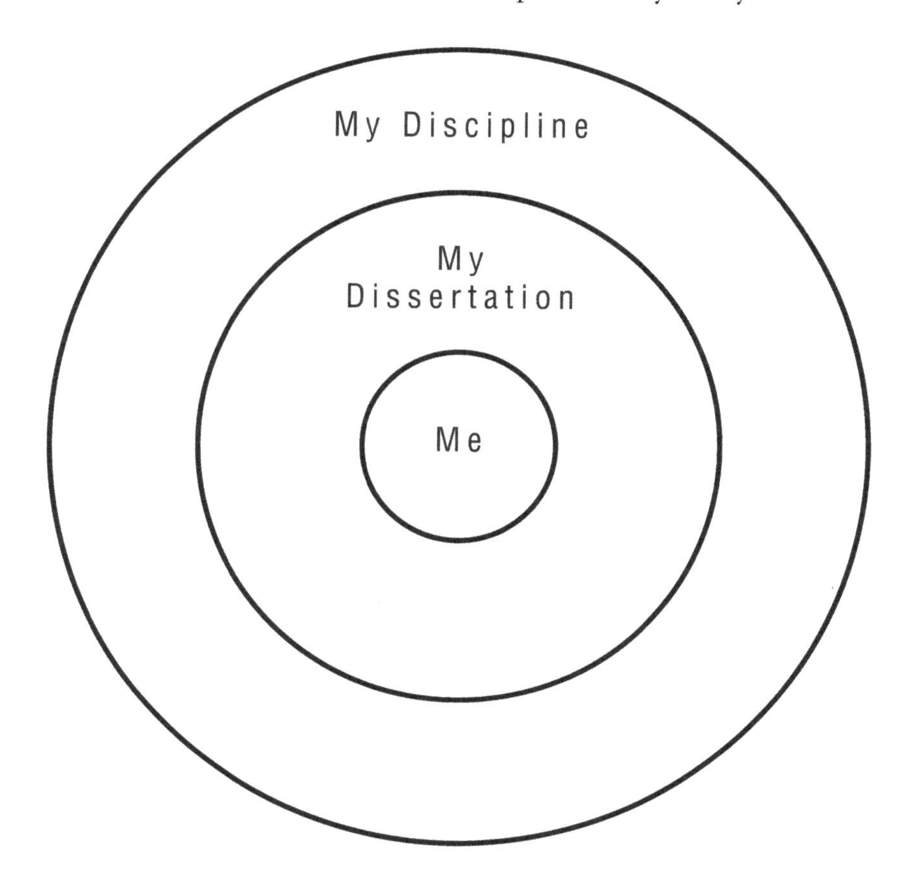

Figure 3.4 Inhabiting a Dissertation Project

From her perspective, she was enveloped by the broad dimensions of the project she was trying to complete, within the much broader dimensions of her field. She was essentially living inside her dissertation, where she spent most of her waking hours reading, thinking about her work, making notes and complex diagrams, trying to expand her comprehension of the subject to the point that she could write about it. But all of this time, thought, and effort simply expanded and complicated the project she was inhabiting, with increasing confusion and isolation. The "whole elephant" she hoped to write about would make explicit that broad reference frame she was expanding: everything she knew and had yet to learn about the subject, everything she understood and didn't yet understand. "You really don't want to live inside your own dissertation project," I told her. "For one thing, no one else will want to live in there with you. You can maybe have a cat or a goldfish." If she wanted to get this project done, I explained, the dimensions in her diagram should be reversed:

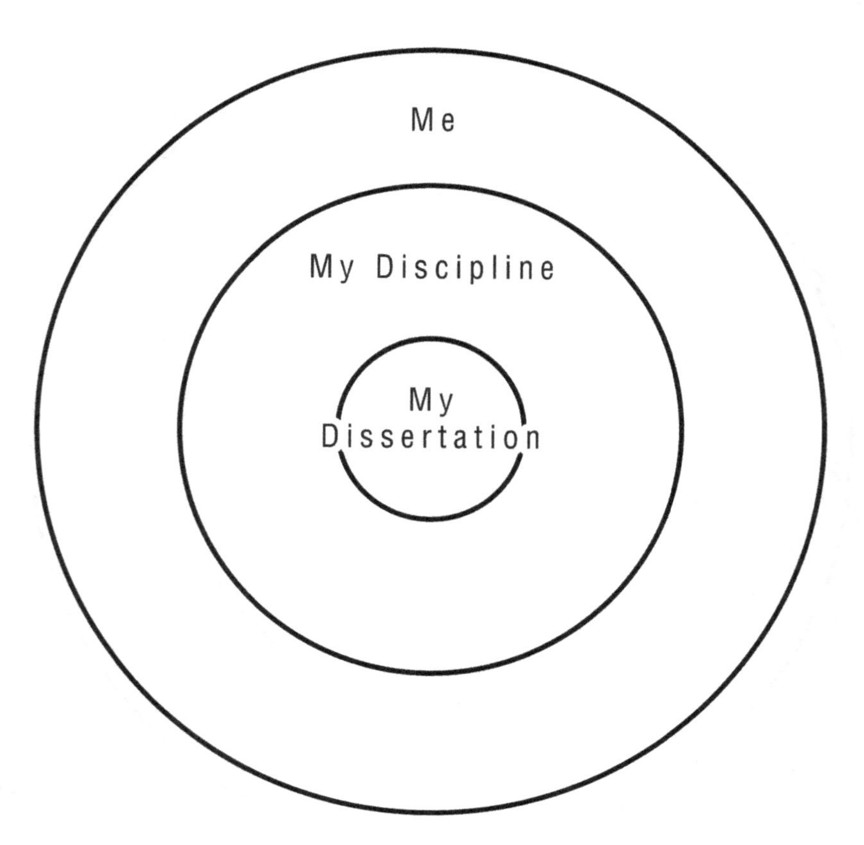

Figure 3.5 A More Productive Alternative

Her dissertation should become just one object she's constructing, within her broader studies of her research field, among other things she spent time doing in her life. To get the scale of this object reduced to viable proportions, I gave her a sheet of paper and told her to take as much time as she needed to write down the central argument of her dissertation there in my office, while I worked on something else. In the dense thickets of our tangential discussions over the past weeks, I had sensed the presence of this argument, and after 20 minutes or so she had it written down in a short paragraph: a viable theoretical position that emerged logically from her field studies.

As we talked further about ways of building a structure around this thesis, Ellen now frequently looked *down* at it, reading it over as a point of reference. When she returned a week later, she had about 20 pages of a first chapter written. She had also noticed an earlier call for proposals, due in three days, for essays in an edited volume related to her research, and because she now had a focused position to write about, she told me she had "whipped off" a proposal in a few hours. Within a couple of weeks this proposal was accepted, to her surprise, and this affirmation seemed to turn her loose as a writer. Writing about a defined position was so much easier than trying to find her way into her dissertation, through the confounding maze of related theory and research, that her sudden productivity felt vaguely fraudulent and slapdash. "Anything worth doing is worth doing badly!" she announced with a grin one day as she tossed the draft of a whole chapter onto my desk. She went on to finish a solid dissertation draft in about four months, and her advisors accepted it with minor revisions.

I wish I could claim that such transformations are typical, quick results of my advice, but even in this case the barriers to productive writing dissolved after several weeks of discussions that were often discouraging. By the time I met Ellen, that implicit, expanding reference frame had come to represent her dissertation project. She didn't feel ready to take a focused position as an author, to tell a specific story, until she had all the pieces of this complex puzzle assembled. In my own frustration and confusion as her informal advisor, I just used my authority to insist that she make the project much littler and easier to complete than she imagined it to be. I simply nudged her across a rhetorical transition she was fully prepared to make: from knowledge consumption to knowledge production.

All the while, however, I was aware that I was compensating for the negligence of advisors who had set this PhD candidate adrift in the dissertation stage and offered no help in getting her research project into focus. I'll have more to say about the roles of advisors in the following chapter. Here I'll just note that they tend to underestimate the difficulties of narrowing and focusing the dimensions of a project much bigger, more complex, and more important than anything you've done before. Without guidance in the opposite direction, you might imagine that your dissertation should convey the full range of your knowledge and potential in the field you're trying to enter. Experienced scholars with long résumés and several projects in the works have trouble recalling what it was like to be immersed as novices in one big project that might determine the trajectories of their careers. Within the whole of an experienced scholar's endeavors, the scale and reference frame of a particular project is relatively small, like crystals forming in a larger medium. For periods of time, scholars might immerse themselves in these projects, in the midst of other responsibilities. Even an ambitious project is nonetheless one thing they are currently doing, among others, and their ability to complete it depends on its conceptual and temporal confinement to certain portions of their lives, interests, and careers. A focus, necessary to make every project feasible, can only occur within a broader field of vision, through exclusion. A good story, which every work of scholarship must tell, becomes coherent and interesting through exclusion as well—what we choose *not* to say when we choose to say something. The parts of a larger story that you leave out can become other stories. In the grand scheme of one's career, articles and books lead to other articles and books, on related subjects or other pieces of a larger puzzle. Nothing you write can be about everything you know and do, and it can't be bigger than you are.

When a dissertation project is essentially your job description for two years or more—the main thing you have to do and the biggest academic project you've undertaken—it's easy to imagine that its breadth and significance should approximate the magnitude of this effort and its importance in your life. Broader and more ambitious projects will then appear to be better ones. As a consequence, dissertation writers often fear that their projects are too narrowly focused and specialized or that the significance of their research questions is too limited, but this is rarely true. *In nearly every case I can recall, struggles to complete dissertations result from trying to do too much, not too little.* When a candidate told me that she planned to study the role of the head administrator of a long colonial regime, I asked, "Which one?"

She proudly answered, "All of them!" Their roles and ideologies in successive periods differed substantially, she explained, and she had begun to see fascinating patterns of continuity and change that required comparison. Most of the substance of her research interests would be lost in a single case.

After skimming the methods section of her research proposal, however, I suggested, "Perhaps two? Or at most three?" The project she proposed was the work of an entire career, requiring archival research on unpredictable sources in three countries. A dissertation based on this material, even if she could gather and analyze it, would require separate and comparative chapters on these figures over a span of more than two centuries. I warned her that she was proposing to make her work extremely difficult, if not impossible, and reminded her that she could pursue further periods and comparisons in future studies, after her PhD. This was just her dissertation. It shouldn't become the definitive work of her career. A scowl and quick departure told me she didn't like this advice, and she eventually, reluctantly accepted it only when one of her advisors also threw cold water on her ambitions.

The problems of breadth and focus I've described arise most often in dissertation monographs on independent research projects. When PhD candidates are working in collaborative research groups and their dissertations will be collections of articles, research questions and reference frames tend to come into focus within larger projects, with direct guidance from advisors. Journal publications are also reliable, readily available models for these components of one's dissertation, for which narrowly focused studies in specialized subfields are the established norm. Many advisors in the humanities and social sciences also assign focused research problems and appropriate methods to their advisees. During my dissertation field research, adrift in a sea of possibilities, I envied a graduate student in history I met whose advisor had given him a specific question to answer about an unstudied period of 15 years.

For determining the scale of dissertation monographs, academic books aren't reliable models, especially if their authors are established scholars. Like other book publishers, academic presses have to worry about publication costs and potential sales. Even highly specialized books need to offer some general interest to scholars in their fields, along with potential use as assigned texts in advanced courses. Most academic books result from years of research and comprehensive knowledge of professional literature on their subjects. This is the main reason for which publishers rarely consider dissertations submitted as book manuscripts. Used as models for dissertation projects, these books often lure graduate students, like the one studying colonial administrators, into excessively broad and ambitious goals they can't meet at the beginning of their careers. Instead, the main purpose of a dissertation monograph, like that of a constituent article in a "paper option," is to demonstrate that you can present, primarily to your advisors, a thoroughly researched and convincing answer to a significant question or an original, convincing argument on a current issue.

As a consequence, the breadth of a dissertation monograph is often closer to that of research article in your field, offering more space than journals do to review background literature, present data analysis, elaborate your arguments, and explore implications for further research. Initial publications based on dissertation research are more likely to be journal articles or conference papers than books, and this is why conference presentations can help to clarify their scope and structure. At this stage, few of you are in positions to produce groundbreaking studies of broad significance in your fields. If you do (and this does happen) the most likely publications for this work will be major journals of general interest to scholars in your disciplines, such as *Nature* or its constituent branches, the *Journal of the American Chemical Society, The Journal of American History, Ecology*, or *American Psychologist*. In most cases, however, the purpose of a dissertation is to demonstrate your potential to become such an accomplished scholar in the future.

The most reliable models for the scope and scale of a dissertation in your field, therefore, are *other completed dissertations in your field*—especially those your advisors have approved. You don't have to read them through. Find several, and for efficiency look closely at their Tables of Contents, Abstracts, and Introductions. These components will quickly reveal the research questions, reference frames, organizational structures, and other dimensions of acceptable dissertations, including ways of introducing and concluding collections of related research articles. Because there are no standard requirements for presenting these collections, you should also consult with your advisors to determine what they expect. When I congratulated one PhD candidate in physics for filing his completed dissertation, he said, "Thanks, but it was no big deal, really. It was basically just my published articles stapled together." In other cases, however, advisors will expect extensive introductions and conclusions to the significance of your research, with thorough reviews of surrounding literature.

Conceptual Balance

Although focused research questions are essential points of departure for dissertation projects you can complete successfully, without serious difficulty, they aren't sufficient. Original and potentially important questions, hypotheses, or arguments aren't always viable bases for dissertation research and writing. Some of these questions are extremely difficult or impossible to answer. Sometimes, information necessary to answer them doesn't exist, is too difficult to acquire, or is too complex to analyze. Viable research questions must also be focused and significant within reference frames in a particular discipline, where they emerge from remaining knowledge gaps and make sense within current theoretical frameworks. These specialized fields and subfields also require particular research methods necessary to establish validity. Arguments or claims based entirely on qualitative methods, for example, won't fully convince scholars who, on theoretical grounds, require quantitative evidence. Every viable dissertation project therefore requires balanced relations among these factors: a potentially significant *research question*, the *sources and methods* used to answer this question, and the *conceptual framework* in which such questions and answers become significant. Because dissertation research is usually highly specialized and addressed to a small audience of scholars in a subfield of a discipline, criteria for this balance can be quite narrow.

To clarify these factors for PhD candidates, the Danish scholar Lotte Rienecker (2003) juxtaposed them in triangular relations between *The Question, The Discipline, and The World*:

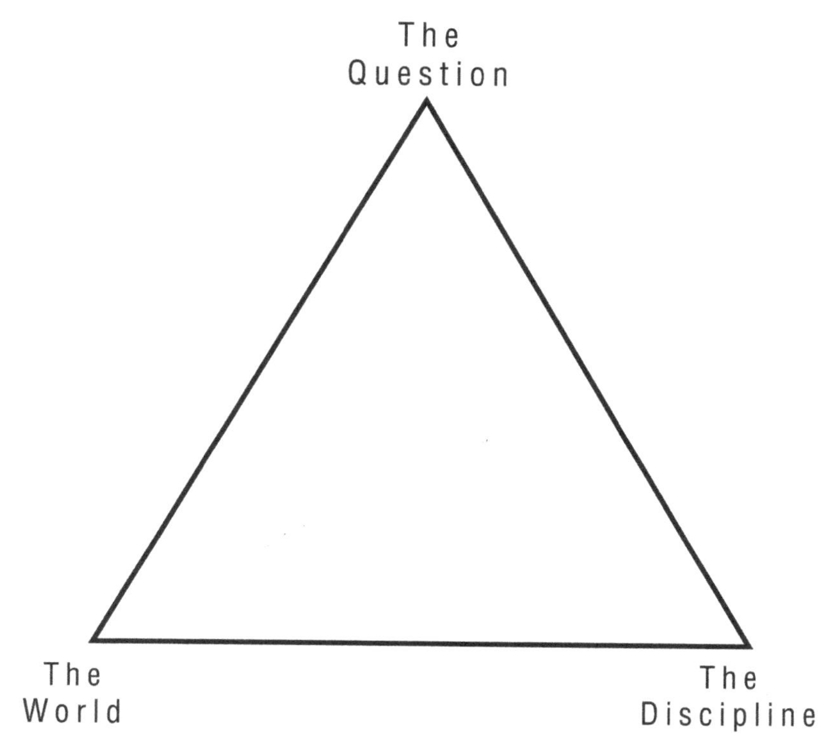

Figure 3.6 Conceptual Balance Triangle

- *The Question*, of course, is the one you place at the center of your research, as your reason for pursuing it.
- *The Discipline* is the conceptual framework—the body of theory, practice, and current knowledge—in which such questions are raised, answered, and become meaningful.
- *The World* represents what these questions are about: the objects of research, phenomena, and sources of information that you hope to understand. These objects of inquiry can be features or phenomena of the natural world, or they may be aspects of human cognition, social or cultural phenomena, or texts of diverse kinds (including archives and data sets, works of art or literature, musical scores, or historical documents).

In this form, our triangle leaves the important role of research methods somewhat undefined. Rienecker includes research methods as features of the discipline, but many of these methods (such as interviews, surveys, microscopy, or mathematical modeling) are broadly interdisciplinary. When I've presented this triangle in graduate and faculty workshops, therefore, participants have often observed that *The Methods* should constitute a fourth point of reference that connects the other three. Particular methods are indeed features and standard tools of disciplines, but they also become appropriate or inappropriate for studying particular kinds of phenomena and for answering particular kinds of questions. To represent these complex relations, a revised diagram might place *The Methods* at the center, as a crucial point of connection among the other three:

Attention to the relations among these factors sharpens our critical perceptions of the strengths and weaknesses of our own projects and those of other scholars. The quality and cohesion of every study depends on the balanced, logical relations between its central question, the conceptual framework in which the question and answer become meaningful, the sources of information necessary to answer this question, and the methods used gather this information. These relations are common bases for critical reading and for reviews of

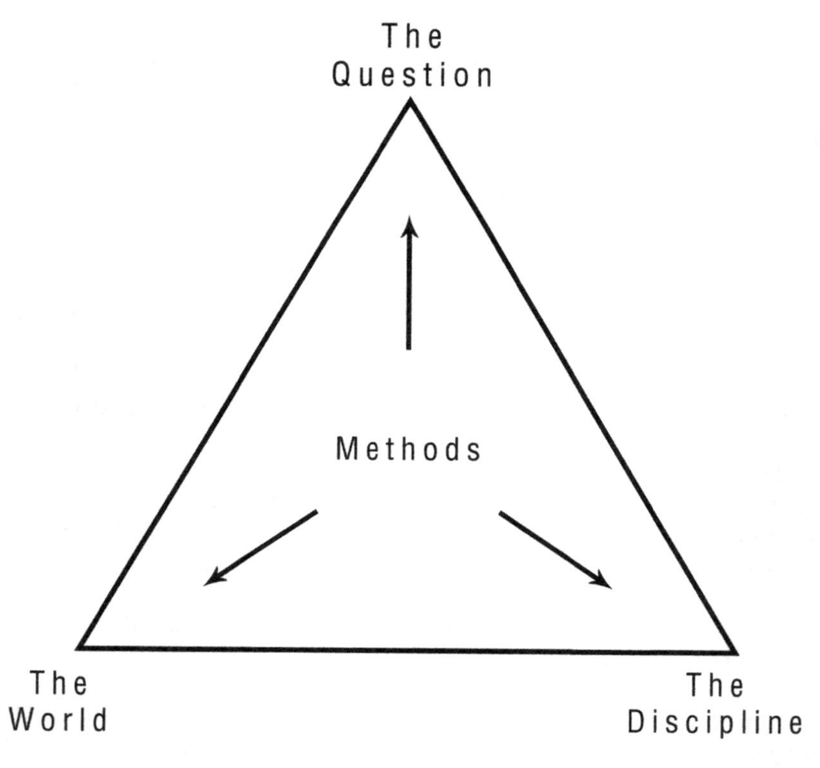

Figure 3.7 Revised Triangle with Methods

published work or submitted manuscripts and proposals. To evaluate this work, readers most often ask relational questions:

- Is the question significant and conceptually grounded in the author's discipline?
- Has the author identified sources of information sufficient to provide convincing answers and knowledge claims?
- Are the methods used appropriate for gathering and analyzing this information, according to standards for validity in this field?

Critical reviews typically point out imbalances or disconnections among these factors:

- The evidence presented isn't sufficient to support the knowledge claims or arguments.
- The methods used don't produce convincing evidence.
- The literature review that rationalized the significance of the question ignores unreferenced sources and findings.
- Alternative theories or sources more effectively account for the author's conclusions.

Ideally, therefore, these elements of a study should cohere though a kind of "tensegrity": a term most often used to describe physical structures in which otherwise disconnected elements are held in balanced relation by countervailing tensions among connecting threads. When any one of these tensors is weak or out of balance with the others, the whole structure collapses. When we read a really "solid," interesting, convincing work of scholarship, therefore, much of our appreciation results from this conceptual balance.

Achieving this balance can be especially challenging for novice scholars, in part because their previous experiences in research and writing, as students, rarely required it. In the process of learning, undergraduates routinely pose insignificant questions, ones they can't answer, or ones that have already been answered. They don't have access to (or the time to access) the information they need to support their arguments. They rationalize their studies with incomplete or outdated sources, use faulty methods, or come up with theories that have been falsified. Standards for evaluating these simulations of scholarship take into account the writer's inexperience and limited time. When graduate students begin to produce real works of scholarship, therefore, the more rigorous standards for balance among these factors, which experienced scholars often struggle to meet, can come as a shock.

Individual abilities and inclinations, strengths and weaknesses, sometimes contribute to these imbalances. Ideally, good scholars should be equally adept at all dimensions of their professions. They should be thoroughly knowledgeable, avid readers of literature in their fields but also innovative thinkers, good at identifying new questions and designing research projects. They should have the methodological skills and patience to conduct this research thoroughly, along with the strong writing and speaking skills necessary to frame and communicate their findings to others. This is a lot to expect from one person, and most of us are stronger in some of these areas than in others. I knew a PhD candidate in the social sciences, for example, who came up with brilliant research questions and experimental designs in his field of game theory, but he hated the processes of rounding up subjects, conducting these experiments, and writing the articles he needed for his dissertation. Graduate students in the humanities often pursue advanced studies because they love to immerse themselves in reading literature, history, or philosophy—the textual *Worlds* of these fields—but are less interested in the theoretical, critical debates that constitute their *Disciplines*. Many scholars in cultural anthropology are drawn to ethnography, deep and thorough immersion in other cultures, while others are primarily theorists who have little patience for the tedium and discomforts of field research. This distinction between experiential learners and abstract thinkers applies also to the sciences, where some students are drawn to field studies or hands-on "benchwork" in the lab and others grasp the subject primarily through concepts and equations. "Put them in the lab," a chemistry professor observed of the latter type, "and they break a lot of glassware."

As inclinations and preferences, these are normal patterns of variation. Nonetheless, knowledge production ultimately requires balanced attention to all dimensions of research and writing in a discipline. Serious obstacles to the completion of dissertations and other projects arise when we get too immersed in some of these dimensions—usually the ones we are best at and most enjoy—at the expense of others. In extreme cases, I've known anthropologists who became so immersed in fieldwork that they never returned. And the graduate students who are terrific at conducting lab experiments sometimes get stuck there on the bench because they are so useful, as members of research teams, to scholars who are publishing the results.

At varying stages in the development of dissertation projects, therefore, most of you will need to push yourselves out of your comfort zones and attend to dimensions of this work that you'll otherwise neglect. And throughout the process, you should occasionally pause to consider whether the relations among these dimensions are in balance and to revise your plans if they are not.

- Do you have a clearly focused research question you can answer, or an argument you can support?
- Is this question significant and conceptually grounded in your discipline?

- Do you have access to the sources of information you need to answer this question or support your argument?
- Are the methods of data collection and analysis you intend to use aligned with these three dimensions of your study?

When dissertation writers do not consider and reconsider these questions of balance, they sometimes reach the late stages when drafts require extensive reconstruction or, in some cases, further research—problems you don't want to discover in your dissertation defense, when solutions can require months of additional work.

Describing the draft of a dissertation in history, for example, the candidate's advisor observed, "She writes about history as though no one had ever written about it before, and everything she says is fresh discovery." Although he appreciated the resulting sense of excitement and revelation, as a part of what makes good historical narration so engaging, this student forgot, it seemed, that she was a member of an academic discipline, engaged with other scholars in collaborative efforts to construct understandings of the past. Including this disciplinary dimension, to establish conceptual balance, required arduous revisions of her draft.

History candidates of the opposite type, this professor noted, "cite ten references for every statement they make," as though nothing they say is valid unless established scholars have already said it. At the extreme, the entire dissertation then becomes literature review, an empty reference frame: not knowledge production but an elaborate affirmation of what is known. These opposite tendencies in graduate writing represent, and probably result from, comparable patterns among student writers: those who come up with interesting ideas they don't substantiate, and those who skillfully summarize what authors have said.

In other cases, however, problems of imbalance result entirely from conceptual or circumstantial developments in the dissertation stage, where ideas and plans can change and get thrown out of balance for a variety of reasons. I've known graduate students whose plans for essential field or archival research were foiled by unforeseen wars or political changes. A few others were unpredictably "scooped" by other scholars before they could publish important findings, or their experimental results falsified their central hypotheses, or their mathematical models didn't work. These developments can create confusion and discouraging delays, but in every case the solution lies in getting the points of our conceptual triangle back into a new kind of balanced relation. And in some these cases, this solution is surprisingly simple. I've worked with several PhD candidates who were struggling with dissertation drafts that had become too elaborate and unbalanced in one dimension or another. They were trying to restore balance by adding weight to the other dimensions, but we solved the problem more quickly when I convinced them that they should simply cut back: delete problematic chapters or sections, abandon or narrow research questions they couldn't fully answer, or ignore large amounts of research material of marginal relevance to their arguments. Nearly impossible tasks of revision then became relatively easy and straightforward.

A candidate in political studies, for example, had submitted a working draft of his dissertation to his advisors, who responded that although his central argument was fascinating, to substantiate it he needed to conduct additional field studies in another country. Due to visa and funding problems, among others, this advice was devastating, to the extent that he considered giving up.

The problem of imbalance that his advisors observed had emerged during his field research on the evolution of a grassroots resistance movement into a political party, when he began to formulate a more general, comparative theory about the factors that bring such transformations about. The central argument of his dissertation was based on this theory, which he supported with his own limited knowledge and related studies of comparable movements in other countries. A dissertation project on the development of one movement in one country then became a more ambitious, comparative, and significant study of such movements internationally. In our triangle, the limited evidence he had gathered from the *World* of political phenomena no longer supported the expanded breadth of his research *Question* and its reference frame in his *Discipline*.

The solution we devised for this problem of imbalance preserved the substance of his comparative theory as a proposed hypothesis, for which he presented his research on one political movement as a pilot case study, with more tentative reference to similar cases deserving further research. This renewed emphasis on the focus of his field studies reduced his obligation to substantiate other cases, which he condensed in a final chapter. These cases led, in his conclusion, to suggestions for further comparative research to test his hypothesis. What he was previously trying to do in his dissertation, still as a fledgling scholar, was recast more realistically as a *future* trajectory for his academic career. When he proposed this strategy to his advisors, they agreed that it was acceptable, and he was able to complete these revisions successfully in a little more than a month.

Interdisciplinary Reference Frames

The previous example also illustrates fairly common misunderstandings and difficulties resulting from consultations with faculty advisors, especially when they represent different research fields. When you talk with advisors about your dissertation projects, you might reasonably assume that their suggestions concern the scope and structure of this dissertation. That's most often true, but in some cases, they may be suggesting what you should do in future studies. When they say, "You really should" pursue further questions, gather additional material, or consider broader ranges of research literature, you might think they are referring to your dissertation, but they might be thinking of your career. Advisors do not always make this reference shift clear, in part because in their own research, one project is usually an extension of others and leads to related, future studies along a broader avenue of research interests. In such conversations, the conceptual boundaries of your dissertation can become blurred. The potential for this kind of misunderstanding increases if your project is cross-disciplinary, your advisors are in different fields, and you meet with them separately. From their disciplinary perspectives, they may have differing views of the scope and significance of your project and envision, in effect, two or three somewhat different dissertations.

An extreme case was that of a candidate whose basic research in physics had significant applications in branches of astrophysics and chemistry. Her advisors, therefore, were in three departments and had never discussed her work with one another. When she met with them individually, they encouraged her to pursue dimensions of her project most relevant to *their* research interests, and she assumed that these diverging recommendations were requirements for her dissertation. In some cases, however, following this advice required further experiments, data analysis, and literature review that would add months to the process. As these "requirements" accumulated, she felt that she was obliged to compile three dissertations, with different reference frames, into one, and the challenges of doing so brought her work to a halt. When she explained her difficulties to me, she had been through several weeks of anguish over the problem without coming any nearer to a solution.

Following long conversations, we concluded that she must ask her main advisor, in physics, to convene a meeting with her doctoral committee to address the problem directly and develop a reasonable set of expectations for the scope of *one* dissertation she could efficiently complete. He agreed to do this, and when her advisors understood the problem, they apologized for the misunderstandings they had created. In some cases, they were just "thinking out loud," they said, about the potential of her research and hadn't meant to compound her difficulties. Collectively, they agreed that her dissertation should focus on her basic research, with less substantial sections on potential applications across disciplines, cast as promising directions for further studies. This plan required very little additional analysis and writing, and she completed this work quickly, with immense relief. The lesson this case offers should be obvious. When you talk with your advisors about your dissertation projects, individually or collectively, try to steer the focus of the discussion to the structure and focus of your dissertation, and ask them to clarify suggestions that complicate or confuse your plans. If you present these plans in writing, this focus will be easier to maintain, and you'll have a reference point for questions about the implications of their advice. In principle, your main advisor or "chair" of your faculty committee is responsible for negotiating, with you and other advisors, a set of reasonable expectations for the focus and scope of your dissertation project. However, busy faculty members often neglect this role and will assume that these expectations are clear to you. If they aren't, you shouldn't hesitate to request clarification. Failures to do so, out of deference or pride, have cost many graduate students months or years of unnecessary struggle with their projects.

The above example raises more general questions about the structures and reference frames of dissertations that are interdisciplinary. The triangular balance I've urged you to establish presumes one discipline in which a single research question about some dimension of the world becomes significant and answerable through research methods appropriate for establishing validity in that discipline.

This conceptual balance would be easier to establish if fields of specialized research were neatly contained within the administrative boundaries of academic departments—if all of the research conducted by members of psychology departments, for example, were distinct from research in biology, linguistics, sociology, and other departments. In reality, fields of research have never fully aligned with the institutional taxonomies of "disciplines" represented by departments. The latter are always somewhat outdated, primarily because administrative changes occur more slowly than the evolution of knowledge. The names of the subfields of traditional disciplines—e.g., biophysics, physical chemistry, social psychology, economic anthropology, or political history—acknowledge that they have one foot in another discipline. Universities gradually adapt to new configurations of research by establishing interdisciplinary programs, in fields such as cognitive science, visual studies, international development, or geographical area studies. Some of these programs eventually become separate departments, faculty members often hold joint appointments in two or more departments and programs, and these disciplinary classification systems vary substantially from one university to another. In relation to these administrative categories, most graduate and faculty research is to some extent cross-disciplinary.

As a consequence, for the purpose of establishing conceptual balance and constructing a reference frame in which you can rationalize the significance of your dissertation project, the *Discipline* corner of the triangle is often the most problematic, in ways that affect other dimensions as well. In the case of the physicist whose research was relevant to two other departments, a comprehensive dissertation seemed to require three distinct disciplinary reference frames (in physics, chemistry, and astronomy), with diverging research questions and methods of data collection and analysis. This is why she felt, with confusion and dread, that she was obliged to write three dissertations in the form of one.

The solution she devised with her advisors was to frame her dissertation primarily in physics, with less extensive, suggestive reference to the relevance of this research in the two other fields. In other cases, however, dissertation projects fall more squarely in the middle of related fields, and it makes more sense to frame and focus the project in the center of a Venn diagram, in the area where these fields overlap:

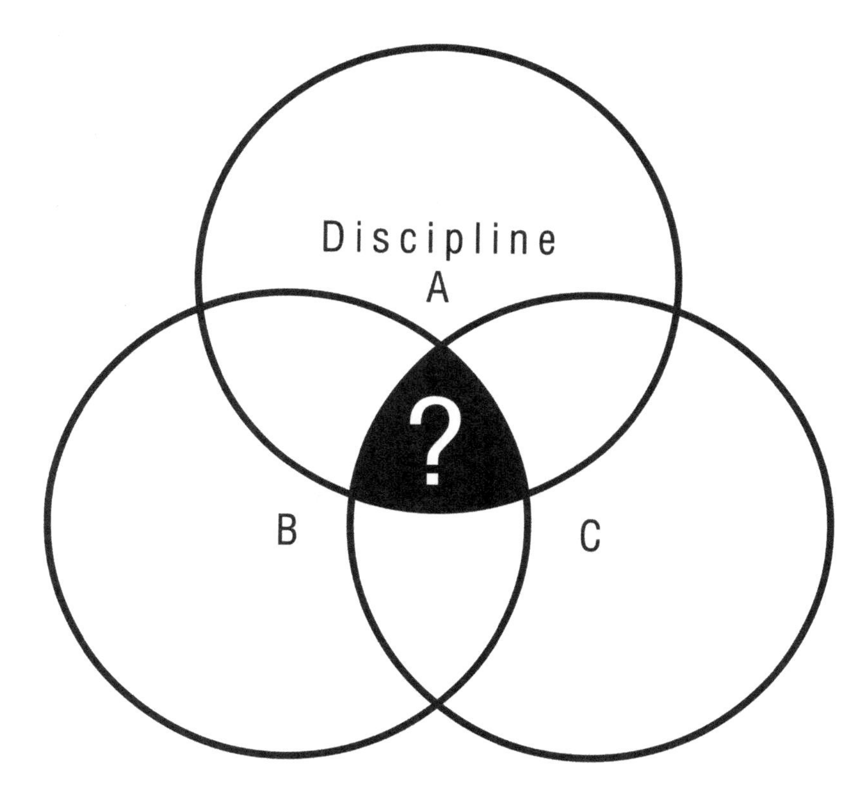

Figure 3.8 Interdisciplinary Focus

The work of a candidate in psychology who is studying aspects of cognition, for example, might be significant in reference to previous studies in branches of cognitive psychology, neurobiology, and linguistics. A study of agricultural development might draw upon research in soil science, plant biology, and economics. In a singular sense, the *Discipline* is then defined not by the candidate's departmental affiliation but by the research questions, contexts, and methods of this project.

The most accurate representations of current fields of research and their professional communities are the journals in which scholars in your field publish their work. Unlike academic departments, these journals respond very quickly to developments and current trends in research, including those in cross-disciplinary fields. When you identify the journals most likely to publish articles on the subject of your dissertation research, look closely at the ways in which the introductions to these articles are structured. Examine how the authors sequence and integrate references to bring the significance of their studies into focus. If your dissertation will be a collection of articles, these journals can provide reliably scaled models for the structure of your work. If it is a monograph, you can expand this structure with more detailed discussion of further references. Cross-disciplinary dissertations and some academic books on your research field can provide further models. If your cross-disciplinary interests make you feel like an outlier in your own programs, you can benefit from attending conferences where people who share your interests assemble.

References

Beau Lotto, R. & Purves, D. (2002). The empirical basis of color perception. *Consciousness and Cognition*, 11 (4), 609–629.

Becker, H. (1986). *Writing for social scientists: How to start and finish your thesis, book, or article*. Chicago, Il: University of Chicago Press.

Bobbitt, J. (1982). Truth and Artistry in the *Diary of Anaïs Nin*. *Journal of American Literature*, 9 (2), 267–276.

Gopen, G. D. & Swan, J. A. (1990). The science of scientific writing. *American Scientist*, 78, 550–558.

Rienecker, L. (2003, June). "Text that works". Paper presented at the Second Conference of the European Association for the Teaching of Academic Writing, Budapest, Hungary.

4 Relations with Advisors

Previous chapters have included many references to the roles of advisors, in graduate education at large and in cases of individual candidates and their projects, because in the dissertation stage, faculty advisors are always implicated in a PhD candidate's progress or difficulties. In graduate workshops, support groups, casual conversations, and social media sites, relations with advisors are also central topics of discussion and commiseration among graduate students. Like the questions sent to advice columnists about marriages, families, and friends, the issues involved in these relations are at once vitally important to individuals, personal, circumstantial, and inexhaustibly varied. Offering some general advice on the subject, for all of you, therefore seems both necessary and nearly impossible.

I've already introduced reasons for which generalization about these important relationships is so difficult. When graduate students have completed other program requirements and become PhD candidates, individual advisors assume primary responsibility for determining the forms of dissertation projects, supervising their completion, and evaluating their quality. Liberated from the structured contexts of schooling at this turning point, candidates are from then on subject to the guidance, expectations, and judgments of a principal dissertation advisor or a small faculty committee, sometimes from two or more departments. In most graduate programs, however, the ways in which faculty members perform these crucial roles are largely unregulated. Like parents, dissertation advisors have considerable freedom to use their authority in ways that are to varying degrees attentive or negligent, strict or lax, authoritarian or collegial. When a graduate student in chemistry described research groups in the field as "dysfunctional families" and I asked what she meant, she replied (with the predominance of male faculty in her program in mind), "You know . . . single parent, authoritarian father, sibling rivalry."

Such analogies to parenting have some historical foundations. In the German postgraduate universities that became early models for American doctoral education in the 19th century, the term of reference to one's dissertation advisor was *vater*: "father." This central figure in the doctoral stage was an established scholar (then almost invariably male) who agreed by individual arrangement to supervise a candidate's research and training as a scholar. The resulting roles were comparable to those of master and apprentice in the guild system. In this relationship, the role of the PhD candidate was often that of a protégé: an individual in training to carry on the senior scholar's research in a kind of academic lineage, and when this bond (or bondage) was formed, individual candidates' experiences resulted almost entirely from the types of parents, or masters, they ended up with. American and European educational systems evolved in their own directions. In the dissertation stage of their doctoral programs, however, vestiges of the traditional master/apprentice relations remained, along with the variety of experiences determined by these critically important, interpersonal relationships that develop in diverse contexts over many years.

The increasing variety of these contexts for specialized research partly explains why the professional roles and responsibilities of dissertation advisors have remained so poorly defined. A dissertation monograph in the humanities is often an independent research project, designed and completed with occasional comments on drafts from faculty members who are pursuing other lines of inquiry. Yet, in the same fields, professors sometimes devote large proportions of their time to close supervision of dissertation work throughout the process. As members of research groups in the experimental sciences or social sciences, PhD candidates may be in daily contact with principal advisors in the development of collaborative projects and co-authored publications. On the other hand, graduate students conducting field studies or archival research in a variety of disciplines may have little or no contact with their advisors for periods of a year or more. When they are writing their dissertations, furthermore, many PhD candidates are living elsewhere, sometimes in other countries, and become increasingly disconnected from their advisors and programs. When I mentioned that I'd met an ABD candidate who was still trying to complete her dissertation in another state, now with a full-time job and a family, a member of her dissertation committee barely remembered her and said, "Oh, right. Is she still around?" These nearly invisible ABDs who hover in the margins of their programs are sometimes termed "ghosts," while some of their peers remain visible and connected, often as research assistants for their advisors. It's difficult to imagine a set of general guidelines for the institutional roles of dissertation advisors and advisees that would apply to all of these conditions.

Because the professional roles of advisors and advisees are so diverse and individualized, both parties tend to describe these relations in personal terms. As I noted in Chapter 1, faculty members usually attribute struggles and failures in doctoral programs to the weak abilities, backgrounds, motivations, or personal characteristics of individual candidates.

In consultations about their dissertation work, graduate students tend to describe the roles of their advisors in personal and interpersonal terms—sometimes as surrogate parents, close friends, colleagues, congenial mentors, remote authority figures, severe taskmasters and critics, or benignly negligent acquaintances, among dozens of other characterizations. Some of these discussions descend into entangled analyses of advisors' personalities, motivations, family lives, relations with other graduate students and colleagues, or positions in departmental conflicts, as though finding the hidden key to this person's being might unlock the barriers to further progress. Sitting near me in a study lounge where I was writing yesterday, two graduate students spent more than an hour discussing, far too loudly, their relations with a faculty advisor I happened to know. They were reporting and comparing things he had recently said to them about their work, things he had previously said to them or to other graduate students, analyzing what these comments really meant, their implications, his hidden motivations and personality. Before I moved out of earshot, I wanted to barge in and say, "Why don't you just ask him, and get on with your work?"

I'm not suggesting that the interpersonal dimensions of these relationships are imaginary or irrelevant. Real friendships or collegial relationships can form between faculty advisors and graduate students. Personality conflicts, misunderstandings, and hasty judgments can undermine working relations, and reaching mutual, interpersonal understandings can be extremely important. Instead, I'm simply reminding you that these are primarily *professional* relations with the central goal—especially for you—of getting your dissertation done successfully. I've had to remind a few faculty members, in turn, that they shouldn't prejudge their advisees' potential for becoming scholars but provide guidance and help to solve problems they encounter in the process. Interpersonal factors may become important means or obstacles to this end, but they shouldn't become ends in themselves or distract us from the purpose of this relationship.

When I sense that interpersonal factors have begun to obscure this goal, therefore, I try to shift the focus of a consultation back to the dissertation work itself and to some fundamental questions:

- What are the current obstacles to progress with your project?
- To remove these obstacles, what kinds of help do you need from your advisors?
- What can you reasonably expect from them?
- What are the best strategies for getting this guidance and support for your project, from them or from others?

These questions return the work you are doing and the help you might need to the center of your attention, where they belong, and they yield a very basic definition of the *professional* roles of advisors in the process:

> *Considering your own professional needs as a PhD candidate, with the goal of getting your dissertation done, you can reasonably expect that your advisors should help you to achieve this goal and to solve problems that arise in the process.*

These expectations will become reasonable only if you make them clear to your advisors. For reasons I'll explain further, it's unreasonable to wait for assistance you haven't asked for. If you do make your expectations clear but conclude that advisors can't or won't provide the guidance you need, you should either change your advisors or find this help elsewhere, from other faculty members, peers, or support services. Deeper analysis of the personal and interpersonal dimensions of the relationship, in the hope of improving it, will be an unproductive distraction from the central purpose of being a PhD candidate: to become something else and get on with your life.

To this end, realistic expectations of your working relations with advisors should take into account two kinds of *unavoidable* imbalance that are built into the structures of these relations.

The most obvious imbalance is that of *power*, linked with status. However friendly or collegial your relations with advisors may be, they remain university professors and members of professional communities, while you remain graduate students. Whether they like it or not, dissertation advisors hold nearly unqualified authority to regulate and evaluate a PhD candidate's progress through this stage. In their institutional roles as faculty members and directors of your projects, they are authorized to determine, approve, reject, or revise the research plans you propose. They can establish schedules and deadlines for this work in progress or, if they choose, leave these decisions up to you. When you submit and defend a complete draft, your advisor must decide whether it's acceptable, unacceptable, or in need of further revisions. Their assessments of its worth as a contribution to knowledge in their fields, along with the amounts of support they provide for your professional development, can strongly influence your fortunes in job markets.

Where does your power lie in these relationships? As a graduate student, you have some power to choose your advisors if they accept this role. If they are agreeable, you may be able to negotiate their expectations or request assistance, and to the extent that they give you freedom in the process, you have the power to use that freedom to your advantage. If a dissertation advisor's expectations are unreasonable and inflexible, or if they abuse their power, you can probably arrange to drop this faculty member and find another willing to assume the role. Like divorces, these decisions to end relationships can be liberating, but they can also be difficult and disruptive, especially in advanced stages of dissertation work. When working relations with advisors break down, regardless of the reasons, graduate students are usually the most vulnerable parties. I've known extreme cases in which PhD candidates had to discontinue their programs when they couldn't find willing replacements for main advisors following disagreements or resignations from their dissertation committees.

Differences in power and status always inflect these relations between advisors and, when they remain unacknowledged, can create misunderstandings and conflicts. Along with their roles as mentors, even the most friendly, collegial advisors must also become judges. Graduate students who imagine that bonds of friendship and mutual regard erase differences in status often feel betrayed and confused when these trusted friends criticize their work or demand revisions with formal, professional detachment. To avoid these misunderstandings or appearances of favoritism, many faculty members adopt policies of maintaining professional distance from advisees. Some graduate students also prefer the clarity of these formal, hierarchical relations.

In other cases, however, such policies obscure the mutual benefits of graduate research and can encourage the abuse of power. In a moment of candor, a director of a graduate studies once told me, "The best reason for maintaining strong graduate programs is faculty development." He was acknowledging that collaboration with graduate students enriches faculty research. Thoughtful professors in graduate programs are aware that while they bring experience and expertise to these relations, graduate students offer fresh perspectives and represent the future of their disciplines. Relative status, while real, has little correlation with the value and potential of one's ideas. I've had dozens of conversations with professors about the brilliance and promise of their advisees' dissertation research, but in their professional roles as authoritative advisors they often fail to convey this enthusiasm. As a consequence, graduate students may feel that their work is undervalued, underestimate its value, or become vulnerable to exploitation. On the other hand, I've known many faculty members who maintain a mutually rewarding, productive balance between these roles, both as authorities over dissertation work and as appreciative colleagues.

A second unavoidable imbalance in these relations is that of *attention*. For you as a doctoral candidate, your dissertation work is probably your main priority and focus of attention. Even if you have other responsibilities as a teaching or research assistant, employee, partner, or parent, completing your dissertation is your main job. Once this work is underway, you'll spend enormous amounts of your time conducting research, reading, analyzing data, writing, and thinking about this project, identifying and trying to solve problems in the process.

For your faculty advisors, however, helping you to get this work done successfully is just one of many jobs they have to do, all competing for their time and attention in extremely busy, fragmented schedules. These other responsibilities might include their own research and writing projects, planning and teaching courses, undergraduate advising, departmental administrative roles, service on university committees, job searches and tenure reviews, peer reviews, and other professional activities, along with commitments in their personal lives. Individuals known to be the most thoughtful, supportive mentors are also the most popular choices as graduate advisors in their programs, so they may have several very different dissertation projects to keep track of at once.

If we made a pie chart of your time and attention as an academic, your dissertation project should represent the biggest wedge. In a comparable chart, even for your main dissertation advisor, it's probably a thin slice. University professors are trained, hired, and promoted primarily for their accomplishments as research specialists, but their actual job descriptions are for "multitaskers," obliged to occupy a great variety of roles that require different skills and kinds of attention. Every faculty includes a few remarkably agile attention jugglers who seem to keep all of these balls in the air without dropping many of them, but these superheroes are rare, and I don't fully understand how they do it. More often, meeting any one of these responsibilities means that you are ignoring others. Even the most responsible advisors will have limited time to think about your dissertation unless you are collaborating on the same research project. If the roles of graduate advisors are parental, therefore, they most often resemble those of single parents with demanding jobs and lots of children. And if you're looking for a nurturing surrogate parent, you may feel like a middle child in this family, always hoping for more attention than you're likely to get. If your advisors seem distracted or can't remember very clearly what you are doing, you shouldn't conclude that they don't care about your work or that it isn't valuable. However supportive and attentive they would like to be, this project is your main focus of attention, not theirs. You can't expect them to be equally aware of its nuances or equally invested in its outcome.

These imbalances are given conditions, and because they are usually implicit ones, in your interactions with advisors it's most important for you to simply take them into account. For the purpose of finding an effective center of balance in these inherently uneven relations of power and attention, you do have some agency. And because you have the most to gain or lose in this endeavor, you should keep your attention focused primarily on completing your own research and writing, thoughtfully and strategically using the agency you have to achieve this goal. In a somewhat ironic sense, you can think of distracted, inattentive advisors as your role models. They're probably attending primarily to their own research and writing as well.

Under these given conditions, most approaches to advising aren't inherently good or bad, realistic or unrealistic. Graduate students who expect lots of help from a dissertation advisor won't get along well with one who believes that good candidates shouldn't need any. Yet this seemingly negligent, irresponsible advisor could be a perfect choice for candidates who don't want or need much supervision. For them, nurturing advisors who want to monitor their progress at every stage will seem overly directive and meddlesome.

Avoidable imbalances in these relations therefore result from differing assumptions and expectations. When these differences remain unacknowledged, unresolved, or unresolvable, they can lead to serious misunderstandings and conflicts. Most of the following advice offers strategies for avoiding these misalignments.

Choose your Advisors Carefully

Across doctoral programs and institutions, the position of dissertation advisor or chair of one's dissertation committee is an official designation, but the pairing of graduate students and faculty members is an unruly process that occurs at various stages and leaves a lot to chance. Graduate students sometimes enter their programs with narrowly focused research interests and intentions to work with particular scholars in that field. Others, perhaps in the same program, enter with open minds about these choices and select advisors at a much later stage. Many graduate programs assign temporary advisors to entering students for the first year or more while they choose concentrations and become more familiar with the faculty. In experimental sciences and social sciences, dissertation advisors are typically the directors of the collaborative research groups one decides to join, often in the first year or two.

The most common criteria for choosing dissertation advisors concern their research interests and professional status. For obvious reasons, these are important considerations that can significantly narrow your options. Accomplished scholars in your areas of interest will be most familiar with the kinds of research you want to do, can potentially give you the most knowledgeable direction, and may be the most useful in your professional development and job searches. Highly productive scholars with lots of funding are most likely to provide support from research grants and fellowships, along with opportunities to publish significant findings. In most fields, certain kinds of research are currently in vogue, and theoretical or political divisions can also influence these decisions.

These are certainly relevant factors, but they shouldn't exclude other considerations, including the varying roles and expectations I've mentioned above. Naively assuming that good relations will naturally develop from their common research interests, graduate students and professors often agree to work together without discussing what this will actually mean. In following months or years, therefore, the most obvious choices may turn out to be bad ones, often for reasons that could have been anticipated. When she returned from a meeting she had arranged with a senior professor closest to her own research interests, a first-year graduate student in the humanities told me that he offered to become her main advisor, but she had decided to reject the offer. Asked to explain his approach to advising, he had emphasized his authority over her work and repeatedly said, "If you work under me . . ." in a tone and view of the relationship that she found ominous.

This sensible graduate student took the initiative to arrange such a meeting and get the information she needed, and I encourage you to do the same. In some programs, comparable interviews between prospective advisors and advisees are standard practice, but even in these cases faculty members do not necessarily explain their approaches or expectations, and graduate students may be too timid to ask. In the majority of programs that leave these arrangements to individuals, professors are usually agreeable to meetings with prospective advisees on request, and most of them will happily answer questions about their roles and expectations. In these meetings, graduate students should explain their research interests, of course, but also the kinds of guidance or instruction they are likely to need. Faculty members should explain their typical approaches to advising, the kinds of help they usually provide, their expectations of PhD candidates, and the amounts of flexibility in their approaches as projects evolve. Following these disclosures and discussions, both parties should know more clearly what they are getting into.

Similar recommendations apply to joining research groups. The advantages of working with a prominent scholar in a highly productive, well-funded project in your research field are obvious, but the potential disadvantages are equally relevant. Like CEOs of corporations, research directors with big grants and multifaceted projects have a variety of management styles. Those who are busy with administrative and professional activities often delegate research supervision and other day-to-day operations to senior graduate students or postdoctoral fellows. The opportunity to work on a stellar professor's team might turn out to resemble a low-level job supervised by middle management, with little autonomy to develop your own research and career plans. Smaller research groups might offer more direct training and attention from faculty, but I know of cases in which assistant professors, desperate to get results and publications for tenure reviews, viewed graduate students primarily as means to this end and delayed the completion of their doctoral research. Before you join a collaborative research group, therefore, you should learn as much as possible about what membership to this group will actually entail. *What are the usual time commitments and responsibilities? How will your roles in the group evolve? How much direct attention and supervision can you expect from research directors, as your dissertation advisors? And how will this collaboration contribute to your own dissertation research and career development?*

You can gather some of this information from meeting with the prospective research director/advisor. In making these and other decisions, however, you can learn a lot from advanced graduate students who work with this professor, from departmental grapevines, and sometimes (more diplomatically) from directors of graduate studies or other faculty members.

Schedule Periodic Meetings to Discuss your Project Throughout the Research and Writing Process

If your advisors don't take the initiative to arrange meetings to check on your progress, don't wait for them to do so or conclude that it isn't appropriate to ask. Well-meaning but busy professors tend to hope, optimistically, that their advisees won't need much attention and assume that if they don't hear from them they must be doing fine. Those who maintain office hours and say "My door is always open!" are often relieved when no one comes through to interrupt their own work. For these reasons, most of them will prefer scheduled meetings in their offices, or perhaps over lunch, to focus on your project. There you are most likely to get sustained, constructive attention and can explain what you are currently doing, discuss questions or problems you've encountered, and explore possibilities you might not have considered. In committee meetings, you can also make sure that your advisors have mutually coherent, reasonable expectations for your project to avoid the potentially hazardous misunderstandings I described in reference to the physics candidate in the previous chapter.

These scheduled meetings are preferable to more frequent, incidental appeals for help whenever a problem or question arises, which might create the impression that you are constantly running into trouble. Because these "quick questions" emerge from immersion in your work, while your advisors are probably immersed in their own, getting useful, reliable answers will take more time and explanation than you might expect.

Be Sure that Your Advisors Have Copies of Your Current, Formal Dissertation Research Proposal

Many doctoral programs and individual advisors require a written proposal toward the beginning of the dissertation stage, sometimes for review in the comprehensive exam, and if your research requires applications for funding, these include detailed proposals as well. Proposals usually resemble research articles in your field without results. They typically include an abstract, introduction/literature review, central research questions or hypotheses, methods, and discussion/conclusion, with the addition of a research timeline. Farther along in the process, dissertation proposals may include chapter outlines.

If such proposals aren't required, you should produce one anyway for reference and clarification of what you are doing, both for your advisors and yourself. If the scope, research questions, methods, or other facets of the project change, as they usually do, you should revise this document as well and give copies to your advisors. In meetings with them, a current proposal can be a valuable point of reference, to keep the discussion focused on your work, to address questions of feasibility and conceptual balance, and to isolate particular problems that need attention. Otherwise, these discussions may meander, and it will be harder for you to figure out their practical implications. Writing and revising these accounts of your project will also remind you that your dissertation is a particular *object* that you are constructing, not just a nebulous, hypothetical endeavor, or a mess of potential problems. Working on your dissertation without them is like trying to build a house without plans.

Because you have the most at stake in this project, you can't safely assume that your advisors' silence means they approve of your research design or that you shouldn't ask for suggestions. I got involved in a messy grievance procedure after a candidate failed his dissertation defense, on the grounds that his murky dissertation resulted from an overly ambitious, incoherent research design. From my perspective, both sides shared the blame for this avoidable disaster. The faculty advisors should have warned the candidate about these design flaws at the beginning of the process, in a proposal review, and he should have asked for this critical review of his plans rather than assuming, as he did, that he knew what he was doing.

In Ongoing Meetings With Your Advisors, Remind Them of What You Are Doing and the Issues You Want to Discuss, Preferably in Advance and In Writing

An undergraduate who described his professors as "walking DO NOT DISTURB signs" told me that before he met with them in office hours, he wrote down lists of the questions he meant to ask. He was primarily concerned about wasting *their* time, but for your meetings with graduate advisors, his strategies can minimize your wasted time as well. Due to the attention imbalance I previously noted, multitasking advisors will recall less about your project than you do, and because the focus of attention should be *your* work, and getting it done, you should remind them. I sometimes encourage candidates to write current one-paragraph abstracts of their projects that advisors and others can quickly read. (If you memorize them, these statements can also be useful at social events when someone asks the awkward question "What do you study?" or "What's your dissertation about?") In advance, jot down an agenda for the meeting, and if you have particular questions or problems you want to discuss, send them to your advisor the day before. There's a reasonable chance, at least, that they will read and think about these issues in advance. For the purpose of focusing attention, diagrams of conceptual problems can be useful as well. What you want to avoid, in any case, is a meeting that begins with the broad question, "So, how are things going?" and proceeds as a search for something useful to talk about.

When You Give Them Dissertation Material to Read, Explain What They Are Reading and Why

When I'm really busy, there's nothing more disheartening than facing a large chunk of someone's dissertation with the attached message, "Here it is," or "Tell me what you think." Graduate students often submit chapter or article drafts with silent expectation, as though they were turning in a student paper for grading. But this work in progress isn't a student paper, and grading isn't the point at this stage. Without knowing what this material represents and the kinds of feedback you hope to receive, advisors are less likely to read it promptly and constructively. The responses you get, in turn, will be less reliable and useful.

If this is a rough, exploratory draft, for example, and you want them to focus on central concepts and arguments, if you don't explain this they may waste their time (and yours) correcting problems of phrasing, with the assumption that you think it's nearly finished. If you don't explain the problems you perceive and want help solving, they may simply point them out to you and essentially tell you what you already know. If you give them a chapter or section out of context, you can't assume that they will understand how this material fits into the dissertation as a whole, and they might criticize the absence of arguments or evidence included elsewhere. More generally, when advisors receive material submitted as though it were a student paper, they often revert to paper grading mode and read judgmentally, emphasizing flaws or offering brief, general assessments, such as, "A good start!" or "Still needs some work."

I'm always grateful, therefore, when graduate students use text editing programs to highlight passages they want help with and explain specific questions in the margins. I might observe other strengths or problems the writers didn't point out, but when I know what they perceive and need help with, even critical responses become more focused, supportive, and constructive, as parts of a productive exchange. With this guidance for reading, I can also read long documents more efficiently. If I know the writer is primarily concerned about the overall structure and conceptual development of a chapter, for example, I can scan it analytically in a fraction of the time it would take to read it otherwise. As a rule, however, you should give advisors the smallest amount of material necessary to get the help you need. If you are concerned about matters of voice and style, a single paragraph or page might be enough to exemplify your questions and is more likely to get a detailed response.

Use Criticism Constructively and Judiciously, as Feedback on Work in Progress

Because their student writing was continually graded, doctoral candidates are sometimes devastated by an advisor's critical response to a draft, which they read as a judgment of its value or of their ability.

This response sometimes results from the judgmental tone of the criticism itself. As students, you have been graded through most of your education. I've noted that as teachers, faculty members are also experienced graders of student work and often assume that role when they respond to dissertation drafts. In addition, most of them frequently respond to manuscripts in anonymous peer reviews, which are routinely skeptical and sometimes ruthless. As authors on the receiving end of these reviews, they've had to learn that to get these things published, you have to become thick-skinned and strategically put this criticism to work toward that end, sometimes with the help of editors or colleagues, even when you feel that comments are unfair. Advisors who bluntly point out flaws in your drafts may believe that you need to learn this lesson as well—that they won't do you any favors by ignoring or sugar-coating problems you need to solve—and they're probably right.

Even the most accurate, useful criticism isn't pleasant. Only the masochists among us enjoy being told that our work is flawed, that we're wrong, or that we should have done it differently. Only the most confident people, with high self-esteem, can avoid feeling a bit injured and personally challenged by such evaluations, and this kind of confidence can become arrogant resistance to necessary changes. It's much more enjoyable to be praised and affirmed, told that our work is splendid or at least very promising. There is a different kind of satisfaction, however, in using critical suggestions to reconstruct and improve work we care about. Most of all, you should remember that regardless of their tone, these suggestions are not judgments of finished products but potentially useful information for improving work in progress. We don't derive this pleasure from the criticism itself but from the ways in which we put it to work for our own purposes. This is not to improve ourselves, exactly, but to raise the quality of this thing we are constructing and reconstructing.

If critical suggestions from advisors or their implications are unclear, therefore, you should ask for clarification, particularly because these readers are also the ones who will evaluate your revisions. If you feel that suggestions are unfair, unfeasible, or simply wrong, try to get second opinions from other readers, such as peers or another faculty member. Sometimes advisors point out real problems in a draft but offer no solutions or unworkable ones. It's possible that you can find better solutions on your own or with the help of others. This is why authors often turn to editors or colleagues when suggestions from peer reviews are contradictory or unreasonable.

Underlying all of this advice is a central message:

> *You can't reasonably expect that anyone, including your advisors, will care more about your dissertation project or take more responsibility for successfully completing it than you do. For this reason, you have to assume primary responsibility for getting your dissertation finished and take initiatives to get the assistance you need in the process, in your own interests and for your own reasons.*

For this purpose, supportive, attentive advisors and other allies can be wonderful assets, but you can't entirely depend on this support. Graduate students can waste enormous amounts of time looking elsewhere for the motivation or confidence they need to get through this complicated process. Because it's a transitional process in which you must try to be (or convincingly seem to be) the kind of scholarly authority you haven't yet become, such insecurities and crises of confidence are normal, and whatever motivational support you can find, from your advisors or elsewhere, is probably welcome. This is why support groups, self-help books, and dissertation "boot camps" are so heavily devoted to morale boosting ("You can do it!") and persistence ("Just keep writing!"). In this stage of doctoral work, common hazards of faltering motivation and confidence can be difficult to conquer without help from others who believe in your ability.

This external support will have lasting value, however, only if it strengthens your *independent* motivation, confidence, and determination to complete your own work. At the ends of dissertation retreats, the looming question is always, "How can we keep this up?" Participants wonder how they can maintain their focus and momentum when they leave this supportive, secluded environment devoted to productive work on their projects and reenter the routines and responsibilities of their normal lives. I don't have simple, prescriptive answers to this question beyond reminders that their ability isn't the real issue. All of them are fully capable of successfully completing dissertations. At best, these "retreats" from their regular lives can only affirm their ability and demonstrate the kinds of focused, sustained attention necessary. The participants who find ways to implement these lessons through their own volition go on to receive PhDs, and others do not. Referring to the close supervision and encouragement she received from her advisor, a candidate in political studies accurately described her reliance on this kind of support as "training wheels." Using them demonstrates some of the skills and experiences involved, but they don't fully prepare you to get along without them. PhDs whose advisors designed and closely directed their dissertation work can face difficult problems of adjustment when they try to establish independent careers, based on their own lines of inquiry.

Assuming responsibility for completing your own dissertation does not mean that you should be able to finish it without help from others, and this is why I also emphasize initiative to find the guidance and assistance you need. As I'll explain further in Chapter 5, professional research and writing are social activities, and for this reason isolation is one of the main causes of difficulty, delay, and attrition in the dissertation stage. Being self-motivated, confident in your ability, and determined to complete a PhD for your own reasons should include awareness of the benefits of collaboration, guidance, and feedback on work in progress, along with the motivation to find this support for your work. If your official advisors can't or won't provide the kinds assistance you need, other faculty members in or outside your programs can be valuable resources, in part because they aren't constrained by the potentially conflicting roles of mentors and judges of your work. For the same reason, other graduate students can be extremely helpful, and I'll have more to say in the next chapter about strategies for developing these collaborative relations. If you run into problems with advisors that you can't resolve on your own, department chairs, directors of graduate studies, or graduate school counselors can sometimes successfully mediate these disagreements or offer strategic advice for resolving them. Due to the power imbalance in these relations, when they break down it may become useful to have made your side of the story known.

Occasionally, dissertation advisors are flagrantly irresponsible, abusive, or exploit graduate work to further their own careers. Considering the imbalance of power, in such cases I usually encourage graduate students to get confidential, strategic advice from graduate school administrators or counselors before they confront the advisor, file official complaints, or take other actions on their own. Grievance procedures and independent attempts to replace main advisors can get very messy and hazardous, as I've noted, and administrative allies in negotiating these processes can reduce your vulnerability. In some cases, department administrators can diplomatically help you to replace advisors with minimal conflict or detriment to your status and progress. Because there are so many variables involved in these cases, however, there are no standard procedures that will reliably resolve such problems. Whatever actions you take should follow careful assessment of the situation, with your own interests in mind and advice from people you trust, to determine available options. A piece that I deliberately omitted from my account of Ellen (the candidate who wanted to write about "The Whole Elephant") will illustrate this last observation and other advice I've offered about these relations. What I can tell you further, I should note, relies entirely on what Ellen told me, and although I have no reason to doubt what she said and saw copies of the journal articles at issue, her advisor's side of the story remains unknown to me.

I did mention that the senior faculty member who was Ellen's main advisor had been happy to discuss her research and ideas but offered little help in focusing these ideas in writing. When she did produce a coherent account of her project and brought it to his office, however, he looked uncomfortable and said, "Oh. Then I guess I should show you this." From his files, he gave her a copy of a recent journal article he had published based on arguments nearly identical to hers, and he pointed out a footnote in which he cited an informal conversation with her. Speechless and confused, she left his office. When Ellen turned to a friend in her program for advice, her friend revealed that she had seen references to footnoted "conversations" with Ellen in two other articles her advisor had published. Considering her advisor's discomfort and failure to disclose these references, Ellen concluded that he was invested in her confusion and inability to write, because he was using her ideas to develop his own writing projects.

When Ellen told me about these discoveries the following day, I asked, "What are you going to do?" And because she looked perplexed, I suggested a few options:

- Go directly to your department chair or to the graduate school to file a formal complaint.
- Threaten to do so and see how he responds.
- First ask him to explain his side of the story.
- Remove him from your dissertation committee and try to find a more honest, helpful advisor.
- Take no action and finish your dissertation on your own or with help from others.

What option would you choose in a comparable situation in your own program? And what would I do? I suspect that my own sense of outrage and injustice would incline me toward revenge, but this course of action could become contentious and disruptive, with unpredictable results. In any case, I couldn't recommend such a decision to Ellen or to anyone else.

What did Ellen do? To my surprise, after thinking for a couple of minutes, she said, "I want him to teach me how to do what he does, when he writes these things." Her fierce look also said, "Or else!" She later reported that when she confronted her advisor with the two additional footnoted articles he'd based on her ideas, he asked her the same question I had asked: "What are you going to do?" And when she explained the collaborative instruction she wanted him to provide, he immediately agreed, no doubt with relief.

This advisor's behavior, the dilemma it created for Ellen, and her strategy for resolving it were all unusual, but they exemplify some of the general advice I've offered here. Considering the circumstances, Ellen acted in the interests of her own dissertation work and career development, taking initiatives to get the guidance she needed in the process. Considering the inherent power imbalance in the relationship, she used the power she had to hold her advisor to his basic responsibilities and establish a productive working relationship, with the central goal of completing her dissertation and related work with a minimum of disruption and delay. If her advisor had refused to meet these responsibilities, of course, other strategies would have become necessary.

5 Getting the Work Done

Disillusionment

To complete a dissertation successfully, you need to envision *what* you are writing, and thus far we've mapped out the central features of dissertation monographs or constituent research articles in your fields. When they're finished, these fruits of your labor should present focused *research questions*, hypotheses, or arguments that fill *knowledge gaps* or address unresolved issues within *frames of reference* to previous research and debate in particular disciplines. The significance and cohesion of this work will result from *conceptual balance* between the central question you raise, the disciplinary framework in which you try to answer this question, the sources of data and other evidence you gather for this purpose, and appropriate methods for doing so. As finished products of similar writing, publications and filed dissertations in your fields can provide models for the structures and styles of your own projects. While you are writing, then, you should have a clear sense for the kind of object you are trying to produce.

Knowing what you are writing differs, nonetheless, from knowing *how* such things get written. This is why the astute doctoral candidate I mentioned in Chapter 1 wanted "to see the writer behind the curtain": the "Wizard of Oz" who was mysteriously producing the kinds of finished work she read and was struggling to write. *What was he doing, exactly, behind the closed door of his office? In the midst of his other responsibilities, how did he get this stuff done?* All she knew for certain at the time was that his writing strategies differed from the ones that got her this far: into her PhD program and to the dissertation stage.

We've also established that finished products can't answer these questions about the process of writing, because they conceal the ways in which they came about. The writing process advocate Donald Murray (1980) wryly observed that "a process cannot be inferred from a product any more than a pig can be inferred from a sausage." (p. 3.) This widely quoted analogy applies more accurately to writing, I'm afraid, than to sausages, from which a food scientist could easily infer a pig. From a published article on this analysis, nonetheless, we couldn't infer how the food scientist got it written: how long the process took, how many versions were involved, or what earlier versions said. And unless we needed to produce this kind of writing ourselves, we wouldn't care.

The best writing of any type sounds like continuous, polished utterance. Like other accomplished performances, it encourages us to imagine that it emerged almost effortlessly in this seamless, cohesive form, like brilliant speech, from the wealth of the author's knowledge, wisdom, skill, or natural talent. Accomplished writing removes all evidence of the confusion and dissatisfaction, the awkward drafts and revisions, that led to a mastery of language and thought that the authors didn't possess at the beginning of the process. If the product of writing represents accomplishment, the process is a means of *becoming* so accomplished: the investment of time and effort to create an illusion of spontaneous ease. Like the audience of an illusionist, readers aren't supposed to see how this trick was performed. Nor, as a rule, do audiences want to know how a good performance came about, any more than diners want to know how their sausages were made. Even in the roles of critics, we're most interested in the qualities of the performance itself. The final versions we read represent what the authors chose, in the end, to say and reveal to us. Discovering what they chose *not* to reveal, in rejected drafts and undisclosed difficulties, seems an invasion of privacy, like snooping in someone's diary or trash bin. To produce such illusions of ease of your own, however, you must remain *disillusioned*, both as writers and as readers: aware that these accomplishments normally result from hidden processes, periods of confusion, second thoughts, and revisions. When it reaches you in the form of polished utterance, every work of scholarship draws a curtain behind it that conceals the long, convoluted history and debris of its production over periods of months or years.

How do scholars get from the beginning of this process to the end? How do they find and use time for this work? Student writers can't answer these questions either, and for this reason you must also become disillusioned about the reliability of assumptions, methods, and uses of time you developed for completing writing projects in the past.

For most student writers who need to get an assignment done, time management is a fairly straightforward problem of finding a block of time (or two or three) to complete the process. Finding this time can be difficult in a busy schedule, but in these "one-night stands" (or two or three), efficient students get very good at compartmentalizing their time and attention, focusing on the task at hand in the time available, and then shifting their attention to another activity or responsibility. In those compartments devoted to completing a writing assignment, students typically begin to write with rhetorical settings that remain pretty consistent to the end of the process. In other words, they begin with an imagined audience (usually the teacher who assigned this project), a conception of its form and length (often defined by the assignment), a sense for the standards they can reasonably meet in this isolated context (the course they are taking), and a voice adopted for this purpose. In coordination with these rhetorical conditions, they also begin with an approximate prediction of the amount of time this work should take, which influences the speed and care with which they produce it. Substantially changing these settings in the process—e.g., beginning with a rough draft in a casual voice and rewriting a more formal version, or shifting mid-process to a new approach to the subject with higher standards—would require additional time that student writers rarely have or don't choose to spend, unless the assignment (or its grade) is extremely important to them.

As a consequence, the typical process of student writing is highly performative from beginning to end. To write efficiently in these narrow time frames, it seems necessary to imagine that whatever you are saying now is what the intended audience will read. This is why student writers usually try, at least, to make the first draft the last, appear to conflate writing with speech, as Nancy Sommers (1980) observed, and view revision as preferably avoidable "afterthought." And this is why student writers often claim in retrospect that they knew everything they wanted to say when they began the process, even though this can't have been true. What these claims really mean is that they were determined from the beginning not to substantially change whatever they said. In the contexts of schooling, these ways of getting through the writing process are not bad or evasive writing strategies but practical ones, conditioned by narrow time frames and institutional emphases on finished products, as objects of grading.

When the time frame of the writing process expands exponentially, from these compartmentalized blocks of a few hours to a year or two, all of these familiar assumptions, conditions, and rhetorical settings become questionable. The time you spend in the writing process, from one week or month to the next, isn't so easy to compartmentalize, and the "management" of this time concerns everything else you do, in the midst of your life. *On a given day, how much time should you spend on this project, and how can you use this time productively? To move the project forward, what should you do on that day, and how much can you expect to accomplish, with what standards?* There is no longer any reason to assume that you should begin the process with the standards and other rhetorical settings you will use toward the end. Nor is it likely that the writing you are producing on a particular day is what the audience will read in the future. The resulting choices are complicated, but in this unfamiliar territory you can't afford to ignore them or rely on familiar, habitual responses. Long-term projects require innumerable, ongoing decisions about what we should say or do at the moment—to work on this section or the next; to use this word or another; to continue writing this version, for now, or pause to revise it; to work on the project today or wait until tomorrow; to keep working, when we run into trouble or get tired, or stop and do something else. Collectively, these decisions affect not only the quality of our work but also the duration and efficiency of the process, potentially by periods of months. As much as possible, therefore, we should make these decisions thoughtfully, with available guidance from writers for whom this terrain is more familiar.

Productive Use of Time: The Behavioral Consensus

In their accounts of the most efficient, effective methods with which scholars get these long-term projects done—and of the most common causes of struggles and failures to get them done—authorities on these questions generally agree. Here is a terse synopsis of their advice:

> *Because these projects require lots of time and sustained attention, you must schedule and spend this time, in regular work sessions devoted to the task. If you obey this rule, you're most likely to complete dissertations or publications successfully. If you don't, you won't.*

Most writing guides and productive writers will tell you this. If you want to get these projects done, set aside regular periods of time to work on them, at least four or five days each week. Stick to your schedule and devote this time to writing and related work on this project, avoiding interruptions and distractions. This advice is so consistent and sensible that it shouldn't require repetition, but it does. So here's another version:

> *If you are a PhD candidate, work on your dissertation is your main occupation: your job. To get this job done, you need to go to work on it as you would in any other occupation, whether you want to be there on a given day or don't. Otherwise, it won't get done and you're likely to be fired. If you were hired to build a house, for example, to know what you were doing you would need plans, knowledge, and skills, but to get the house built in a reasonable time frame you would also need to work on constructing it consistently with sustained labor every work day, even when you were tired, weren't in the mood, or wanted to do something else.*

Although this necessity seems obvious, large proportions of PhD candidates, like unreliable builders, don't show up for work, delay completion of their projects by months or years, or fail to complete them altogether.

I emphasize these delays in doctoral studies because I'm writing on behalf of graduate students, who must contend with unfamiliar challenges in the process. If you imagine that all of your advisors and other scholars in your programs have surmounted these obstacles, however, think again. Equally large proportions of college professors write and publish infrequently, delay work on writing projects essential to their careers, work on these projects intermittently with fragmented attention, miss deadlines for submissions, and publish less than they feel they should. Boice (1990) noted that "Estimates typically attribute some 85% of publications to some 15% of those who could potentially write them" (p. 7). Some unproductive scholars have lost interest in research and decided that they no longer want or need to write for publication. Some, with heavy teaching loads and other responsibilities, can't find sustained time for such projects. But many others continue to struggle with the problems of time management, procrastination, weak motivation, insecurities, and misconceptions that afflict many PhD candidates. Individual writers can offer countless circumstantial explanations and excuses for these distractions and delays, but the most common, underlying problem is their failure to work on their projects consistently, with focused attention. The writing guide that makes this argument most directly is *How to Write a Lot*, by Paul J. Silvia (2007). Silvia is a professor of psychology, writing primarily for faculty colleagues, but most of his advice applies equally to PhD candidates across disciplines, and his book is widely used in writing courses and support services for graduate students.

Although Silvia is a psychologist, his diagnoses and advice for solving writing problems largely dismiss the personal, mental, and emotional dimensions often used to explain writing difficulties. From his perspective, because failures to get writing done are essentially behavioral and methodological problems, their solutions lie in behavior modification. Work on long-term writing projects can be tedious or frustrating, and on a given day there are probably other things you would rather do. But if you need to get these projects done, you need to behave accordingly, with strict work schedules, clearly defined goals, and methods of measuring your progress. In an early chapter on "Specious Barriers to Writing a Lot," Silvia argues that our most common excuses for not writing—that we can't find time, aren't yet ready, need better equipment or work environments, or don't feel sufficiently inspired—are fallacies with behavioral remedies. "Instead of *finding* time to write," for example, "*allot* time to write" regularly, at times when you're most fresh and free of distractions (p. 12). The only real solution for a tendency such as procrastination, in turn, is to stop procrastinating and get to work. Productive writing doesn't result from inspiration, Silvia argues, but from steady labor. As you might predict, he views "writer's block" as a fiction: "The cure for writer's block—if you can cure a specious affliction—is writing" (p. 46). If you're afraid that you can't write or feel bad that you aren't, getting some writing done will make you feel better.

In *The Clockwork Muse*, the sociologist Eviatar Zerubavel (1999) emphasizes a similar regimen of scheduled writing, with clearly defined goals and systems for measuring progress. Like Silvia, Zerubavel views the belief that writing results from inspiration to write as a fallacy.

More often, the reverse is true: inspiration results from writing. "In reality," he observes, "writing is virtually inseparable from the development of our ideas. In other words, much of our thinking actually takes place while we are writing!" (p. 48). In a chapter titled "A Mountain with Stairs," he emphasizes that work on long-term projects should be divided into smaller and more manageable tasks, defined by outlines and plans. On a given day, you should not feel that you are working on your dissertation as a whole but on composing or revising a specific section. "Boot camps" for dissertation writers place similar emphases on the development of productive work habits, with regimens of daily writing sessions, incremental goals, and measurements of progress in work environments free from distractions. Their underlying premise, or hope, is that the behavioral and attitudinal modifications established in these sessions will persist when their recruits break camp and resume their former lives.

Do These Behavioral Explanations and Solutions for Writing Problems Work?

Almost all of the participants in dissertation boot camps make significant progress on their projects during these events, which usually last a week or two. While under the rules and conditions of these environments, writers do get a lot done. What happens afterward? I'm not aware of aggregate data on completion rates of participants, but individual program directors report positive long-term effects. In the less regimental dissertation retreats I led for several years, 60–70 percent of the participants eventually completed their PhDs, and most of these participants were long-term ABDs, many of whom were considered unlikely to finish their projects. To the limited extent that I know, those who didn't finish were unable to find the time or motivation to maintain the focused attention they developed during the retreats.

Robert Boice—a psychologist with behavioral views similar to Silvia's—has maintained a longstanding clinical practice for struggling academic writers, with a primary focus on professorial faculty, and has conducted a variety of comparative studies of writing behaviors. Unlike Silvia, however, Boice views impediments to productivity such as writing blocks, anxiety, procrastination, and perfectionism as real psychological conditions (often rooted in misconceptions or past experiences) amenable to behavioral remedies. He argues that unproductive, detrimental methods he calls "binge writing," for example, result less from laziness or disorganization than from mistaken beliefs that delaying work on a project fuels the pressure and intense concentration necessary to generate brilliant, creative writing and thinking in long, exhausting "binges" of productivity. Such writers believe that without this pressure and urgency, the time they spent writing would be unproductive and the results would be unexceptional. Boice suggests that these beliefs among scholars (as well as poets, novelists, and other artists) are rooted in romantic notions of "creative illness," fed by examples of all those famous authors who seemed obsessed and afflicted by their creative passions. In the rationale for binge writing, it follows that to produce lots of comparably brilliant work, worthy of your time, you should postpone writing until the need and inspiration to write intensifies and you feel that euphoric fire in the belly that focuses the mind.

To test the validity of this belief, Boice (1997) conducted a comparative, longitudinal study of methods and outcomes with two groups of assistant professors. One group consisted of habitual binge writers who worked on manuscripts in intense marathon sessions only when they felt sufficiently inspired. The other group consisted of "regular writers" who worked on their projects frequently (at least three days each week) for shorter periods and with modest expectations, as though going to a routine job. Boice monitored these methods and measured the effects in productivity and other outcomes over a two-year period. The bingers, he found, produced much less writing and were less likely to finish their projects. Contrary to their beliefs, the work they finished was considered less creative by their peers. Patterns of "creative illness," however, were confirmed. Binge writers were far more vulnerable to writing blocks, depression, and other mood disorders, and apart from their euphoria while writing, they expressed far more negative feelings about writing and themselves as writers. The "regular writers," in contrast, found writing "mildly pleasant" and more often thought about their projects when they were doing other things. As a consequence, they usually began writing sessions with a clear sense of what they should do.

In another study, most clearly summarized in his book *Professors as Writers*, Boice (1990) tried to answer the related question of whether productive writing results from inspiration or the opposite: that inspiration, creative ideas, result from writing itself. In this experiment, he divided 27 faculty members into three groups of nine, given different rules for using the same 50 scheduled writing sessions. One "abstinence" group was told not to write unless they felt compelled to do so by creative ideas they needed to express. The second group was told to write when they were in the mood to do so. Members of the third, "contingency" group were told they must write a required amount in each session. If they failed on a given day, a prewritten check (the "external contingency") was sent to an organization they disliked. Members of the first two groups were happy with their assignments and expected their freedom to inspire lots of creative ideas. Members of the third group were generally disgruntled and anticipated drudgery.

It isn't surprising that the "contingent" group produced more than three times as much writing as the second, "spontaneous" group or that the "abstinence" group produced very little. More significant are the numbers and frequencies of "creative ideas" they listed, occurring every day for the "contingency" members and every other day and once a week for "spontaneous" and "abstinence" writers, respectively. Furthermore, "contingency" writers expressed the most enjoyment of and satisfaction with their assignment and were surprised that they looked forward to the scheduled sessions, with ideas they wanted to express.

My own anecdotal evidence generally confirms these principles and findings. I've known many scholars in that 15 percent of professorial faculty who publish a lot. Most of them are also very busy with teaching, administrative roles, and other professorial responsibilities. Yet almost all of them schedule regular times to work on writing projects, often early in the morning before they go to campus or in the evenings. Those who can't make this time regularly during academic terms sometimes postpone writing projects for sabbatical leaves, summers, and breaks when they can work nearly every day. As a rule, they view this work not as drudgery or euphoria but as a rather ordinary routine. Doctoral candidates who appear to sail through the dissertation stage, without delay or serious difficulty, fit the same pattern. They just go to work on their projects most days, at preferred times and places and with moderate expectations, and methodically deal with problems as they arise. Like Boice's "regular writers," they often find this work "mildly pleasant," sometimes tedious or frustrating, but rarely either thrilling or agonizing.

What Does "Regular Writing" Mean in Practice? How Often and for How Long?

PhD candidates who view dissertation work as their occupations and have a lot of time available often feel that they should put in their eight-hour shifts (or longer) every day and thoroughly immerse themselves in these endeavors. In many cases, however, a lot of this time is unproductive, and writers can get unnecessarily bleary-eyed, exhausted, and isolated. One hazardous response to the expanse of time stretching ahead of you is to postpone writing, waiting for the right frame of mind or sense of authority, until you feel "ready" for this work. But the opposite hazard is to become a victim of duty, feeling that you have to fill all that time with hard work.

Among the writing guides I've mentioned and others, no one recommends that you should work all day or all night, over several uninterrupted hours. Instead, the most important terms are "moderate" and "regular." The title of Joan Bolker's (1998) popular self-help book, *Writing Your Dissertation in Fifteen Minutes a Day*, is an admittedly optimistic tease, but she notes that 15 minutes each day is better than none. Most authors recommend daily sessions of one to three hours, depending on your circumstances and tolerances. If you schedule one of these sessions in the morning and have some momentum, you might productively resume writing later in the day. Meanwhile, do something else you enjoy or need to do, and don't feel guilty about setting the work aside. In fact, there's a peculiar satisfaction in stopping when you still have things to say, before you've run out of steam. If you know where the work is going next, write a note to yourself where you left off. When you return, then, you'll have an immediate sense of direction.

The emphasis on "regular" sessions is extremely important for a couple of reasons. If you schedule regular sessions several days a week, the work will feel familiar and normal, less urgent, with more reasonable expectations attached. The other benefits are continuity and efficiency. When I've set a project aside for more than a couple of days, I have to spend the first 15 minutes or longer reading over what I previously wrote, and I often get embroiled in editing or revising of questionable value. One dissertation writer continually interrupted his writing for days or weeks because he felt he needed to read and think more, and when he returned, what he had written seemed stale and he usually started over with different ideas, but not necessarily better ones. Here's a version of my advice to him:

> *You have to think of your writing as a little fire you build and have to keep going. You may have to leave it to get more fuel, but not much, and not for long. If you go off for two days or a week, you'll always return to cold ashes. It will be dead, and you'll have to build a new one.*

I should note that most of this advice applies primarily to work on individually authored dissertation monographs or research articles that candidates produce largely on their own. If your dissertation work is situated in a research group and co-authored, time frames may be very different, with diverse implications that can offer advantages or disadvantages. For time management and focus, a potential advantage is that these groups sometimes provide structured schedules and guidance for publications, so the process is mentored by co-authors and divided into stages. Candidates then know when analyzed results, section drafts, or revisions should be finished and can expect constructive feedback from colleagues. A potential disadvantage is that work for the research group at large can become a full-time job, even with overtime, and leave little time and attention for the candidate's own dissertation work. Under these circumstances, my only advice is that you must keep the priority of your own research, writing, and career in mind and do everything you can to clear time for this work. As I suggested in the previous chapter, you should make these needs clear to your research directors as well, even if doing so seems uncomfortable. Allowing you sufficient time to complete your dissertation is one of their professional responsibilities.

Can it Be This Easy?

Two or three hours a day, on average. Perhaps five days a week. Sounds like a part-time job.

For everyone except compulsive writers (such as Stephen King or Georges Simenon) actually writing—producing texts—*is* a part-time job. Professional journalists usually spend more time gathering material for articles than on writing them. Faculty members have lots of other jobs they need to do, including the research activities that lead to writing projects, and most of you have other responsibilities as well, often as teaching or research assistants. Two or three hours of focused writing day, on a regular basis, should be sufficient to get dissertation projects done in a few months. Limiting the time you spend on projects, even if you have more available, is also sensible preparation for demanding academic careers, in which finding even a couple of hours for this work can be difficult. For reasons we'll consider in the next section, most people can't tolerate much longer periods of sitting, trying to produce or revise writing, without becoming restless and uncomfortable, distracted and inefficient.

Unfortunately, the romantic traditions of creative illness and sacrifice that Boice describes still flourish in many academic environments, though their adherents usually don't. The ethos of some programs encourages graduate students to assume that dissertation work will be a grim ordeal that requires long hours of intense concentration, like a lonely and arduous vision quest. Moderation is often viewed as a symptom of mediocrity, and candidates who have joined these cults of suffering feel guilty if they aren't working all day and into the night or take a day off to enjoy themselves, even when the long hours they spend aren't very productive. These are stereotypes of PhD candidates in the humanities, especially, but there are similar communal pathologies in other fields, surrounding research as well as writing. One unhappy PhD candidate in the "hard sciences" told me that joining his research group was like taking vows of seclusion and renunciation in a monastic order. He was expected to remain in the lab every day even when there wasn't much going on, and in one slow period when he asked for permission to travel for a couple of weeks with his girlfriend, his advisor scowled, considered the request, and said, "Well, I won't tell you you can't come back." When he returned from his travels with a clearer head, therefore, he found a more congenial advisor and research group. Even if you can't so easily escape from such oppressive environments, I encourage all of you to question suggestions that you can't be a serious, successful scholar if you aren't slaving away for long hours and suffering.

If I've convinced you that such moderate amounts of time are enough to complete your dissertation successfully, with requisite patience and persistence, pause to consider how you can best schedule this time in the midst of other things you want and need to do. And when you've put in this time for the day, turn your attention to those other things just as fully. Spend time with family or friends. Get some exercise. Begin to work on other projects you find interesting. Sleep and eat well, with pleasure. Keep in mind that the writing practices you develop now should become sustainable components of a healthy and satisfying life.

What Could Possibly Go Wrong?

How can you complete a dissertation efficiently? In addition to a clearly structured sense for what you are writing and why it's significant in your field, we've now added compelling arguments that you must maintain regular but limited periods of time to work on specific parts of your projects with focused attention and modest, reasonable goals for what you can accomplish on a given day. You're aware that in these long-term projects, persistence and patience are greater virtues than sacrifice or burning passion, which is likely to flame out pretty quickly and leave you exhausted. If you follow these principles, what could go wrong?

Nothing, perhaps. The advice I've summarized thus far is sensible, and if these strategies work for you and you are satisfied with your progress, there may be no reason for you to delve more deeply into the reasons for which they don't work for everyone. Here and in a further chapter on writing blocks, I don't want to make you hypervigilant about problems you don't encounter and don't need to worry about.

Some unanswered questions remain, however, about what productive scholars are doing, exactly, in those periods of time they devote to writing. Advocates of strict writing schedules usually presume that these sessions will produce sufficient quantities of writing to move a project forward, and Boice's "external contingencies" require the production of at least three pages per session. In 60 of these writing sessions, you would accumulate at least 180 pages, enough for many dissertations, and Boice's research indicates that these pages will contain lots of "creative ideas."

But a dissertation isn't just a large pile of pages full of creative ideas. It's a continuous, coherent story about your research on a specific subject and its significance in a specific field of scholarship. Those sentences, passages, and pages must eventually form a structured, linear sequence addressed to particular kinds of readers in a consistent voice, and pages you compose that don't serve this purpose must be reconsidered, revised, or perhaps discarded. To evaluate what you've written thus far, you must spend time reading it, and revisions sometimes require further background reading or data analysis. On particular days, how should you use the time you've set aside for this work? How can you use it most productively?

I raise these further questions because I've known many dissertation writers who routinely show up for work and put in their time, as recommended, without making much progress. Some of them try to write but produce very little. Others write lots of pages of drafts that don't fit together into a coherent whole and writing more of them doesn't solve the problem. In those first months of my dissertation work, I was doing what Silvia, Boice, and others suggest. I dutifully spent several hours every day with moderate expectations as recommended. I produced lots of pages, containing some "creative ideas."

Nonetheless, I was moving in circles, not really getting anywhere. Later on, when I was making real headway, I often wrote much less each day or spent the time revising and editing previous versions, but I worked with a very clear, satisfying sense that I was moving forward. Productivity in the writing process isn't so easily quantifiable as counting pages, numbers of creative ideas, or amounts of time. And although the eventual product will be a linear sequence of sentences and passages, sections or chapters, the process isn't linear. Moving forward often entails going back, reading and revising what you've previously written, pausing to think about what you've said or will say next, and then going ahead, in overlapping spirals. This kind of writing isn't just the headlong addition of new words to the strings of utterance before them, as in conversational speech. The multitude of activities and decisions actually involved in this recursive process create lots of potential traps—opportunities for getting sidetracked or derailed, moving in circles or exerting futile effort, like that of a stalled dissertation writer who told me, after working for several weeks and getting nowhere, "I feel like I'm standing on something I'm trying to lift."

How can we explain and solve such problems? If the usual, behavioral recommendations don't work or you can't follow them, they can make you feel worse about your struggles, because the most obvious remaining explanation is that there's something wrong with *you*: that your personality is flawed or that you lack sufficient ability, motivation, or discipline for this work. And feeling bad about yourself isn't likely to help.

More constructive understandings of these remaining problems result from awareness that they result from the normal, inherent difficulty of what you are trying to do. Even if you follow the usual advice, there's no reason to believe that the process of completing a specialized work of scholarship over a period of months should be easy or that running into trouble is abnormal. This kind of work isn't just a matter of putting in your time and following standard procedures for turning out standardized products, like a job on an assembly line. While it's true that anyone who is literate can just sit down and write continuously, as in "freewriting," what they produce won't automatically become something like a dissertation or a publishable research article. If there's anything abnormal about such an endeavor it isn't you; it's the complexity and difficulty of what you are doing. To understand and solve these problems, we need first to go "back to the basics" of what writing is and what writers are actually doing. Then we can reconsider some of the most common rules for productive writing with a deeper understanding of what they mean in practice, why they can be difficult to follow, and why they don't always work.

The "basics" I have in mind are not the grammar and syntax of a language, which writing shares with speech, but the distinct characteristics of writing itself, which I defined in Chapter 2 as *the use of shared symbolic systems to communicate across time and space.* Like speech, all writing actually occurs in a succession of present moments. In comparison with face-to-face, interactive speech, however, the potential power of writing, its advantages and disadvantages, and most of the difficulties we encounter in the process result from the fact that when we're writing, *the audience for this communication isn't present.* Whenever and wherever someone actually reads what we wrote, in turn, it's unlikely that we will be present. In most cases, we don't know when and where that communication will occur; and if this writing is published, we won't even know who most of these readers are or how they respond. The power of this medium to communicate across time and space therefore creates a variety of unknowns, uncertainties, and strategic decisions we have to contend with in the present.

In this respect, all writing (and not just "creative" or "expressive" writing) is a work of the imagination. Those rhetorical decisions about audiences, standards, appropriate voices, and forms for communication with these audiences are strategic predictions. This is why the injunction *Spend this time writing!* can't account for the problems we encounter in the process. Whether this time we spend is productive or unproductive, agonizing or rewarding, depends on what we choose to imagine at the moment. This basic fact may seem obvious, but most teachers and authors of writing guides tend to ignore its implications.

In his explicitly titled essay "The Writer's Audience is Always a Fiction," Walter Ong (1975) was one of the first scholars to acknowledge that what we must imagine in the process of writing includes not only the invention of content but also of our readers. In the hypothetical case of a student completing an assigned paper, Ong notes:

> The problem is not simply what to say but also whom to say it to. Say? The student is not talking. He is writing. No one is listening. There is no feedback. Where does he find his "audience"? He has to make his readers up, fictionalize them.
>
> (p. 11)

Writing this paper in his dorm room, we'll say, this student will probably imagine his teacher reading through a stack of these papers later, somewhere else; or the assignment may have told him to imagine a different audience, such as his classmates or a particular author.

Dissertation writers might imagine that they are addressing their advisors or other scholars in their research fields, but in any case, these hypothetical readers are not present, not yet reading what we say, and the process of getting this work done *requires* their absence. If they were really there, we would just talk with them. And if what we wanted to say required a much slower process of composing and revising this communication in writing, their actual presence, peering over our shoulders and waiting, would interfere with the process. Noting the irony of this necessary absence, Ong observes, "I am writing a book which will be read by thousands or, I modestly hope, by tens of thousands. So, please, get out of the room. I want to be alone. Writing normally calls for some kind of withdrawal" (p. 10). While the purpose of academic writing is social, in ways we'll explore further, the present experience of writing is necessarily private and potentially isolating.

What we must "invent" in the present includes not only the substance of this writing, the absent reader, and the eventual form of the product, but also *the writer*: the particular version of ourselves, the *persona* or voice, with which we choose to address this audience. Advice that you should *Just write!* or *Be yourself!* doesn't acknowledge this necessity. With the possible exception of private writing such as diary entries, for which you are your own audience, you're always choosing particular voices, certain levels of diction and formality, for the occasion. When writing in the most familiar forms and circumstances, these decisions seem almost automatic and unconscious, but you make them strategically nonetheless. In quick messages to people you know well, for example, you may feel that you are just writing and being yourself, but in messages to a close friend and then to a parent or acquaintance, even on the same subject, you'll adopt different tones and choose different words. You may feel that you don't have to think about these decisions, but sometimes the ways in which we hastily imagine our readers and present ourselves turn out to be wrong, especially when we hit the SEND button too quickly, without reading over what we've said and considering its possible effects.

In comparison with face-to-face interaction, this delayed communication with absent, imagined readers offers potential advantages and creates potential difficulties that affect individuals differently. Some of these differences result from personality types or dispositions. Extroverts who thrive on social interaction often find written communication disorienting and difficult, especially when the process is long and the stakes are high. While they're writing, they feel deprived of the immediate visual and verbal responses that tell them whether the audience understands, agrees or disagrees, is impressed or offended: cues that stimulate expression, bolster their confidence, and tell them how to perform. I recently met with a dissertation writer in the sciences who seemed very confident, expressive, and articulate in our lively conversation about her work; but when we began to talk about a chapter draft, she became self-conscious and flustered. Although her conversational explanations of her research project were extremely clear, her writing was bogged down in long, tangential explanations of questionable relevance, and she confessed that when she was writing she didn't feel that she knew what she was doing, what voice she should use, or what her readers would understand, because she was alone. When I read part of her chapter aloud, however, she could hear the voice she was using, more easily imagine someone reading, and recognize the changes she needed to make. Listening to the sound of her writing helped to reconnect it with the qualities of speech. Reading a draft aloud to a friend, giving a conference presentation, or getting feedback from readers on work in progress can also help to socialize and clarify what can otherwise feel like silent guesswork or lonely muttering in an empty room.

For introverts and slow processors, on the other hand, the reader's absence can be a blessing. In that delay, free from the disarming pressures of immediate performance, they have time to consider and revise what they will eventually say to readers. The writing process gives them time to "compose themselves": to construct a persona they feel more confident about presenting to others. That bubble of solitude that writers inhabit in the present offers composure. This is why the poet William Stafford (1978) described writing as "one of the great, free human activities" (p. 20). While you are writing, you are completely free to say, revise, or delete whatever occurs to you. Because your readers are not present and remain imaginary, no one can read or judge what you are now saying unless you choose, in the future, to let them read it.

We lose this sense of freedom and composure, however, if we imagine that what we are saying in the present is immediate performance, as student writers do when they're trying to make the first draft the last. Potentially liberated from their performance anxieties, shy writers will then read what they've just written and think, "Does this sound stupid? Am I making a fool of myself?" as though they were already being judged. For all of us, regardless of our dispositions, productive writing strategies result from awareness of what we are actually doing in the present.

For the purpose of adopting a voice and persona, advice that you should "just be yourself" or "write what you know" can be particularly confusing for graduate students who feel that they haven't yet become the confident authorities their writing should represent them to be: that there is no authentic voice and version of oneself that meets these standards. One common result of this perception is a sense of fraudulence, of pretending to be someone you are not and to know more than you do. A related effect is procrastination: a tendency to postpone writing until you have become sufficiently accomplished and ready to write, as someone you actually are. If you feel that you are pretending to be someone you are not, what you say will seem to represent a minefield of potential blunders.

When will you be fully prepared to write effectively as an authentic version of yourself? Because further preparation for this kind of writing is always possible, the logical answer appears to be, "Not yet."

Illogical as it may seem in these moments, the real answer to this question is, "Always." In the present moments when writing occurs, you are always free and ready to write as some version of yourself, without risk. Although you can choose to imagine future readers and finished products, in reality no one else is reading or judging what you say. You may not like what you've written and want to change or delete it in following moments, but you are free to do this as well. As you continue to write and revise, your persona as the writer, what you know, what you have to say to imagined readers, and the authority with which you can say it—all of those fixed qualities we associate with finished products—will continually change. If you postpone writing and revision because you don't feel sufficiently accomplished, this dynamic process of becoming an accomplished writer can't occur. If you wait until you feel ready for this movement, you won't get anywhere.

I should emphasize again that this necessity of using the writing process to become accomplished applies to all scholars, not just to insecure novices. What I'm describing is the way accomplished works of scholarship actually come about in practice, in the hidden realms of uncertainties, second thoughts, and revisions from which these illusions gradually emerge. The illusions remain compelling in part because most of us prefer to maintain them, both in writing and in professional speech. "My professor talks like a book," a couple of undergraduates have told me in reference to course lectures, and they probably assume, by inversion, that these professors can "Write books like they speak," with spontaneous ease and authority. Apart from the likelihood that these lectures were prepared in advance and delivered before, to previous classes, the illusion is easily falsified. If these scholars could write this easily, they could complete books and articles in periods of days or weeks, not months or years.

Prepared speech, however, as in an academic lecture or conference talk, can be a useful way to think of what you are doing when you write. One reason for which writers imagine that they are already performing, and become vulnerable to stage fright in rehearsal, is that the experience of being on stage, performing before an audience, never occurs in writing and therefore seems no less hypothetical than everything else we imagine in the process. When you know that in a future moment you will actually be on stage, speaking to a real audience in a given amount of time, you probably welcome whatever time you have in advance to compose, revise, and rehearse. You wouldn't choose to deliver this speech without preparation or feel that you should be ready for this performance at the outset. You would use this time, instead, to compose and reconsider what you wanted to say and to experiment with different voices, levels of formality, and styles of delivery, without feeling that the voice you happen to be using is the one your audience will hear or that you are already being judged. As a means to the end of accomplished performance, the writing process is essentially the same, except for the disorienting fact that when the performance of your writing occurs, you won't be there. In this slow process, thinking of your writing as prepared speech can also maintain a more reliable sense for the sound and flow of your writing, which will be read and "heard," after all, as continuous utterance.

With this awareness of what we are actually doing in the writing process, we can evaluate some other common recommendations that dissertation writers often tape to their desks or screens, but with clearer understanding of what they mean and why they can be hard to follow.

Silence Your Inner Critics!

You can best understand this advice in light of Walter Ong's premise that "the writer's audience is always a fiction." If you must always invent your audience while you're writing, why would you choose to imagine a harshly judgmental critic rather than a friendly, supportive reader who is interested in your work?

In trying to follow this advice, however, you should remember that in the present moments of writing, all of these imagined readers, whether friendly or hostile, are "always" fictions, for all writers. In these moments, the supportive readers we imagine are no more real than the judgmental ones, and considering how they might respond to what we're saying isn't an abnormal psychological affliction. It's what writers normally do. The opportunity to imagine how our writing will sound to others, before it actually reaches them, is part of the creative freedom of the process. If you hear these voices, you shouldn't feel you're an insecure neurotic. Like other rhetorical decisions about form, content, voice, and style, however, the sense of audience should be a matter of strategic choice. Applied as a general rule, furthermore, advice that you should silence these inner critics can be limiting or misleading. Imagined readers who tell us we're stupid or incompetent should certainly be silenced. When we're trying to evaluate drafts for revision, however, those "inner critics" can tell us things we need to know about ambiguities, errors, or alternative strategies. We can't reliably revise our work if we've suspended our own critical perceptions.

For this reason, a more realistic version of this advice is that you should *Imagine audiences that are presently useful to you.* When you are composing new sentences and passages, it can be useful to suspend a sense of other readers altogether and just listen to the sound and meaning of the writing itself as it unfolds. Imagining how others will read and respond is more useful for revision, and when you are proofreading final versions, even a cranky English teacher from the past can sometimes be useful. This is why some composition scholars suggest that the process is initially *writer-based* and becomes increasingly *reader-based* in later stages of revision and editing. In other words, when they are still writing essentially to themselves, to figure out what they want to say, writers are most inclined to set aside concerns about other readers, in part because it's unlikely that anyone else will actually read these versions. In later stages of revision and editing, when they can more realistically think of what they are doing as a finished product, they're more likely to imagine how their work will sound to intended readers.

Avoid Distractions!

Most of us kick ourselves for our lack of discipline when we ignore this advice and interrupt writing to answer emails or text messages, get seduced by internet sites beckoning from the very devices on which we're supposed to be writing, or get distracted by any number of little chores and diversions. Such choices seem, and can easily become, irrational and self defeating. If you make a list of the things you might be doing at the moment in order of their importance in your life, continuing to work on your dissertation is likely to rank higher than pausing to rinse out your coffee mug, tidy up your workspace, give your cat some attention, or check what's happening on Instagram. Before you kick yourselves too hard, however, you should pause to consider what it is about writing that so often invites us to do something else.

One relevant factor is that writing requires a tolerance for delayed gratification, and for dissertations or publications, the delays are very long. Work on these long-term projects offers certain kinds of satisfaction, through engagement with the subject and the pleasure of saying something about it, but a sense of quick accomplishment isn't one of them. As the philosopher John Perry observed in his online essay "Structured Procrastination," (n.d.) when we aren't doing something we think we should be doing, we aren't doing nothing. We're doing something else, including things that might be useful and more immediately gratifying. Washing the dishes, replying to a message, or reading something relevant to a dissertation project brings immediate rewards. Sitting in a chair, staring at a computer screen, struggling to compose a new paragraph or rewrite an old one does not bring immediate rewards, especially when the imagined end of this project lies months in the future. The signal for an incoming message beckons because we know we can get this message read and reply to it in a matter of minutes. Or we tell ourselves that we can write with a clearer head if we get all of these little chores out of the way. We then get distracted by trying to remove distractions. When I expected them to show me new pages of dissertation chapters, several graduate students have announced, with a sense of accomplishment, that instead they had thoroughly cleaned and reorganized their workspaces, so they were finally ready to get to work. This is why writing guides tell you so insistently to turn off your phone and email or remove web browsers from the computers you use for writing. Because these and other distractions offer immediate gratification, they're hard to resist. Recommendations that you should focus on completing small parts of your dissertation, with reasonable daily goals and rewards to yourself for meeting them, serve related purposes. If you presently feel that you are working on the whole dissertation, moving at a snail's pace toward a remote destination, you'll feel that you aren't getting much done and can find any number of reasons to do something else instead.

A second factor that interferes with sustained attention is the fact that writing is not just mental work but also *embodied* activity. Academics tend to think of writing as the disembodied work of the mind or intellect that occurs in a realm disconnected from their physical presence and surroundings. Physical activity, attending to their bodies, means doing something else, such as going for a run or a walk, taking a yoga class, or working out at the gym. Stereotypical absent-minded professors are "lost in thought," adrift in time and space, and the spouse of one of these disembodied beings told me that he once emerged bleary-eyed from hours of writing in his study and asked, "Have I had lunch yet?"

When you are writing, nonetheless, you are also physically present somewhere in particular, still breathing and moving, and writing results from actually being there at the moment in that place, doing something. Like everything else that we do, writing is "psychophysical" activity, and one of its challenges is that our bodies and minds have limited tolerance for sitting (or standing) in one place, just moving our fingers on a keyboard and staring at a screen. This is why experienced writers recommend that you limit writing sessions to a couple of hours, and even in that time we're likely to get restless and uncomfortable. If you observe writers at work on their laptops in public places, you'll see that most of them are hunched forward, their heads and shoulders drawn by their attention toward their screens and keyboards, and you know they'll end up with stiff necks and backs. Sooner or later, their bodies are going to call for equal attention and say, *Wake up and look around! Notice where you are! Get up and move!*

And that's what you should do. You can't really solve this problem by forcing yourself to stay put, because you'll soon become distracted by your own discomfort. Sustainable writing practices shouldn't feel like self-sacrifice or punishment. Writers who sit in one place for hours aren't necessarily getting more done than those who work for shorter periods, take frequent breaks, or pause to stretch their bodies and take in their surroundings. Although writing is usually a solitary activity and requires sustained attention, it isn't synonymous with sitting still, and there's no rule that to get writing done you can't do anything else. My own tolerance for sitting in front of a screen, trying to write, is very low. After 20 or 30 minutes, at most, I feel compelled to get up and move, and this physical restlessness usually correlates with a loss of voice and forward movement in the writing I'm trying to produce. The whole process of figuring out what I want to say, whether it makes sense, or how it will sound to readers starts to become abstract and arbitrary. In other words, I find that I'm getting stuck, and I want to move my body in part because my writing isn't moving either.

But these interruptions don't mean that I stop writing. Before I get up, I usually pause to register what I was trying to say, and then when I'm walking, driving, or doing something else I essentially talk to myself, letting sentences materialize. The movement of walking, especially, seems to elicit the flow and cadence of written utterance as it will be read, and while I'm moving I can more easily hear what works. Over the years, I've cultivated a memory for sentences, whole paragraphs, or outlines of following sections I've composed in this way, and as soon as possible I write them down. On a long-term project such as this one, my work sessions often consist of these sequences: 20 minutes or so of sitting somewhere, ten minutes of walking, resumed sitting (often somewhere else), and so on. I always carry a notebook, so I can stop almost anywhere to record sentences and ideas I want to use.

Most of this writing-in-motion is solitary but talking to people about our work can also be productive writing activity. When we try to explain what we're doing in conversation, an audience is really there. What they immediately understand or find confusing can elicit more effective ways of saying things to imagined audiences when we return to the keyboard. These discussions remind us that what we're producing is not just an intellectual construct, assembled in our own minds, but also a form of delayed communication with others.

Avoid Revising and Editing While You Compose Drafts

In principle, this is good advice, especially for perfectionists who get embroiled in fussy tinkering to make every sentence perfect before they move on to the next. The tendency to combine revision and editing with the generation of drafts often results from lingering habits of student writing, under time constraints that encouraged us to avoid substantial revision. The effort to get everything right in the first version usually means we are imagining that what we're saying now represents the finished product and performance. In long-term projects that require revision, this probably won't be true, and interruptions to fix everything can be a waste of time. Pausing to read over, revise, and proofread what we've just written also makes composing very slow. Switching back and forth among these very different writing activities and roles—as *writer*, critical *reader*, and *proofreader*—disrupts our sense for the sound and flow of the language we're using. When we've just written something, furthermore, we aren't very reliable judges of its quality or of the way it will sound to other readers. What we've said might sound perfectly clear because we just said it and know what it means, or if we've struggled to get it said, it might sound awkward or ambiguous. If we read the same passage a day or week later, from a more detached perspective, our assessments are usually more accurate.

In theory, therefore, the most efficient strategy is to separate these roles and activities. Assuming that you've previously figured out what you want to say, as the *writer*, you should compose an initial draft version as continuously as possible, set it aside, and return to it in the more clear-headed role of a *reader*, perhaps with feedback from other readers, to determine what you need to revise. While you're making substantive changes as a *rewriter*, possibly in a series of drafts, you should avoid getting tangled up in correcting typos or making small changes in diction and phrasing. The role of a *proofreader* is most efficient at the end of the process when you're reasonably certain that a draft is almost finished. This sequence of neatly compartmentalized activities is useful in theory, as I said, because it clearly differentiates activities that can easily become muddled and counterproductive when we aren't aware of their different functions. For the purpose of developing methods that work for you, therefore, this advice is most useful as a set of conceptual tools for making strategic choices. In practice, many experienced writers use versions of this sequential approach: producing rough drafts fairly quickly and continuously, ignoring clumsy sentences, leaving blanks or notes to themselves for later revisions, and postponing detailed proofreading until the end of the process.

As a set of procedures all of you should follow, however, this advice is misleading, and if you can't follow it, you shouldn't feel that your methods are wrong. For reasons of their own, productive writers move through the process in a great variety of ways that offer alternatives. All of them face the necessity of reading over, revising, and editing what they compose, but these activities don't necessarily occur in a compartmentalized sequence of stages. Although it's very difficult to determine what writers are actually doing, I suspect that few of us can compose new sentences and passages for very long without pausing to read what we've written and, when we're dissatisfied, make changes. I certainly can't. While I'm composing drafts, I frequently ignore the recommended procedures and interrupt composing to revise and edit passages before I move on. I go through these recursive loops of composing and revising when I'm rewriting further drafts as well.

Are my methods wrong? They might be wrong for you and for other writers, but they work for me in their admittedly convoluted ways, and they represent deliberate choices I've made, based in part on factors of personality and preference. I'm aware that I could compose drafts more quickly if I didn't pause to read and revise previous sentences, but I'm not trying to make the first draft the last and avoid further revisions. Instead, I loop back to read and revise to create a smooth runway from which further writing can take off, like a glider, in a clear direction. If I can avoid getting bogged down in these changes, the time I spend reading, remembering, and clarifying what I've said pays off in forward momentum. If I don't do this, and the path I've created remains rough or crooked, I feel I'm stumbling ahead and don't get very far. To use another analogy, I feel like the new sentences I'm composing extend into empty space like a string from what I've already said, and because I can sense when the writing I've left behind it is tangled, I go back to straighten it out.

This way of writing only works for me when I'm making these changes primarily for myself, without trying to be done or to avoid further revisions. While I'm composing and revising, though, I'm not imagining that you (in this case) are already reading and judging what I've said. I go back to untangle and clarify sentences primarily because doing so makes the long, potentially tedious process of completing a project more pleasurable, interesting, and rewarding. I can't enjoy the freedom of writing in the moment if I imagine that I'm being stampeded or judged.

This is one alternative way of getting academic writing projects done, but there are many others. Because revision is an unavoidable necessity in this kind of writing, all scholars have to develop strategies for making changes in working drafts—deciding when they should revise and what they should do with the resulting debris of deleted and potentially useful material. Like other creative endeavors, producing the linear, coherent structure of finished writing from the masses of ideas and information at hand is a messy process. Some writers (and cooks, builders, or artists) can work happily and productively in the messes they've made, which they clean up at the end of the process. Others can't and frequently pause to tidy up.

As a consequence, I can't give you a reliable formula for dealing with the necessity of revising what you write, and neither can anyone else. After many years of consultations with writers, I still haven't identified revision strategies I can confidently recommend to everyone. When I ask scholars to explain how they draft and revise books or research articles, they usually describe their methods as idiosyncratic preferences that they adapt, to varying degrees, to specific projects, and they often say they wouldn't recommend their approaches to other writers, including their advisees. This is why guidance through this potentially bewildering, recursive dimension of the process can be especially difficult to find. Two scholars in the same field, working on the same type of project, are likely to use very different methods that wouldn't necessarily work for their colleagues. Across disciplines and forms, the range of practices expands further. For those of you who haven't developed effective revision strategies, however, the most hazardous approach is simply to drift into the process with the hope that a finished dissertation will somehow materialize at the other end. If the methods you're using don't work, you first need to examine what you are doing, and why, and then experiment with alternatives. Here I'll briefly describe some variations.

Draft Management

When student writers are assigned a "rough draft" with a certain deadline, get suggestions for revision, and produce a finished paper, these versions exist as separate documents. Most writing guides also refer to drafts as distinct, separable versions of your work. In practice, however, the term "draft" can have diverse meanings. All of us have to develop ways of orchestrating and keeping track of changes to work in progress, but these methods don't necessarily yield a sequence of documents.

One Draft

For reasons I've explained, student efforts to produce finished writing in one draft rarely work for professional academic writers. Still, the idea of producing brilliant work almost spontaneously, with sufficient knowledge and inspiration, remains alluring, in part because you wouldn't have to face the messy business of managing drafts if there were only one. Because you might find the idea tempting, I'll give you an unusual example that reveals some of the costs.

Known for his highly polished, literary, interpretive style of ethnographic writing, the anthropologist Clifford Geertz is widely admired by writing teachers, and his work is often included in anthologies of academic writing, as models for student writers. Geertz delivered prepared speeches in a similar erudite style that invites us to imagine that, like those professors who "talk like a book," he could just sit down and write the same way. By his own account, he did produce essays and books in single drafts, without much further revision, but an interview about his writing, published in the *Journal of Advanced Composition* (Olson, 1991), reveals some of the implications of this strategy.

Admitting that he thought it was "a very bad way to do things" and that he "would not advise that other people write this way," he said, "I don't write drafts. I write from the beginning to the end, and when it's finished it's done" (p. 248). Even when writing a book, Geertz explained, he began with an outline but largely ignored it. "I never leave a sentence or a paragraph until I'm satisfied with it; and except for a few touch-ups at the end, I write essentially one draft," revising sentences "in a sort of craft-like way of going through it carefully, and when it's done it's done." Although his intentions to avoid further drafts were similar to those of student writers, Geertz wrote with extremely high standards within a large reference frame, including about 12 years of field research at the time, in which he only produced extensive notes. Drifting into the writing process without detailed plans, he maintained cohesion by dismantling and reconstructing sentences until they met his standards for finished work. With these methods, before his death in 2006, Geertz published a dozen influential books and dozens of articles and reviews.

Before you try to emulate this model, however, consider its costs. Geertz wasn't just sitting down and spilling out brilliant writing. If your standards for finished writing are high, he acknowledged, the process is almost unbearably slow, and meeting those standards in long time frames requires extremely high motivation, patience, and persistence. "I usually write about a paragraph a day," Geertz estimated, over long periods of unencumbered leaves at places like the Institute for Advanced Study, Princeton (p. 248). Writing at this snail's pace with comparable standards, few of us could maintain the motivation and direction necessary to continue. Most of us would become mired in this work, confused or discouraged, and essentially blocked.

Evolving Drafts

What I've said about my own methods thus far might suggest that they resemble Geertz's, to the extent that I frequently read and revise passages until they meet my immediate standards for cohesion and flow. And sometimes this revision-while-composing is very slow.

In the larger scheme of things, however, my methods are very different and much more common among scholars. Although I spend a lot of time cleaning up the messes I've left behind, in order to move on, much of the resulting debris gets pushed forward as well. Now, for example, when I'm approaching the end of this chapter, I've gone back to rewrite previous sections of it several times, deleting passages I don't want to use there but might (or might not) use farther on or in another draft. If this material is potentially useful, I paste it at the end of the document, and later I sometimes cut and paste it back into a passage I'm currently composing. Going back to read the current version from the beginning, furthermore, I've twice thought of new approaches altogether and begun to write another version from the beginning, leaving the old one below as a stockpile of material I can cut and paste into the new version as it develops. As a consequence, many pages of cannibalized drafts accumulate below the one I'm currently composing. Every document I've been working on for some time therefore becomes a model of descending entropy. It usually starts out pretty smoothly and coherently, maintains cohesion up to a certain point where I'm working now, and then starts to fall apart into an incoherent jumble of spare parts. When I stop writing for the day, I usually mark this turning point with asterisks, so I can find it easily when I return. And when I finish a draft, with this mess of unused but potentially useful junk at the end, I often cut out the leftovers and paste them into a new document labeled "Scrap Pile."

In this fashion, the chapter draft gradually evolves until I'm willing to leave it as is. Even then, however, I know I'll have to come back to it eventually, read it over, and make further changes. When people ask me how many drafts I wrote for a book or article, I don't have an answer. I've known several other writers who can't answer the question either, because writing and revising are ongoing, overlapping dimensions of work on a single document.

Multiple Drafts

When a biologist told me that he had 36 drafts of a recent research article on his computer, therefore, I wasn't surprised that he had spent so much time revising it. From evidence of other scholars, I know that this much revision isn't unusual. I was more surprised that he could *count* these versions of the article. Unlike my evolving drafts, these were separate documents. When graduate students show me drafts of dissertation chapters or articles stored on their laptops, many of them also have two or more complete versions in separate, labeled documents.

These writers prefer to complete a draft before they substantially revise it. In some cases, they note handwritten changes on a printed copy before saving the old version to a new document they revise. This approach is most sensible when the basic structure of a chapter or article is established from the beginning, as it usually is for research articles in conventional formats. Even if central arguments, research claims, or results substantially change, other portions of previous drafts usually remain intact. Revision seems more methodical and manageable, and in the succession of documents you can observe incremental improvements. Ideally, the changes you need to make should become increasingly local and minor as the work approaches completion, though peer reviews or feedback from advisors sometimes require more substantial revisions to drafts you thought were nearly done.

Standard word processors present some basic visual and cognitive challenges for revision, especially for writers who are reorganizing drafts from one document to the next. Because the screen displays a limited portion of the text you are working on, you can easily get lost in your work, like someone in a labyrinth or a fog, due to limited visibility. To remedy this problem, some writers use two or more screens for cross-reference, each displaying a different version or section of the work at hand. Others use editing software systems such as Scrivener, with which you can display and transfer portions of text from different documents on a single screen.

A significant advantage of separate, complete drafts is that you can more easily get feedback from other readers at any stage of work in progress. Scholars who rely on advice from colleagues or co-authors need to have separate documents that clearly represent what they've done thus far. One of my evolving drafts, on the other hand, won't make much sense to anyone else, unless I extract completed portions or postpone feedback until the draft is done.

Piecework

Writers who are working on the same type of project, such as a dissertation monograph, conceptualize what they are presently doing in different scales. In other words, some imagine that they are working on the whole dissertation, others that they are writing one chapter or a particular section. Although these conceptual variations are hard to observe, the sizes and numbers of the documents they create offer some tangible evidence. Graduate students occasionally show me massive draft documents, of 200 pages or more, representing the whole dissertation. At the other extreme, writers' computer screens are littered with dozens of labeled files, representing small sections at varying stages of completion.

Both of these extremes can create problems in maintaining cohesion. If you are working on a chapter toward the end of a long document, it's difficult to remember and locate what you previously said, to ensure continuity and avoid repetition, and writers can feel lost in the enormity and complexity of the whole endeavor. Dividing the work into lots of small, manageable pieces, in turn, increases the risk that, in the later stage of assembly, they won't fit together. Writers who break down the task into lots of separate components can benefit from a greater sense of immediate control and accomplishment in the work at hand. Turning their attention to one small, clearly delineated part, they can get this task done, perhaps, on a given day, and move on to another. This benefit applies to all levels of subdivision, including larger chapters, but it depends on the strength and clarity of the overall design. You'll lose this sense of productive engagement if the central focus and structure of the project remains ambiguous or subject to change. In piecework of any kind, reliable construction of a part always requires a clear, coherent design of the whole.

The piecework approach to the writing process is most common in experimental fields of the sciences and social sciences, especially for research articles, where larger components (such as the *methods* and *results* sections) and subsections are clearly defined. In many cases, these pieces can be drafted at different stages of the project. Introductions and methods, for example, might be composed while results are still coming in or data analysis remains incomplete. Results are often divided into subheaded components, and some of these can be written up before others. Some of them will also need more revision than others. Treating these as separate writing tasks and documents therefore makes sense.

If the project is collaborative, furthermore, individual co-authors might compose different parts of the whole and exchange drafts for feedback and consistency. Separate document files facilitate these exchanges and further revisions, through which the proportions and styles of components gradually mesh into a coherent whole.

Fleshing Out a Skeletal Draft

Regardless of the sizes and numbers of constituent documents, successive drafts sometimes begin with a detailed outline that is incrementally fleshed out in later versions. I've known several doctoral candidates who successfully used versions of this method, which some of them learned from faculty advisors or peers. Although it's most common for research articles in the sciences, the strategy can be adapted to articles or dissertation monographs in other fields as well. Novelists sometimes use versions of this process, beginning with plot structure outlines similar to storyboards.

Because successive drafts flesh out a skeletal structure, this approach begins with a detailed plan, comparable to a blueprint, usually in the form of an outline of sections or chapters and subheadings. This plan can change, of course, as the project develops, but changes in the underlying structure also require coordinated revision of its components to maintain cohesion and proportion through the process. The sense that you are fleshing out a consistent, articulated skeletal structure allows you to move from one part of the project to another, with more control over the inescapable messiness of revision, along with a measure of your progress, like that of a sculptor adding clay or plaster to an armature.

In practice, this incremental process can also methodically regulate those changing rhetorical settings of your standards and sense of audience in the present, because successive drafts move deliberately from "writer-based" toward "reader-based" versions and levels of formality. A basic outline of headings and subheadings, for example, can lead to what traditional English teachers called "sentence outlines," with brief explanations of their contents or central points. For example, a PhD candidate recently showed me drafts of a dissertation research article with sections in various stages of completion. The introduction and methods sections were nearly finished, in full paragraphs with references. Because she was still analyzing data for parts of the results section, these subheads were followed by bulleted lists of points: brief statements or phrases she would later flesh out into full explanations. In separate documents she had created several technical illustrations that she could revise as necessary, with further results, and paste into appropriate sections when they neared completion. Though complex and unavoidably time consuming, the whole process seemed very orderly and constructive. A graduate student who used similar methods for research articles explained that after outlining her "scientific story" with notes on references she'll use:

> I continue to flesh out the draft until the meat of the paper is there. First, I write the methods and results sections. I next write the introduction. I remind myself what my original scientific question was. I then proceed to reread the first drafts and clean up major problems in flow, before tackling the discussion section. I then copy and paste each section into a separate document and rework it before recombining the entire paper and reading it aloud to make sure it makes sense together. At this point I typically send the paper on to my advisor. We send this back and forth many times, a main difference from my undergraduate experience, before bouncing it around any other co-authors and submitting it for publication.

Which approach will work best for you? For reasons I've explained, I can't answer this question for you. Ways of writing and revising that make perfect sense in theory don't work for some writers, and individuals develop productive strategies that seem bizarre or disastrous to others. My main point, instead, is that you should never feel stuck with methods that aren't working. In new writing projects, there's no virtue in continuing to do what you're currently doing or have done in the past. There are always options.

The Social Dimension of Scholarship

Walter Ong's assertion that written communication with others requires "withdrawal" from them reveals a paradox that requires clarification especially in dissertation work, when PhD candidates begin to write as members of professional communities. For the purpose of communicating with thousands of readers, as Ong said, he needs to be alone. While writing in that bubble of solitude, where other people are potential distractions, though, he isn't just muttering to himself. What he's saying emerges from and will become professional discourse, in networks of communication among people with related interests. While we're writing, these people aren't present, but we can imagine them most easily and reliably when we know who they are, what they know and believe, how they communicate with one another, and what they find interesting. All of those rhetorical factors we've considered—concerning audiences, purposes, standards, and forms of discourse—are inherently social.

These two dimensions of writing, private and social, correspond with conflicting images of eminent scholars as solitary, contemplative figures and as active, influential members of what writing specialists have termed "discourse communities." When they are absorbed in their own research and writing projects, your advisors may disappear behind closed doors or from campus altogether to prevent distractions from their work. Because they vanish, you might conclude that your projects require comparable seclusion from social interactions and academic responsibilities.

When they appear to be missing in action, however, most of these scholars are communicating with specialists in their fields at other universities, exchanging drafts of work in progress, attending conferences, giving presentations on their research, and participating in current debates. These interactions extend far beyond their home departments and campuses. "My field," one biochemist told me, "is a beehive of communication." Every project he works on is the subject of ongoing conversations, conferences, and electronic exchanges, including manuscript drafts and reviews. Even when scholars are working alone, behind closed doors, what they are writing is deeply entangled with other dimensions of their professional lives, within and beyond their own institutions. When I visited the office of an engineering professor for consultation about the work of one of his graduate students, I remarked, "This looks like the office of an editor." There were two computer screens on his desk and another on a table behind him, all displaying written documents he was working on, and his desk was covered with piles of manuscripts, correspondence, and professional journals.

With a laugh he replied, "Well, that's because it *is* the office of an editor, among other things." Two of the documents on his screens, he explained, were drafts of his own articles, co-authored with members of his research group. The other was a submitted manuscript of an article he was reading as an editor of a professional journal in his field. Some of the manuscripts in the piles on his desk were also submissions to this journal. Others were peer reviews he had solicited from scholars, to be forwarded to authors with his editorial synopses and recommendations. Everything going on in that office and in his research facilities nearby involved interactions with others, and the complex social networks involved extended to institutions across and beyond the United States.

These examples are from the sciences, where research and writing are most obviously collaborative, but similar activities are typically social, collaborative endeavors in the social sciences and humanities as well. In a discussion of faculty writing practices, an English professor observed, "In every writing project, I reach a point when it's no longer just my own—when I need help from other people." He was referring most explicitly to feedback from colleagues on early drafts and to later advice from editors and manuscript reviewers. However, in a broader sense the social dimensions of writing were there from the beginning of the process, when reading, conferences, and other exchanges generated questions or critical perspectives that motivated a writing project: *the sense that something needs to be said in response to what others have said.* In every field, scholars position themselves in relation to the positions of other scholars. Even a monograph, therefore, is not a monologue but a dialogue: the product of ongoing conversations in which our own contributions of ideas, findings, or arguments become meaningful. Those other participants in the conversation establish a sense of audience for the work that clarifies its focus and purpose. The activity of composing should then feel like response within networks of exchange, not like talking to yourself—aimless utterance into a void.

Because they involve a lot of collaborative assistance, these interactions also compensate for individual weaknesses. A well-written publication doesn't necessarily mean that the author is a skillful writer. Extremely successful scholars with tin ears for language have occasionally asked me for feedback on early drafts of articles or grant proposals full of errors, disorganized passages, and clumsy, ambiguous sentences. I initially wondered, "How do they get their work published?", but the answer was right at hand. They were doing interesting research, of course, but they were also willing to ask me and other colleagues for help.

For quick confirmation of these social networks in which scholarship occurs, scan the *acknowledgements* sections of books in your field. These sections typically begin with humble statements of gratitude, such as "This book could not have been written without the help of . . . ," followed by credits to the many people who contributed, at different stages, to the long process of getting it written and published. These may include supportive friends and family members, colleagues and other scholars who read draft versions, editorial staff who helped to steer the manuscript through publication, research assistants or data analysts, library and archive staff, specialized consultants, field research contacts, or organizations that provided funding. Some of these sections list more than a hundred individuals and organizations involved with the project in diverse ways. "Long-term relationships" with writing projects aren't just relations between an author and a subject; throughout the processes of research, writing, and revision they develop through relations with others in real social networks.

For comparison, then, look at the *acknowledgments* at the beginnings of filed dissertations. As a rule, these maps of the author's networks are much shorter and more closely confined to the author's program and advisors, university, and research context. These differences suggest that for the purpose of completing and publishing works of scholarship, the authors are socially disadvantaged. Still in the "liminal," transitional process of becoming scholars, they haven't yet developed professional relationships and identities comparable to those of their advisors and other faculty who are established members of larger research communities. In this early stage of their careers, it's likely that available networks of support for their projects are more limited, and in cases of extreme isolation, the noisy beehives of communication in their fields might be reduced to the drones of their own voices.

You don't want to let that happen, but the structures and trajectories of higher education can limit the social dimensions of scholarship in ways that privatize dissertation writing. Although undergraduates write in the social contexts of their courses, the priorities of competitive grading tend to define writing as independent effort and individual performance: what they can do on their own. Due in part to demands from employers and professional schools, collaborative learning has become increasingly common in some fields of undergraduate studies, but individual assignments and grades are still the norm in most courses, and academic integrity codes suggest that unauthorized help with assignments represents cheating or plagiarism. Behind the scenes, students work together on their assignments much more than their teachers realize, but much of this collaborative learning remains clandestine and vaguely illicit. When I led one advanced physics class, in the professor's absence, I asked the mixture of seniors and first-year graduate students to describe the most valuable learning experiences in the course. Following an uncomfortable silence, one student said, "Working on the problem sets together," and others nodded in agreement. They were reluctant to admit this, they explained, because they weren't sure they were allowed to help one another and were too timid to ask.

The early stages of doctoral programs, in which graduate students complete course requirements, sustain this emphasis on individual performance, and so do qualifying and comprehensive exams. Graduate courses and cohorts of peers can provide social networks, support systems, collaborative relations, and a sense of identity within the university. In the dissertation stage, however, this social fabric often unravels. Now pursuing their own specialized research projects, candidates disperse, often to field sites, archives, and other remote settings. If and when they return to campus to complete their dissertations, the social environments of their programs have changed. Most of their friends and peers from earlier years are absent or absorbed in their own projects, and new collaborative relations can be difficult to find. Having returned to campus from two years of field research, one anthropologist told me, "When I come into the department now, I feel like a ghost."

Unless programs actively sponsor collaborative dissertation groups, professional development seminars, and other measures to socialize this final stage of doctoral work, candidates tend to resign themselves to the necessity of completing dissertations on their own, with varying amounts of guidance from advisors. Although the resulting isolation is a widely known cause of attrition and delay and an impediment to further career development, many graduate advisors continue to believe that candidates need to work on their projects in seclusion. One reason, perhaps, is that faculty members crave unencumbered time, free from teaching and other professional responsibilities, to complete their own research and writing projects. Taking the value of their professional networks and collaborative relations for granted, they often assume that graduate students face the same problems. Candidates who internalize these values feel that they should seclude themselves from social and professional distractions: that their transformation into scholars should ideally occur, like the metamorphosis of caterpillars into butterflies, in a cocoon where they experience challenges of scholarship as personal struggles.

From my perspective, this was the underlying flaw in the Mellon Foundation's ten-year Graduate Education Initiative (GEI), thoroughly described and assessed in the book *Educating Scholars: Doctoral Education in the Humanities* (Ehrenberg et al., 2010). This ambitious project supported initiatives to improve PhD completion rates and times in 54 humanities departments at ten universities, from 1991 to 2000. The GEI gave individual departments considerable freedom to design their own "interventions," including workshops to "reduce isolation," promote "collaborative work," or develop "job/profession preparation"—components that graduate students often considered the most valuable features of the GEI. But fewer than half of the participating departments adopted these initiatives, and some of those dissolved over the term of the project. Instead, participating departments used the bulk of GEI funding to provide fellowship support that relieved PhD candidates from the constraints of teaching assistantships or part-time jobs on the assumption that they needed more time to focus on their dissertations. But these opportunities for withdrawal did not yield substantial benefits. Over the ten years of the GEI, completion rates across these departments slightly improved, but completion times did not.

Some of the reasons became apparent in focus groups of PhD candidates that a graduate school dean and I assembled a few years ago, to identify "unmet needs" in their dissertation work. Their most common response was that they felt isolated and needed more collaborative assistance from other scholars and peers. More specifically, they had difficulty finding what I call "incremental readers" to give them feedback on work in progress. We were surprised that these complaints were consistent across disciplines, including fields of the sciences in which the candidates' research had been highly collaborative. In the process of dissertation writing, however, these working relations in labs or field sites often dissolved. A few of the participants reported, with expressions of envy from others, that their programs sponsored dissertation seminars or colloquia, promoted peer collaboration, encouraged their involvement in professional organizations, and included them in group presentations at conferences. A few of them had also benefitted from workshops sponsored by the campus teaching and learning center, but these events did not lead to further collaborations. Because other graduate students they knew were busy with their own projects, asking them to read and discuss drafts seemed intrusive. On the whole, therefore, participants described dissertation work as a lonely and somewhat bewildering process.

What can you do to avoid or solve these problems? As individual PhD candidates, your abilities to change your program environments and institutions are limited, but you can take initiatives to enrich your own experience and facilitate your progress within and beyond these environments.

These initiatives begin with realistic assessment of what you actually need and deserve for the purposes of completing your PhD and furthering your career goals. If you assume that you can best complete this work in a social vacuum or that you should postpone career development until you finish your dissertation, you should seriously question these assumptions. Because knowledge production occurs in social networks, extensive reading in your research field, accumulating knowledge of its literature, won't automatically make you a part of it, any more than reading lots of novels will make you a novelist or a literary scholar. Because program environments, specialization, and writing itself tend to encourage isolation, within a shell of hypothetical connections, developing real connections with other scholars requires deliberate effort. Here are some suggestions:

On Campus

Use Available Resources

Contact offices of the graduate school, teaching and learning center, and writing program on your campus to learn about available programs and services for doctoral candidates. These often include a variety of workshops or seminars on dissertation writing, publication, and professional development; consultation and peer tutoring services; and help in joining collaborative support groups. Investigating and using these resources doesn't mean you are needy or inept. Participants often report that their main benefit was the opportunity to meet and share experiences with graduate students in a variety of fields.

Contact Faculty Members in Related Disciplines

The fragmented social environments of doctoral programs tend to encapsulate PhD candidates in subfields of their departments and relations with their official advisors. I'm often surprised that candidates in neurobiology or sociology, for example, haven't met scholars on campus who pursue related inquiries in cognitive psychology or human development, anthropology or political science. These cross-disciplinary interests are extremely rich and underutilized resources for graduate students who feel that those other departments are foreign territory. When you've identified scholars in other departments who have related research interests, spend a little time investigating their work. If there are common issues you would like to discuss, contact them to explain what you are doing and arrange a meeting or ask, perhaps, if you can sit in on graduate seminars they teach. Departments also sponsor lecture series, and you might benefit from attending these and meeting speakers. Faculty members usually welcome these cross-disciplinary discussions, and your ventures into other departments will seem stranger to you than to them.

Form Collaborative Writing Groups

Some doctoral programs encourage and help to assemble small groups of dissertation writers, and if yours does, I encourage you to join one. Because participation involves reading and responding to other members' drafts, candidates often doubt that the benefits outweigh the costs of time and attention away from their own work. When these support groups function well, however, they can be enormously helpful. In addition to constructive feedback and perspectives on your work, shared experiences help to normalize and solve the unavoidable problems of dissertation writing. If your program doesn't sponsor these collaborative groups, your graduate school office might do so. Otherwise, you can take the initiative to form one in your program or related fields. Department offices can give you contact lists for dissertation-stage candidates on campus, and you can send out open inquiries without concern for imposing on anyone.

These groups usually work best when they are small, from three to five members. Two PhD candidates in one department ignored my advice and formed an extremely successful group that grew to more than 20 graduate students from all levels, but they subdivided collaborations to smaller groups and mentoring pairs, and administering its operations consumed a lot of their time. Even in small groups of three or four, however, I encourage you to begin with a meeting to establish some principles and ground rules you can all agree on. Graduate students often abandon these collaborations because the "chemistry" among members didn't work, but these problems usually result from misunderstandings about goals and purposes. Constructively reading, responding to, and discussing work in progress requires a combination of goodwill and honesty that needs to be established as a matter of principle, to avoid harsh criticism, injured feelings, or timidity. The purpose of collaboration isn't judgment or correction but potentially useful observation. When I help to form these groups, therefore, I recommend a set of rules for writers and readers, concerning their freedom and responsibility:

> As *Writers*, you are free to show members work at any stage of the process, but you must tell them what this writing represents (Is it a very rough draft? A portion of a chapter you think is nearly finished?), the kinds of help you hope to receive, or the problems you're trying to solve.
>
> As *Readers*, with this guidance for reading in mind, you are nonetheless free to make any observations that might be useful to

the writer, including strengths and weaknesses, stylistic patterns, or alternative perspectives the author hasn't considered. Be sure to include what you like about the draft and find most valuable.

As *Writers*, then, you should welcome all of this feedback, but you are completely free to ignore advice you don't agree with or don't want to follow.

Find Writing Partners or Incremental Readers

Some writers prefer collaboration with one other person or more incidental feedback on a particular draft. Graduate schools sometimes have lists of candidates who are looking for writing partners, with information about their fields and research interests. If they can't help, you can simply ask individuals in your program or related ones if they are willing to exchange and discuss drafts or just read yours.

As the members of our focus group explained, finding readers for work in progress can be difficult and daunting, because everyone is busy. If you need feedback on your work, however, you should do your best to get it and accept the possibility of getting turned down. The acceptance of this risk resembles that of publication. If you don't submit manuscripts, you won't get published, but you have to accept the strong possibility of rejection.

Beyond Campus

I've noted that professionally active scholars in your fields develop social networks far beyond their own universities. They maintain and expand these networks by attending and giving talks at professional conferences, visiting other campuses and research facilities, accepting appointments as visiting professors, serving as editors or reviewers for journals, and maintaining informal communications with disciplinary colleagues around the world. These connections and opportunities lead to others, such as invitations to give talks, join panels, submit or co-author publications, serve on organization committees, or apply for research grants and fellowships. When I urge you follow their examples and develop your own professional networks, I'm aware that graduate students rarely have comparable resources for this purpose. With the resources available, nonetheless, you should do what you can to become active, visible members of your research communities.

Attend Conferences and Propose Presentations

Those of you who are members of research groups funded by research grants may be included, even in the first years of doctoral studies, in conference panel presentations or poster sessions with funding from research grants. For those of you who are working individually, these professional activities require more initiative. Unless the conferences are nearby, attending them is expensive, and presentation proposals have to be submitted months in advance. It's easy to convince yourselves that you aren't ready to present your work or that you can't afford the time and expense.

Because you represent the future of your disciplines, however, these organizations welcome participation from PhD candidates, and most of the large ones have funds you can apply for to defray travel expenses. Some have branch organizations or satellite conferences for graduate students. Getting there and presenting your work is almost invariably worth the effort. At sessions in your area of specialization, dispersed members of your research community converge in the same rooms, where you can meet them and discuss mutual interests. PhD candidates who give brief talks about their dissertation work can benefit enormously from the necessity of focusing on its core significance and getting feedback from audiences. While we're working on our projects alone, most of us have wondered, "Who cares?" Speaking to real audiences, discovering that they are interested in what you're saying, can boost your motivation and confidence.

Contact Other Specialists in Your Field

Professional conferences are great places to make initial contacts with other scholars, including graduate students who share your interests. That's one of their main purposes. But you can also make these contacts through messages in which you introduce yourself, tell authors what you find interesting about their work, and explain what you are doing. These initiatives sometimes lead to further exchanges or offers to read work in progress. If there are scholars at nearby schools whom you would like to meet, or if you are traveling in the vicinity of more distant universities where they teach, contact them to propose a brief meeting.

Publish as Much as Possible

For the two PhD candidates I mentioned who formed a large writing group, one of their main incentives was the observation that newly minted PhDs who applied for jobs in their department had substantial lists of publications and presentations on their résumés, much longer than their own. Because their program faculty members weren't actively encouraging advisees to publish, they took matters into their own hands, and much of the work in their group was devoted to publication and résumé-building. In competitive markets for academic jobs and postdocs, these credentials have become increasingly important.

Completed dissertations and *potential* for scholarship are no longer sufficient, but you can't necessarily rely on your advisors to push you in this direction.

Full research articles in reputable journals are most valuable, of course, but all kinds of publications and presentations in your field will be useful to your career development. These can be brief communication articles, responses to previous articles, talks or colloquia at other schools or in your department, participation in conference panels, or poster presentations. Beyond their value as credentials, publications help to establish your identity in research communities and often stimulate communications with readers, along with further opportunities to publish or collaborate.

References

Boice, R. (1990). *Professors as writers: A self-help guide to productive writing*. Stillwater, OK: New Forums Press.

Boice, R. (1997). Which is more productive, writing in binge patterns of creative illness or in moderation? *Written Communication*, 14 (4), 435–459.

Bolker, J. (1998). *Writing your dissertation in fifteen minutes a day: A guide to starting, revising, and finishing your doctoral thesis*. New York, NY: Owl Books.

Ehrenberg, R. G., Zuckerman, H., Groen, J. A., & Brucker, S. M. (2010). *Educating scholars: Doctoral education in the humanities*. Princeton, NJ: Princeton University Press.

Murray, D. M. (1980). Writing as a process: How writing finds its own meaning. In T. Donovan, & B. McClelland (eds.), *Eight approaches to teaching composition* (pp. 3–20). Urbana, Il: National Council of Teachers of English.

Perry, J. (n.d.). Structured procrastination. [Web log post]. Retrieved from www.structuredprocrastination.com

Olson, G. (1991). The social scientist as author: Clifford Geertz on ethnography and social construction. *Journal of Advanced Composition*, 11 (2), 245–268.

Ong, W. J. (1975). The writer's audience is always a fiction. *PMLA*, 90 (1), 9–21.

Ong, W. J. (1982). *Orality and literacy*. London, England: Methuen & Co.

Silvia, P. J. (2007). *How to write a lot*. Washington, DC: American Psychological Association.

Sommers, N. (1980). Revision strategies of student writers and experienced adult writers. *College Composition and Communication*, 31 (4), 378–388.

Stafford, W. (1978). *Writing the Australian crawl: Views on the writer's vocation*. Ann Arbor, MI: University of Michigan Press.

Zerubavel, E. (1999). *The clockwork muse: A practical guide to writing theses, dissertations, and books*. Cambridge, MA: Harvard University Press.

6 Writing Blocks

What Is a Writing Block?

I became particularly interested in writing blocks because many of the graduate students who turned to me for help were mired in the process of writing dissertations, master's theses, or other important projects, exerting lots of effort without making substantial progress. Similar problems had occasionally surfaced in the undergraduate courses I taught, when highly motivated, capable students were unable to complete assignments, but these cases were unusual. Among doctoral candidates, entanglements in the process of writing and revising dissertations are fairly common, and almost everyone involved with PhD programs knows of several who have struggled for years or given up. As my interest in these obstacles to productive writing became known, primarily through departmental grapevines, dozens of graduate students who were encountering such problems turned up in my office in the hope of finding solutions.

Almost all of the help I could offer (and can offer here) was based on insights I gathered from these capable but struggling writers themselves, not from any coherent body of knowledge about their difficulties. When I looked for published research and theory on "blocks" in the writing process, I found very little material relevant to the specific problems these graduate students described. In my own profession of rhetoric and composition, as I've noted, earlier research interests in the writing process had largely dissolved by the 1990s. Because writing specialists were primarily concerned with undergraduate instruction, the few studies of blocked writers available usually concerned student writers who were unable to complete course assignments. Mike Rose's (1985) edited collection of essays, *When a Writer Can't Write*, suggested useful directions for further research and clarification, including distinctions between cognitive and emotional causes of writing blocks, but these lines of inquiry soon dissolved. Scholars invested in the study of texts had little interest in writers who failed to produce any, and occasional accounts of "writer's block" in literary studies concerned the agonies or dry spells of famous novelists or poets such as Conrad or Coleridge, not students or scholars.

The term "writer's block," most often used to describe these afflictions, conveys the common assumption that blocking is not a real writing problem but a type of "mental block": a mysterious psychological condition, aversion, or anxiety that undermines ability and stifles normal expression. When teachers say that students "can't write," they usually mean that the writing they produce isn't very good, not that they can't produce writing. If a writing problem doesn't yield a text, where we can observe it, the problem must be hidden in the writer's mind: the expertise of psychologists, not writing teachers. This is one reason for which capable graduate students who can't produce dissertations are often referred to campus mental health clinics for psychological counseling. But apart from Robert Boice, whose behavioral approach I discussed in Chapter 5, very few psychologists have studied writing difficulties. Boice acknowledges the real insecurities and misconceptions that can undermine writing ability, but John Silvia, as I noted, maintains a common belief that "writer's block" is an imaginary problem that simply results from not writing. The equally simple, behavioral solution for not writing, he argues, is to write.

When graduate students are bogged down in complex dissertation projects, however, telling them that their problems aren't real or are just in their minds isn't very helpful. The message writers usually receive is *You're just being neurotic. Get over it, or see a therapist.* And in a less judgmental sense, the suggestion that the problem is in the writer's mind isn't useful because it states the obvious. Apart from the physical activities of typing or handwriting, almost *everything* we are doing when we write is going on in our minds, because writing is a work of the imagination. When the process of writing is long and complicated, what we imagine that we are doing creates all kinds of possibilities for getting into trouble.

The troubles my students were getting into, furthermore, didn't represent consistent psychological patterns or personality traits that defined "writer's block" as mental condition or a "blocked writer" as a type of person. John Daly's (1985) accounts of "writer's apprehension" or "anxiety" suggested that blocks often result from fears and aversions to writing itself, but few of these graduate students seemed to be afraid of writing. The stereotypical image of the blocked writer staring helplessly at a blank page was also false. Although the writing they produced wasn't moving them forward in the process, some of these graduate students produced lots of informal writing and drafts, with steady investments of time and effort. The behavioral remedies of strict schedules and production goals didn't solve their problems.

In most cases, furthermore, these blocks in the process were not longstanding, general conditions. Most of these graduate students had written successfully and productively in their undergraduate and even graduate courses, as students, and many of them still completed shorter or less important writing projects without much difficulty. Although anxiety, distress, depression, or loss of confidence were often complicating factors, it was very difficult to determine whether these emotional conditions were causes or effects of their writing difficulties. Struggling unsuccessfully for years, in some cases, to get a dissertation written can be depressing and demoralizing for anyone.

Because prevalent assumptions about "writer's block" failed to account for complex writing problems among doctoral candidates, I published a book that was based on what I learned from these writers, titled *Understanding Writing Blocks* (2001). Over following years, however, these understandings have continued to evolve. Although most of the premises of that book remain unchanged, here I'll return more concisely to the foundations of my current views of these problems, with a narrower focus on the challenges of dissertation writing and related works of scholarship.

To define these problems, first of all, I use the term "writing block" to describe a category of *obstacles to movement through the writing process*, not a category of writers, personality types, or psychological conditions. Even with this narrower definition, individual writers who are working on difficult projects encounter obstacles in the process for so many reasons, in such diverse circumstances, that I've often questioned whether the term "block" represents a meaningful category. After all, running into trouble, getting confused, and feeling temporarily immobilized are *normal* writing experiences for scholars. Arguments fall apart or lead to an impasse. Pieces of the puzzle are missing. We raise questions we can't answer, or the answers we present sound unconvincing. To move forward, then, we have to go back, and in those loops of revision most of us feel at times that we're regressing, stalled, or going in circles. Forward progress doesn't mean that we're always charging forth with clear-headed confidence, leaving a trail of terrific writing we won't need to change. That isn't a reasonable standard for normal academic writing; it's just a rare bit of luck or a fantasy. If the term "block" has any useful meaning in practice, therefore, it must represent a category of particularly stubborn obstacles to movement that writers run into consistently and can't easily overcome.

To further clarify this category of writing difficulties, we should add that they afflict *capable, motivated writers* who have the knowledge, skills, and incentives to complete the task at hand. If I tried, without years of preparation, to write a publishable article in a field I know little about, such as biochemistry or astrophysics, I would struggle and fail, but the underlying problem would be my lack of ability, not a writing block. In contrast, those of you who have reached the dissertation stage of a PhD program are almost invariably capable of completing dissertations. We can further define a writing block, therefore, as *a pattern of interference with the use of our ability*. These obstacles in the process appear to disable *capable* writers.

Because a dissertation is the ultimate requirement for a PhD, almost all of you who are trying to complete dissertations are also motivated to invest the necessary time and effort. Various people have told me that they "have writer's block" (as though it were a communicable disease) because they feel they should really get around to writing a book they have in mind but don't or occasionally start, give up, and do other things instead. These are not blocked writers. Nor are several capable graduate students I've known whose progress slowed or stopped because they lost interest in their work, got involved in more rewarding endeavors, or began to feel that the benefits of a PhD weren't worth the costs of time and trouble. These writers sometimes say they are blocked and initially appear to be, until I realize that they are looking for motivations to continue, not for productive ways of doing so. For motivational factors as for emotional ones, however, it's often difficult to distinguish causes from effects. Loss of motivation can cause writing difficulties, but loss of motivation and confidence can also result from the frustrations of trying to move ahead without getting anywhere.

With these distinctions in mind, we can more fully define a writing block as *a particularly stubborn obstacle in the writing process that impedes progress and prevents capable, motivated writers from using their ability productively*. Blocked writers typically want to write, sometimes desperately, and expend lots of effort to get beyond these obstacles, without success. Similar to the graduate student who said "I feel like I'm standing on something I'm trying to lift," they typically describe their difficulties in terms of movement and immobility. They say that they feel *stuck, stalled*, or *paralyzed*, that they aren't *getting anywhere* or are *just going around in circles*, or that they're *lost* or *wandering*. Describing what happened when she tried to compose a draft, one of these writers said, "I freeze, like a deer in the headlights." And the political theorist who said "Reading doesn't leave tracks," to explain why she continually stopped writing to read, revealed that she thought of writing as a hazardous trail of evidence from which critical readers could locate her position and identify her weaknesses. It felt safer, then, to remain still and silent.

These obstacles to movement can arise at any stage of the process, from the generation of notes and plans to the editing of final drafts. I once advised an unusual college senior who couldn't stop revising and proofreading course papers that were essentially finished, even after he had missed deadlines. As a last resort, I had to walk with him to a department office to make sure that he put a very late research paper in the professor's mailbox, and I was still concerned that he might return to remove it. He was blocked at the very end of the process, at the point of releasing his work to the audience.

In most cases, however, these impediments to movement occur when writers are composing or revising drafts. Sometimes they represent longstanding difficulties that have disabled writers in all kinds of academic work, including undergraduate courses. More often, they arise specifically in new kinds of writing projects that are particularly challenging and important, such as dissertations, proposals, or research articles. When writers identify the nature and cause of a block, the barrier that seemed intractable sometimes vanishes and they begin to write with comparative ease and speed. In other cases, writers who understand the problem conceptually must struggle for months to solve it in practice. To remove such obstacles, in every case, we need first to understand when they occur in the writing process and why.

Why Do Blocks Occur?

Through his dissertation research on college students at UCLA, published in a research article and then in a slender book titled *Writer's Block: The Cognitive Dimension*, Mike Rose (1984) began to formulate some promising foundations for identifying and removing writing blocks through instruction. When capable writers can't produce writing, Rose observed, "we are puzzled and often resort to broad affective explanations, e.g., 'He's afraid of evaluation,' 'She's too hard on herself'" (pp. 1–2). The title of Rose's earlier article on his research—"Rigid Rules, Inflexible Plans, and the Stifling of Language" (1980)—conveys his alternative explanation. Among the undergraduates in his study, writing blocks usually resulted from cognitive problems: writers' *misconceptions* of what they were doing and how they should do it. In many cases, ineffective strategies for completing college assignments resulted from adherence to "rigid rules" or methods students had learned in high school, such as the belief that all essays should divide a thesis into three parts or that every sentence should be perfect before you write the next. When inflexible conceptions of writing conflict with present realities, writing can seem impossible. A case in point is the freshman I mentioned who couldn't write an analysis of six short stories because she believed that an essay must consist of three parts, introduced by an apt quotation.

If blocks result from particular misconceptions, the solutions lie in identifying these cognitive barriers to the use of ability and providing alternative concepts appropriate for the tasks at hand. Rose found that in most cases he could effectively provide this help in one or two conferences with individual students. In a few cases, however, his cognitive diagnoses did not solve the problem, and he concluded that deeper, "affective" problems, possibly requiring psychological counseling, prevented these writers from implementing revised strategies.

Obstacles to writing dissertations are rarely this easy to identify and remove, but Rose's explanations of these problems remain useful. One valuable insight is that "cognitive" blocks, resulting from misconceptions of writing, are most common in academic transitions, when writers must adapt previous writing strategies to unfamiliar contexts, expectations, and forms of discourse. In these transitions, inflexible, dysfunctional conceptions of writing result in a wide range of difficulties among capable writers. This is why college freshmen considered to be good writers in high school often seem to be weak writers in their undergraduate courses, where expectations can fundamentally change, and previously successful writing strategies can also fail to work in higher levels of undergraduate work. Throughout this book, I've argued that advanced graduate students encounter a further set of transitional challenges, from student writing to scholarship, in which fundamental conceptions of writing must change. In undergraduate and graduate studies, capable writers can also encounter blocks and related difficulties in transitions from one field of academic writing to another. I consulted for several months with a former engineering professional who was unable to complete acceptable writing assignments in his social science graduate courses, required for a PhD he hoped to pursue for a new career. As an experienced writer of technical reports and instructions, he believed that good writing was as clear and concise as possible, with lots of bullet points and direct statements of fact. "If it's important to say DON'T HIT THE RED BUTTON!", he argued, "you make sure people will get that message. You don't bury it in a long paragraph." The sensible rules for good writing in engineering were at odds, however, with the expectations of his professors in social and educational philosophy, where convincing arguments unfold from long passages of referenced discussion. Until he revised his fundamental conceptions of assignments, he couldn't meet length requirements, and his advisors told him he lacked the "basic skills" for graduate work. "I feel like I'm back at square one," he complained, and in some respects he was.

This engineer's professors in the social sciences didn't explicitly tell him how arguments in their fields are constructed, even after they had read his failed attempts. They just assumed that he should already know or should learn on his own and concluded that he was a bad writer. If most of the cognitive problems that block capable writers can be solved through instruction, as Rose argued, instruction should also *prevent* many forms of blocking and other difficulties that result from misconceptions and maladaptive writing strategies. With Karen McClafferty, Rose (2001) published an article titled "A Call for the Teaching of Writing in Graduate Education," based on professional writing workshop courses the authors taught for graduate students in diverse disciplines. In the context of a little writing "community," class discussions of the students' work in progress addressed many causes of rhetorical confusion I've discuss in this book, including the construction of reference frames in literature reviews, questions of voice and audience, and revision strategies. Discipline-specific graduate seminars on writing proposals, research articles, or dissertations can prevent a wide range of difficulties and delays among graduate students in these fields. Habitual strategies that no longer work can be very difficult to identify and revise on one's own, and for this reason graduate students who discuss these issues with faculty and peers in department seminars, informal writing groups, or collaborative projects can revise their methods more effectively. These were also the main conclusions of Barbara Lovitts's extensive research on the causes and preventions of difficulty and failure in doctoral programs, presented in her books *Leaving the Ivory Tower* (2001) and *Making the Implicit Explicit* (2007). The proportions of doctoral candidates who spend years struggling unsuccessfully to complete dissertation projects would shrink dramatically if all of their programs assumed responsibility for teaching them how works of scholarship are written.

Because this preventive instruction hasn't become a standard component of most doctoral programs, extracurricular services—such as writing and learning centers, graduate school advisors, psychological counselors, and leaders of dissertation "boot camps"—must try to solve the problems of large numbers of PhD candidates who have become stalled in the writing process for months or years, with compounding effects. Over time, what begin as preventable "cognitive," rhetorical problems often lead to anxiety, loss of confidence and motivation, depression, aversion, and other "affective" conditions easily mistaken for personality traits and causes of blocking. When they've developed, these implications of blocking become complicating factors that demand attention as well. If the underlying cause of a writing block is a misconception about this kind of writing, however, treatments of its psychological effects, such as boosts to confidence or motivation, won't reliably solve the problem.

Although the causes and effects of their problems are often hard to distinguish, I can roughly estimate that about 75 percent of the blocked writers I've advised were initially immobilized by maladaptive writing strategies and misconceptions of the task at hand. These were essentially *rhetorical* problems, and in this sense, most "blocks" in advanced academic writing aren't a peculiar category of writing difficulties. They are extreme effects of the transitional challenges I've discussed throughout this book, which can be read as an attempt to remove all kinds of conceptual obstacles that undermine ability and progress in dissertation work. The teaching strategies I used in consultations with blocked writers didn't differ substantially from those I used to identify and remove other obstacles to the productive, successful completion of dissertations.

Many of the examples I've offered in previous chapters were also those of blocked writers or of misconceptions that, if left unchanged, can bring further progress to a halt. Ellen, who was trying unsuccessfully to write about "the whole elephant"—everything related to her dissertation research—was severely blocked but began to complete chapter drafts with remarkable speed after she produced a focused statement of her central argument and resolved conflicts with her advisor. As a foundation for a narrower, explicit reference frame, this "thesis statement" converted a vast, bewildering maze of potential implications into a manageable task of construction. Graduate students who try to compose dissertation drafts before they have identified focused research questions are most likely to get lost and eventually mired in the process of writing and revision. In Rose's category of "inflexible plans," dissertation proposals that seem focused and significant in coherent outlines are often too broad and ambitious to implement. If her advisors hadn't persuaded her to revise her plans, the historian who was determined to study all of the colonial administrators over a couple of centuries would have reached an impasse in her research and writing.

Related kinds of rhetorical writing blocks result from adherence to plans that are conceptually unbalanced. When research questions, theoretical frameworks, available sources of evidence, and methods for gathering it are out of balance, dissertations can seem impossible to complete. The progress of the candidate I mentioned who had developed a significant comparative theory on the evolution of political movements came to a halt when his advisors told him his research was insufficient to support his theoretical model and arguments. Until he redefined his dissertation as a case study and modified his claims, completing was nearly impossible.

Even when their dissertation proposals are conceptually balanced and constructed around focused research questions, candidates can become entangled in the process of writing introductions or literature review chapters, because they confuse what I termed *implicit* and *explicit* reference frames. Because they view literature review as a demonstration of their general knowledge and authority, they are trying to write thoroughly annotated bibliographies of all of the important literature in their research fields. Since much of this literature is at best tangential to their own research questions, both writer and reader are soon lost in those labyrinthine "squiggles" of loosely related implications, in which the significance of the author's own research became increasingly obscure. In these cases, the best recourse is to start over with awareness that a literature review is not an inventory of research and theory in your field, used to demonstrate the breadth of your knowledge. It's a narrative account of the research that leads to and illuminates the significance of *your* study. The typical structures, lengths, and reference systems for literature review vary considerably from one field to another, but you can easily find reliable models for your own work in research articles, books, or filed dissertations. With this conceptual change, the obstacle often vanishes.

To the extent that these particularly stubborn obstacles to movement through the dissertation stage result from rhetorical, transitional misconceptions, the advice I've offered in previous chapters should prevent writing blocks or remove obstacles you've already encountered. If you've identified a focused research question, have conducted research that is conceptually balanced, understand how works of scholarship in your field are structured and produced, and follow my advice for getting the work done (with persistence and patience), you should make steady progress through those unavoidable loops of writing and revision. Because isolation compounds all of the difficulties I've described, your progress will occur more smoothly and efficiently through discussion of your work with advisors and peers, collaboration, and feedback from incremental readers.

In some cases, however, this kind of rhetorical, conceptual advice doesn't prevent or remove writing blocks. There are other causes and implications of blocking, including ones I don't fully understand and can't resolve. Misconceptions don't always account for writing blocks, and in some cases the writers themselves seem to fully understand the causes of problems they can't solve or work through very slowly, over periods of years. As I've noted, this kind of academic writing is something we do in the midst of our lives, not just in isolated segments of time. In important, long-term projects, the entangled effects and causes of writing problems are hard to distinguish, but three categories will provide some clarification.

Performative Blocks

I've emphasized that regardless of the background knowledge, plans, and other preconceptions we bring to writing, it's something we do in present moments. Whether we write quickly or slowly, continuously or hesitantly, with ease or excruciating effort, depends on the way we presently think and feel about what we are doing. For anyone who is reasonably literate, even in a foreign language, these variables have little or nothing to do with ability. As the title of Alexandria Peary's perceptive blog on writing affirms, "Your Ability to Write is Always Present" (http://alexandriapeary.blogspot.com), and her recent book *Prolific Moment: Theory and Practice of Mindfulness for Writing* (2018) explores the profound implications of this fact for all writers. My current understanding of performative blocks, along with previous discussions of the conditions writers attach to this moment, relies heavily on Peary's insights.

In freewriting exercises with a group of writers, when we remove all other rhetorical conditions, all of them can write continuously at about the same speed. It's important to note that all of the blocked writers I've known can do this as well. The problem isn't that they "can't write," and if they believe it is, freewriting is a useful way to disillusion them and begin to identify the real causes of their difficulties.

When we're working on complex, high-stakes writing projects such as dissertations, the underlying fact that we are presently able to write remains true, but further conditions we attach to this moment override our ability to write continuously and slow us down to varying degrees:

What we're writing at the moment should make sense to an imagined audience.
It should be grammatically correct.
It should logically extend a previous train of thought, lead to another, and fit into a larger plan.
It should meet imagined standards for finished work.

When the words and sentences we've just produced fail to meet these conditions we've imposed on them, dissatisfaction leads us to pause, think *about* writing, try to revise what we've said, prepare to meet those conditions more successfully, or stop trying to write and do something else. Among the rhetorical conditions we set for ourselves in the moment, those "slide switches" for motivations and standards largely determine the ease and speed with which writing occurs. When the standards we're trying to meet are very high and our immediate motivations to produce writing are relatively low, as I've explained, writing can become extremely hesitant, laborious, or seemingly impossible. The effects of "stammering" or "freezing up," as writers sometimes describe them, are comparable to those of performance anxiety or stage fright, except that the writer isn't really on stage, performing, and isn't necessarily anxious.

When we think of what we're writing as performance, when it fails to meet our standards, and when our perception of this disparity is stronger than our motivation to continue writing, the type of block that occurs requires an amendment to our previous definition. In these cases of blocking, as in others, capable writers who are motivated to complete the project seem disabled by an obstacle to movement through the process. The underlying cause, again, is a *misconception*: the illusion that what they are writing now or have just written is a performance that should meet their standards (or those attributed to imagined readers) for the finished product. The more specific cause of a performative block, however, is *dissatisfaction*.

In an interview included in his book *Writing the Australian Crawl*, the poet William Stafford (1978) offered a similar definition when Sanford Pinsker observed Stafford didn't seem to be "troubled by writing blocks." Like most writers who aren't troubled by them, Stafford initially replied, "Writing blocks? I don't believe in them." When Pinsker prodded him further by saying, "You may not suffer from them, but surely other people do," Stafford pinpointed the cause of this suffering:

> No, I've never experienced anything like that. I believe that the so-called 'writing block' is a product of some kind of disproportion between your standards and your performance. I can imagine a person beginning to feel that he's not able to write up to that

> standard that he imagines the world has set for him. But to me, that's surrealistic. The only standard I can rationally have is the one I'm meeting right now. Of course I can write. Anybody can write. People might think that their product is not worthy of the person they think they are. But it is.
>
> (pp. 116–117)

Stafford made a related observation in another interview, with Cynthia Lofsness: "There are never mornings when I can't write. I think there are never mornings when anybody 'can't write.' I think that anybody could write if he would have standards as low as mine [Strange laughter]" (p. 104).

By his own accounts, Stafford was free from such maladies because he remained mindful that he was writing in the present, with low standards, without imagining that he could control how future readers might judge what he was saying. That would become their job, not his. *Easy for him*, you might argue, *as an established poet, free to say whatever comes to mind.* To avoid performative blocks as an academic writer, however, you don't have to be like William Stafford. I noted that Clifford Geertz wrote at a slow crawl with extremely high standards. How did he avoid becoming blocked? He didn't imagine that he was performing. Mindful of his freedom in the present, he maintained sufficient motivation to continue tinkering with sentences until they met his standards.

If this definition of a performative block is accurate, solutions seem both obvious and realistic: while reminding yourself continually that you are presently free to write whatever you choose, and are not yet performing, lower your standards and raise your motivations to levels that sustain productive writing. To implement these solutions, you just need to be mindful of what you are actually doing. You shouldn't need to become a different kind of person, to badger yourself with carrots and sticks, or to persuade yourself that you are capable.

Even with this general awareness, however, performative blocks can be difficult to overcome in practice. Years of experience as a student writer can instill persistent habits of trying to make the first draft the last, even when you know this is unlikely, unnecessary, and unproductive. If you're haunted by criticism from the past or imagine future readers too vividly, it can be very hard to maintain awareness that what you are presently saying isn't being judged and can't be until you choose to release it to an audience. Even if you know in principle that good writing of this kind almost invariably results from worse writing and that the process is a means to the end of accomplishment, a way of *becoming* accomplished, it can be difficult to read a rough draft as work in progress as an opportunity for revision, not as disheartening evidence of your weak ability and unreadiness to write. When the sentences you've just produced aren't working to your satisfaction and you have months left to complete a project, without clear deadlines, giving up for the day can be almost irresistibly tempting. Because writing is necessarily work of the imagination, maintaining this disillusioned awareness of what you are actually doing in the present can be extremely challenging, but it remains, nonetheless, the key to productive, satisfying movement through the process.

When dissertation writers are continually interrupted by dissatisfaction with what they've written, I can only remind them, just as continually, that this isn't performance. These are nothing more than words and sentences to go on with. They can be retained, dismantled, revised, or discarded without consequence. The sentences you've written can be *played* with. To break their paralyzing grip on the writer's sense of ability and worth, I've occasionally commandeered laptops and scrambled these sentences or inserted nonsense. *You see? It doesn't matter. Now what will you do? Restore them? Change them? Write something else? You're completely free to do whatever you like.* To remove performative blocks, I'm afraid that I don't have any other tricks up my sleeve. And this isn't a trick. It's simply reiteration of what's true.

Causal Disabilities

As primary causes of interference with writing ability, the misconceptions and dysfunctional strategies I've described thus far concern writing itself. Over time, however, the frustrations of struggling unsuccessfully to produce a dissertation can have a wide range of emotional and even physical effects that further complicate writing problems and may appear to cause them. These potential effects include anxiety, depression, other mood disorders, low self-esteem, and social isolation. The stress of unproductive writing can also cause strained relationships, insomnia, or vulnerability to illness. I recall two cases of blocked writers who developed severe skin rashes that vanished when they began to write productively.

When they further undermine efforts to write, these effects provide convenient causal explanations: that otherwise mysterious blocks must result from underlying psychological conditions, personality traits, or illnesses. Performative blocks, for example, then appear to result from "perfectionism," even when the writers aren't perfectionists in other aspects of their lives. Writers who become distressed by their difficulties are often labeled "stress cases" or neurotics. Those who become depressed or exhausted from futile efforts to write can't do so, it seems, because they're chronically depressed or fatigued. Unable to find other explanations, troubled writers themselves often come to the same conclusions.

Because I've often consulted with blocked writers for a year or more and delved into the histories of their difficulties, I've learned to distrust these amateur diagnoses and even some professional ones. In some cases, causes and effects of blocking become so entangled that trying to distinguish them seems pointless. When struggling writers are severely distressed, I've strongly recommended psychological counseling but learned, more often than not, that they were already receiving this professional help. In several cases, they had been diagnosed with and were taking medication for clinical depression or anxiety disorders that had first developed in their dissertation work and were "cured," it seemed, when they neared completion of their projects. I've also known a couple of clinical psychologists who specialized in the stress of graduate work and were counseling some of my students. These implicit collaborations added valuable psychological dimensions to the assistance I could provide as a writing specialist. The question of whose expertise addressed the real causes of these problems seemed irrelevant. Whether my students needed other kinds of help or not, they came to me for help with their writing difficulties, so I assumed that the causes and solutions for these problems had something to do with writing itself. Biographies of accomplished authors who suffered from a great variety of mental problems remind us, in turn, that these conditions do not always prevent productive writing.

But sometimes they do. Chronic depression or anxiety disorders can make sustained attention to writing extremely difficult or impossible for reasons unrelated to one's conceptions of writing. So can personal crises and emotional traumas. In these cases, writing blocks are the effects of underlying conditions that require counseling and other professional help before individuals can begin to write productively. The kinds of writing assistance I can provide are then of little use, if any, and because futile attempts to write can worsen feelings of anxiety or despair, postponing writing projects is sometimes the best recourse. A PhD candidate who suffered from long periods of severe depression made the causal role of this malady unmistakably clear in her own case:

> I am not an older than usual graduate student by choice. I suffered my first major depression when I was 17 and watched my life slide away from me for the next decade and more. I was not a professional writer at that age and I am pretty certain that the journal I kept as a teenager wasn't the catalyst for this depression. But I did develop a habit over the years of packing my productivity or my creativity into the brief windows between the blackness . . . out of necessity, not because of a lack of self-discipline! I never thought this was brilliance and I would have given up these cycles in a heartbeat if the chemicals in my brain had allowed it. With time, anyone can learn habits to mitigate their suffering; steady, moderate work habits are certainly a part of that.

Most of the graduate students I've advised who were struggling with these underlying conditions were aware of the effects on their efforts to write, disclosed these problems to me, and were receiving other professional attention. We could therefore work constructively on their writing with awareness of the factors involved. Although academic writing remained extremely difficult for them, a few of these students were writing profusely in journals *about* their writing problems, with insights much deeper than mine, and with the benefits of these understandings, some of them were able to complete PhDs. Clearly, misconceptions of writing were not the causes of their blocks.

In other cases, however, the unfamiliar transitional challenges and pressures of dissertation work can amplify latent, undiagnosed mood disorders and other tendencies that weren't significant problems in the past. Continuing to write productively then becomes inexplicably difficult. If dissertation writers without a history of depression become severely depressed, for example, are writing problems the causes or effects of this malaise? Without other professional help (or sometimes even with it) neither the writers nor I can reliably answer this question.

Underlying cognitive factors, such as learning disabilities and attention disorders, can also induce certain kinds of writing blocks. When Mike Rose (1985) defined blocks as "cognitive" problems, which he distinguished from "affective" causes of blocking, he was referring to misconceptions: dysfunctional, maladaptive ways of thinking about the task at hand. But cognitive factors also include the differing ways in which people's minds generally work, and some of these cognitive patterns make writing more challenging than others.

Cognitive obstacles to writing sometimes result from the relentlessly linear nature of writing, both as a way of thinking and as a medium of communication. The concepts we convey in writing may consist of categories and subcategories we can represent in schematic clusters or tree diagrams, but in the end, we must convey these conceptual structures in a string of words and sentences, using transition phrases and other cues to maintain linear cohesion. If a general assertion has several related, branching implications, for example, we usually introduce and present these in a list, with additive markers such as "First . . . ," "Second . . . ," and so on.

All of us have to contend with this limitation of written communication: the necessity of translating our complex, multidimensional thoughts and understandings into linear, narrative sequences. Writing is a particular way of thinking and communicating thought, but those who claim that writing is a "window to the mind" (or that unclear writing always represents unclear thinking) are wrong. With the full range of our senses, we perceive and think in ways we can't convey in writing. Diagrams, other illustrations, or equations can help to convey two- and three-dimensional concepts and relationships, but these are also components of a linear sequence that proceeds from the first word of a text to the last. Because the way we fully understand a subject is usually much more complex than what we can say about it in writing, constructing the order of such a sequence involves exclusion as well as inclusion. Learning to produce conceptually complex works of scholarship therefore involves training our minds to think about what we're doing in this linear way, not just as thinkers but also as writers.

Learning to convert multidimensional understandings into the logical sequences of writing is unusually difficult for some people. When I taught courses for undergraduates considered to be weak writers, students in fields of design, such as architecture, often turned in papers that seemed disorganized, as though they wrote without plans. In conferences, however, they sometimes showed me elaborate diagrams of labeled clusters and intersections, like those of complex molecules or geodesic domes. Some of these plans were very thoughtful and interesting, but it was nearly impossible to convert them into a series of logically connected passages, from a point of departure to a destination. For writers most inclined to think in these multidimensional and visual ways, efforts to write can be laborious and frustrating. The necessary exclusion involved in linear, narrative communication feels like a loss of substance, a fragmentation and distortion of one's real understanding.

As the culminations of long processes of learning and thinking in a field of inquiry, dissertation projects can magnify these cognitive tendencies and resulting frustrations. Constructing those introductory narratives I've described as "explicit reference frames," about the specific significance of your research, involves enormous amounts of exclusion. From much broader fields of research and debate, with potential relevance to an expanding maze of related concepts and questions that extend across disciplines, viable dissertations must carve out particular lines of inquiry about particular questions. Writers most inclined to conceptualize their dissertations as representations of their broad, multidimensional understandings can become hopelessly lost in the effort to reduce these understandings to a coherent narrative. The resulting cognitive blocks represent versions of what Rose (1980) called "inflexible plans." I've worked with a number of candidates who knew that they were blocked by the complexity of their own intentions but were unwilling to revise and simplify their projects. Doing so, they felt, would sacrifice too much of what they considered important to say and too much of the time and thought they had already invested. In one case, I pointed out that a stalled writer could quickly finish his dissertation by deleting the two chapters he was struggling to write and the related claims and reviews in his introduction. He agreed that his advisors would accept the simplified version, be he would not.

Solving these problems in practice requires certain kinds of preventive training and intellectual discipline, through which writers acknowledge the limitations of written communication and learn to think about writing, as early in the process as possible, as linear narrative. For this purpose, I often resort to old-fashioned sequential outlines: lists of topics and subtopics, with explicit transitions, so the initial plan for writing just describes the feasible structure of a text, not the writer's whole understanding of the subject. These strategies don't invalidate or presume to change the ways in which writers are inclined to think. They are simply ways of contending with the narrower, inescapable demands of thinking as a writer.

Another inescapable demand of writing is *sustained attention*, and for this reason, attention disorders can also create obstacles to productive writing. In the end, a work of scholarship is a complex, continuous story about one's research that maintains internal cohesion, and producing it requires hours of sustained, focused concentration. Avoiding distraction in the process can be challenging for anyone, for reasons I've explained, but cognitive problems with attention present special challenges. Students who were mired in writing projects or struggling to maintain cohesion have often told me they were diagnosed with ADHD (Attention Deficit Hyperactivity Disorder) or other patterns, such as dyslexia, but the effects of these conditions weren't always apparent to me. When I wrote *Understanding Writing Blocks*, I believed these were ambiguous causes of blocking and interference with ability. One writer I described in the book, who told me she was diagnosed with ADHD, seemed to be *too* focused on particular ideas, passages, or decisions. Absorbed in a writing project, she became serene, the opposite of hyperactive, and lost track of time. Because her slow progress seemed to result from *riveted* attention, not distraction, I doubted that an attention disorder was relevant to her writing block.

The real problem, however, was that I didn't understand the complexities and varying effects of attention disorders, which I associated with hyperactivity and scattered attention. In response to my book, Lesle Lewis, who teaches at Landmark College for students with learning disabilities, offered valuable clarification of these common misunderstandings. In a research article published in the *Journal of Teaching Writing*, Lewis and Peg Alden (2007) described diagnostic patterns and treatments for attentional writing blocks in greater detail. The diagnostic questions and strategies they include in this article will be useful to any of you who suspect that attention issues (whether diagnosed or not) contribute to your writing difficulties.

Lewis and Alden emphasize that attention disorders are cognitive problems (not motivational ones) that exacerbate common challenges of academic writing. The capable, highly motivated undergraduates they interviewed for the study described familiar problems of time management, procrastination, and distraction; of developing feasible plans and maintaining cohesion; and of making innumerable decisions in the process. Most of these writers also had "expansive, creative minds" that generated lots of complex ideas with compounding implications and resulting choices. As a consequence, one of the most consistent obstacles they encountered in the writing process was that of "selectivity" at all levels: from the choices of specific topics, viewpoints, references, and logical sequences to those of particular words and phrases. For writers with attention difficulties, all of these choices, which I've also called "excusions," can pose time-consuming dilemmas. When my student was adrift in serene reflections that seemed the opposite of hyperactivity or distraction, she was mulling over endless alternatives. Thinking *about* writing continually distracted her from getting writing done. Interesting alternatives to what she was currently saying complicated other choices, including ones she previously made, so the whole project was in continual flux. One of the students Lewis and Alden interviewed said that writing was like "raking leaves when it's really windy" (p. 121).

Because these underlying cognitive factors exacerbate challenges that all thoughtful, capable writers must contend with, their symptoms aren't reliably diagnostic. If they were, we might conclude that attention disorders were primary, epidemic causes of difficulties and delays among PhD candidates. Chronic indecision in the process, for example, isn't a reliable symptom of ADHD. Paralyzing indecisiveness often results from insecurity: fear of making wrong decisions, revealing ignorance, and being judged. Further deliberation then results from *caution*, as a search for safer alternatives. In contrast, writers with attention problems are usually driven by inquisitive *fascination* with the complexities of the subject: extremes of the intellectual qualities that teachers and advisors encourage. Our weaknesses, as I remind writers continually, are usually our strengths taken to excess.

With these writing problems as with others, therefore, it's most important to identify the particular difficulties you've encountered, their possible causes, and potential solutions. For this purpose, Lewis and Alden provide a detailed list of diagnostic questions and specific strategies. These conceptual tools, useful for all writers, represent the general category of "metacognition": thinking about the particular ways you are thinking. If you are lost in dithering over choices, for example, it's useful to identify the particular decisions that impede progress and deliberately make them. Because blocked writers are typically lost in their own thoughts about their work, talking with friends about your project can help to reveal a path forward that others can follow. And because slow, deliberative writing tends to become congested and awkward, freewriting exercises can help to restore the natural flow of language and reduce arduous, hesitant deliberation over every word.

Even with such diagnostic tools focused on writing, I don't have the expertise to determine in individual cases whether attention problems are underlying causes or effects of writing difficulties. Knowing, with the help of experts, can help you to understand and overcome the obstacles you face, but the diagnosis of a "learning disability" or any other disorder shouldn't represent a hopeless limitation of your ability. It shouldn't make you feel powerless or immobile. We can't change the hardwiring with which our minds tend to work in certain ways, but we can find productive ways to compensate for or bypass tendencies that create obstacles, often by using other, enhanced abilities. I knew a writing teacher and author of short stories whose conditions of dyslexia and ADHD made reading, writing, and other schoolwork extremely difficult, to the extent that he routinely failed English classes. Because he read so slowly and methodically, however, he also read very deeply, and the resulting appreciation for language led him into professions his teachers thought he would avoid. I noted that the problems with linear sequences associated with dyslexia, including reading and spelling, often accompany strong abilities to visualize and analyze complex schematic systems. With these evident cognitive patterns, my oldest son found ways to negotiate daunting challenges of schooling, and when he finished college in computer science, one of his first jobs was in the field of language software, including the development of electronic spelling and proofreading systems: the very tools he needed.

Circumstantial Blocks

If writing blocks represent types of interference with writing ability, not types of writers, these obstacles to movement through the process are not necessarily caused by the misconceptions or underlying mental conditions we've considered thus far. External, circumstantial factors can also undermine a writer's ability and block expression. The literary reference most often cited in accounts of "writer's block," for example, is Tillie Olsen's collection of essays *Silences* (1979), which examines the ways in which writers are "unnaturally" silenced by external conditions and expectations. These essays emphasized social and cultural barriers such as gender roles and responsibilities, prejudices based on race and class, censorship, fear of punishment, deprivations of space and time, and the sense that one's thoughts can't be voiced or won't be heard. Olsen presents many examples of writers who found ways to break through these obstacles, but doing so requires courage and sacrifice.

Olsen was writing some 40 years ago, primarily about literary expression rather than scholarship, but some of the conditions she described persist in academic communities. In some fields and programs, gender stereotypes, for example, still influence faculty assumptions about the ability and potential of women in ways that can undermine their confidence, limit the fields of research they enter, or impede their progress toward a PhD. These assumptions and their effects are often subtle, but sometimes they are startlingly explicit. Just a few years ago, a PhD candidate in one of the physical sciences told me that in a department meeting a senior professor made the bizarre statement that he didn't understand "why anyone without a penis" would go into his field. When I reported this to my wife, her apt reply was, "What exactly do they do with it? Stir things?"

Even without such overt prejudice, representing a small minority of any kind in a program—whether of gender, race, ethnicity, nationality, or social class—can make you feel disadvantaged and subject to challenges that other graduate students don't have to face. Graduate students can feel similarly marginalized by research interests that are weakly represented or discredited in their departments. I've known a few PhD candidates who discontinued their studies or transferred to other universities because they couldn't find program advisors who would support their dissertation projects. Many others lose motivation because the only advisors available have little knowledge and interest in their fields of specialization. Within their disciplines at large, every doctoral program represents particular strengths and weaknesses, favored positions in theoretical arguments, and methodological biases. Candidates on the wrong sides of these imbalances, such as those who use qualitative methods in highly quantitative programs, can feel isolated and stigmatized.

If you feel immobilized or defeated by these conditions, it's especially important for you to expand your professional networks beyond your programs, to scholars in your own university and elsewhere who understand and appreciate what you are doing. Those reference frames that validate the significance of your research represent broader communities of real people with similar interests. Contacting and meeting them can provide the confidence and incentives you need to complete your projects.

Circumstantial blocks can also result from unreasonable or conflicting expectations of advisors. The physicist I mentioned in Chapter 3 was immobilized by conflicting, interdisciplinary expectations that were impossible to meet. Although the challenges she faced made her feel helpless and inept, the misconceptions that caused her writing block were not hers but those of her advisors. The solution for this block was therefore a meeting to clarify *their* mutual understandings and expectations for a dissertation she could reasonably complete. Identifying the real source of this misunderstanding was crucial.

PhD candidates often create comparable problems for themselves by trying to meet *imagined* expectations for dissertations that are too broadly focused, profoundly significant, and complex. Writers may attribute these expectations to their advisors or to the world at large, and they sometimes feel unrealistically obliged, in this work, to reconcile conflicting interests and positions that their advisors don't expect them to resolve. If what you are trying to do, and feel you must do, seems impossible, stop to consider the real origins of these expectations. *Did you invent them for yourself? Are you just presuming that this is what your advisors expect? Or are they explicit requirements for your dissertation?*

Moving ahead with your work requires definitive answers to these questions. If the first is true, you should revise your project and do something possible instead. If the second is true, you should meet with your advisors to determine and negotiate what they really expect from you. If the third is true, you should meet with your advisors to explain your difficulties and try to persuade them to revise their expectations. If these efforts fail, you may need to find more reasonable advisors, with help from your department or graduate school.

Even when dissertation designs and expectations are reasonable, apparent writing blocks can result from personal circumstances that interfere with sustained attention, such as financial problems, family responsibilities, demanding jobs, or illness. Having completed my PhD while raising three young children, with intermittent part-time jobs to relieve our financial constraints, I understand these circumstantial challenges of finding time and attention for writing. It's easy for others to say that getting your dissertation done should be your main priority, but much of the time it isn't. Other responsibilities are more immediately important or unavoidable, and when you do find time to return to your writing, you often feel exhausted and distracted. In that period when my life seemed impossibly complicated, I met an old alumnus who told me that when he was a student, decades earlier, the attic of my department building was used as a bunkhouse for single graduate students who worked as building custodians in exchange for one of the beds lined up in rows, as in military barracks. It seemed like a grim, austere way to get through graduate school, but in some ways, I was envious.

Circumstantial factors can be particularly challenging for ABD candidates who have taken leaves of absence and established lives elsewhere, with families and full-time jobs, often as adjunct faculty with heavy teaching loads. The immediate realities of their lives and responsibilities become increasingly remote from the academic environments in which they pursued PhDs, and finding time to complete their dissertation projects requires discipline and sacrifice. One of the participants in a dissertation retreat I led was then living in another city as a single parent with a demanding administrative, non-academic job. Although most of her dissertation was finished, she told me that it now seemed like part of a life she no longer lived. When she tried to reenter it, assemble the pieces, and remember what she was doing and why, it had become surreal. She felt guilty for wasting time she could be spending with her children or in other immediately meaningful and productive ways. She was therefore immobilized by a conundrum: completing her PhD would potentially allow her to improve circumstances that prevented her from completing her PhD.

For those of you who face comparable obstacles, the only viable solutions are those offered by Boice, Silvia, and other authors who recommend very moderate, regular periods of time devoted to writing projects. If your lives are extremely busy and otherwise disconnected from your doctoral work, you won't *find* this time; you'll have to *make* it deliberately and use it for writing. As I've explained, if the writing sessions you schedule are regular, they can be fairly short—perhaps an hour or two. Make a space where you can work on this project regularly and methodically, like a jigsaw puzzle, and then ignore it. And try to think of this project as one thing you are currently doing, with engagement and pleasure, not as an onerous burden you drag around or a looming shadow from your past.

Analysis, Resistance, and Release

I've defined writing blocks as obstacles to movement through the processes that interfere with writing ability, but blocks aren't general conditions with general solutions. They occur in particular kinds of writing, at particular times in people's lives, for a variety of particular reasons. My conversations with blocked writers therefore begin with lots of questions that I've raised in this chapter and in others—questions you can also ask yourselves.

If you are stalled in the process of writing your dissertation (or some other project) and feel unable to move forward, when did this problem first occur, in what kind of writing, and in what stage of the process?

What kinds of writing can you complete more easily, and why?

What makes writing more difficult in this project?

Do you feel that you're stuck, unable to write much of anything, or that you're caught in loops of writing and rewriting, moving in circles, writing a lot without getting anywhere?

Do you have the central question or argument of this project in focus, with a viable plan for its structure, or are you just muddling through, trying to figure out what you want to say?

How much time do you devote to writing in a given week, and how do you distribute this time?

Do you avoid or postpone writing until you feel pressured, inspired, or guilty and then work in what Boice calls "binges," or do you work in regular, consistent sessions of shorter periods, with moderate expectations?

Of the types of blocking I've described, which seems to be the most probable cause of your difficulty?

Do you think it results from misconceptions of what you are doing or dysfunctional rules for writing? If so, what do you think they are?

When you are trying to write, do you feel that you're already performing or that what you're writing now should represent accomplishment?

Do you have reasons to believe that an underlying condition, such as a mood disorder or a learning or attention problem, make writing particularly difficult?

Do you think there are circumstantial causes for this problem, such as misunderstandings with your advisors, unreasonable expectations you feel obliged to meet, or life circumstances that make time and attention for writing difficult to find?

To the extent that you use these and other questions to identify the causes of a writing block, you can more easily solve the problem. Until you know what the obstacle is, just pushing against it, exerting more effort, won't remove it. On the contrary, *less* effort or a different kind of effort is more often the solution, though it's very hard for me to convince blocked writers that this could be true. In itself, writing, getting words and sentences on a page, shouldn't be hard. Like walking, it's just a matter of letting yourself fall into empty space, with faith that your ability and coordination will support this *release* into motion and carry you forward. It results from letting go. If you exert lots of effort to make this happen or micromanage your coordination, without trusting that it will work on its own, you are making writing harder than it needs to be, like someone who feels that in order to take a step she needs to deliberately operate all the muscles, connective tissues, and neural networks involved. Trying to do that, you won't get anywhere.

This is why I often (but not always) feel that for all their effort, or because of it, blocked writers are exerting resistance to writing as a release into motion. Referring to a "train of thought" that rolls along on its own momentum, one of them said that she felt, when she was *trying* to produce academic writing, that she was actually trying to pull the train backwards rather than just hopping on, as she could in the journals in which she easily described this experience. Even when she got an academic project rolling, as soon as she began to think of it as one, as a performance of knowledge, that conception turned her around. She couldn't see where her thoughts were going, and she felt that she was deliberately, arduously operating the language, fabricating sentences disconnected from what she was thinking. She termed this activity and effort "notwriting": not just not writing, but also devoting time and effort to writing that can't produce any.

Regardless of the particular causes of this resistance and counterproductive effort, in the present moments when writing occurs, we either release ourselves into motion and let writing happen or we don't. In these moments, when we begin to think about the future ends of what we're doing, especially in high-stakes projects, we also tend to think of "release" as letting the work go to the imagined audience. That idea of letting go is what makes writing seem risky and hard, even though it isn't. I've known writers who feel that way even when they're working on early rough drafts that they *know* no one else will see. The barrier between "notwriting" and writing, resistance and release, seems tissue thin. Sometimes, with just a slight change of awareness and surrender, the barrier dissolves. Released into motion, these writers move through the process with increasing confidence, coordination, and ease.

References

Daly, J. A. (1985). Writing apprehension. In M. Rose (ed.), *When a writer can't write: Studies in writer's block and other composing-process problems* (pp. 43–82). New York, NY: Guilford Press.

Hjortshoj, K. (2001). *Understanding writing blocks*. New York, NY: Oxford University Press.

Lewis, L. & Alden, P. (2007). What we can learn about writing blocks from college students with output problems, strong writing skills, and attentional difficulties. *Journal of Teaching Writing*, 23 (1), pp. 115–146.

Lovitts, B. E. (2001). *Leaving the Ivory Tower: The causes and consequences of departure from doctoral study*. Latham, MD: Rowman & Littlefield.

Lovitts, B. E. (2007). *Making the implicit explicit: Creating performance expectations for the dissertation*. Sterling, VA: Stylus Publishing.

Peary, A. (2018). *Prolific moment: Theory and practice of mindfulness for writing*. New York, NY: Routledge.

Peary, A. (n.d.). Your ability to write is always present, http://alexandriapeary.blogspot.com.

Olsen, T. (1979). *Silences*. New York, NY: Delacorte Press.

Rose, M. (1980). Rigid rules, inflexible plans, and the stifling of language: A cognitivist analysis of writer's block. *College Composition and Communication*, 31 (4), 389–399.

Rose, M. (1984). *Writer's block: The cognitive dimension*. Carbondale, Il: Southern Illinois University Press.

Rose, M. (ed.). (1985). *When a writer can't write: Studies in writer's block and other composing-process problems* (pp. 43–82). New York, NY: Guilford Press.

Rose, M. & McClafferty, K. A. (2001). A call for the teaching of writing in graduate education. *Educational Researcher*, 30 (2), 27–33.

Stafford, W. (1978). *Writing the Australian crawl: Views on the writer's vocation*. Ann Arbor, MI: University of Michigan Press.

7 A Note to International Students

While I'm writing this book and address it to "you," like all writers I have to imagine my readers on the basis of my knowledge and experience. The sense of audience I'm using for this purpose results to some extent from reading, but it's based primarily on the many graduate students I've known, at Cornell and other universities, primarily in the United States. Along with other factors—such as my intention to write a small book—the knowledge and experience I have to work with limit what I can reliably say and the categorical distinctions I can include. Because I chose to focus on patterns of transition and difficulty that arise in dissertation work among PhD candidates at large, I've noted some categorical differences in the nature of this work across disciplines, for example, but I haven't distinguished categories of graduate students on the basis of their nationalities, cultural, and educational backgrounds, or fluency in English.

The reason certainly isn't that the graduate students I have in mind, as I write, represent a homogeneous group in these respects. Slightly more than half of those enrolled in my graduate courses were designated international students, and many others who were American citizens or residents were born in other countries and were native speakers of other languages. This cultural and linguistic diversity isn't peculiar to my courses. Currently, 48 percent of the graduate students at Cornell are international students, a proportion considerably higher than the national average of about 25 percent, which is also substantial. Since I began to teach these courses, 30 years ago, new enrollments of international graduate students in the United States have steadily increased, by 5–10 percent annually over the past decade, and similar trends have occurred in Canada, the UK, European nations, and Australia.

When I imagine you, my real readers, therefore, I'm thinking of graduate students from every part of the world who speak many different languages and previously studied in a great variety of educational systems, all converging in academic environments that thrive on international and cross-cultural exchange. The graduate programs and fields of inquiry you enter in these research universities have also become increasingly global. University faculty members come from diverse countries. Scholars in several nations are often working on the same problems, publishing in the same professional journals, and collaborating across geographical, cultural, and political divides. They assemble at international conferences, teach and study at foreign universities, and travel abroad for research, guest lectures, and consultations with foreign colleagues. In these peculiar cultural environments, almost everyone is from somewhere else, and feeling atypical is typical.

When diversity reaches these levels, cultural stereotypes and categorical distinctions quickly dissolve into more complex realities. To this point, I haven't tried to address the distinct challenges that "international students" encounter in their graduate work because I wouldn't know where to begin. Some of those I've known were native speakers of English or fully bilingual, attended high schools or colleges in the United States, or had lived in this country as children. To the extent that using English as a foreign or second language presents challenges for large proportions of international graduate students, I can recognize and address patterns of difficulty in the practice of teaching, but I'm not formally trained for this kind of instruction, and these patterns are so complex and varied, according to individual levels of fluency and language backgrounds, that in this book I can't summarize, much less provide, this kind of instruction.

Nor do I need to do so, because help of this kind has become widely available. In response to rising undergraduate and graduate enrollments of foreign students, universities throughout the United States and in other countries have developed extensive language programs and support services, staffed by specialists in applied linguistics, international education, and related fields. Hundreds of textbooks and other materials are now available for teaching English as a foreign or second language and for self-study, for students at different levels of education and fluency. Specialists in this kind of teaching understand the particular challenges that English presents and offer instruction that advisors and general writing courses can't fully provide. Although courses for international graduate students focus primarily on language instruction, they usually include valuable guidance for other dimensions of graduate studies, academic writing, and professional development that doctoral programs often fail to offer, including teaching skills and oral presentation, writing methods, the organization of theses and dissertations, or reference systems and citation. International graduate students therefore have access to types of assistance that their "domestic" peers often need but can't easily find.

If you need this kind of instruction, therefore, my main advice to you is that *you should investigate the resources available on your campuses and use them strategically, to your own advantage*. Staff members in these language programs—often listed as English for Academic Purposes (EAP)—are usually available to assess your needs and recommend courses, workshops, tutorial services, or materials for self-study. You can also find extensive lists of available texts for international students on the Consortium on Graduate Communication's website, www.gradconsortium.org, under the heading "Resources." Potentially useful references for self-study in these lists include comprehensive guides for international students, such as *Academic Writing for Graduate Students: A Course for Nonnative Speakers of English* (Swales and Feak, 2012), writing guides for specific disciplines (such as the series of guides published by Oxford University Press), books on journal article or proposal writing such as Belcher's (2009) *Writing Your Journal Article in Twelve Weeks*, work that focuses on English grammar and syntax, and advice for adapting to the unfamiliar environments of graduate programs.

You should also use available resources with a sense that you are fully entitled to do so, because they exist entirely on your behalf. Needing help in becoming fluent in English doesn't represent personal weakness or disadvantage; it's an inherent, institutional problem. Research universities in the United States and elsewhere welcome the internationalization of their students, faculties, and disciplines. They promote and advertise their cultural diversity and inclusiveness, but they remain embedded, nonetheless, in particular cultural and linguistic environments to which students with diverse backgrounds must adapt, and their most common obstacle is the necessity of using English as the primary medium of learning, communication, and scholarship. You should think of this problem as a structural weakness in graduate education, not in your own ability or potential as a scholar.

I emphasize this way of thinking because a large proportion of international students in my classes (though certainly not all of them) feel disadvantaged by their difficulties with English in comparison with peers in their programs who are native speakers. I can honestly point out to them that *collectively*, in terms of outcomes, they are not disadvantaged, since they are more likely to complete their PhDs, not less (Sowell, 2008). This general reassurance, however, is rarely reassuring. National averages, some have pointed out, can't predict their individual fates or struggles, and in some cases my students have become anxious or annoyed, because I seem to be telling them that their difficulties with English aren't real handicaps and shouldn't need special attention. To overcome these language problems, a few have argued, they have to work harder and get more help.

To make my point clearer and more convincing, I have to admit that there's some truth to these arguments. To varying degrees, incomplete fluency in English, combined with other adjustments to a foreign academic environment, can create additional challenges to the ones I've described in previous chapters. Solving these problems can require additional kinds of instruction and attention that native speakers of English may not need.

For reasons I've explained, however, acknowledging that you need help can be an advantage in itself, as long as it doesn't erode your confidence or lead you to push yourselves in the wrong directions. International students are significantly more likely to use resources offered by campus writing programs, teaching and learning centers, libraries, graduate schools, and their own departments because they admit that they need and deserve this assistance and are less likely to feel stigmatized by the admission. In turn, native speakers of English are often *disadvantaged* by the belief that they should be able to complete this difficult, unfamiliar process on their own or that asking for help is a sign of weakness. Regardless of our linguistic backgrounds, all of us produce clumsy, ambiguous sentences and make errors, and getting help from others is a normal, necessary part of the writing process among scholars. *Avoiding* this help is abnormal and counterproductive.

In order to solve problems strategically, however, we need to understand as precisely as possible what they really are. When I ask international students to explain the kinds of help they *think* they need, they frequently express concerns about errors and worries that their writing "sounds foreign." When I find out what they're trying to do and read samples of their work, in some cases remaining errors in grammar and usage are the main problems they need to work on, in projects that are otherwise focused and cohesive. When we're using a foreign language, however, concerns about error tend to assume exaggerated importance that can obscure more fundamental problems that have little or nothing to do with our fluency. Learning to avoid or correct errors won't solve these problems. Their writing is unclear, perhaps, because they haven't figured out what they want to say, because they are trying to say too much, because their work is conceptually unbalanced, or because they haven't identified a significant knowledge gap and research question: common challenges for graduate students at large. In some cases, we then ignore patterns of error altogether and work on what's really important. *When you assess your writing, on your own or with help from others, don't assume that the main problems you need to work on result from your use of English as a foreign or second language.* For the purpose of producing works of scholarship, graduate students are all in the same boat, regardless of their backgrounds. Native speakers of English may be struggling with the same problems you are, for the same reasons, or with problems you've already solved.

A related reason for which difficulties with English don't categorically disadvantage international students will seem like an odd, almost sacrilegious thing for a writing teacher to say: *in itself, one's individual writing ability or fluency doesn't necessarily undermine success in academic work.* I don't mean that writing quality isn't important or that academics are bad writers, with low standards for clarity and style. Instead, as I've noted, lots of prominent scholars with "tin ears" for language complete PhDs and publish extensively because they have significant things to say and, in saying them, get lots of help with their writing from friends and colleagues. This assistance is a normal, acknowledged dimension of the writing process and doesn't diminish assessments of a scholar's accomplishments.

I don't mean to trivialize the significance of errors or the difficulty of avoiding them. Most of the graduate students in my classes who weren't native speakers of English had studied English extensively in their home countries or elsewhere, had a solid grasp of grammar and syntax, and had sufficient working vocabularies to express what they needed to say. Most had taken or were taking further EAP courses for graduate students. Remaining patterns of error and usage problems in their writing resulted from grammatical features of English most alien to their native languages or from patterns of idiomatic usage: peculiar forms of expression that can't be explained by coherent rules. These lingering patterns of error vary from one language background to another. Native speakers of East Asian languages, for example, have particular difficulty with accurate use of the definite article *the*, which native speakers of English learn to use as children but can't explain. Why did I just say "*the* definite article"? The rules, such as they are, are so complex that I once interviewed a job candidate in linguistics who had written her entire dissertation on the subject. Preposition usage is also idiomatic and often counterintuitive. I can't easily explain why I say my home is *on* a particular street, when it's really beside or along it, or why saying that I live on *the* street would mean that I have no home at all. Some English nouns can be pluralized and others can't, but there are no reliable rules to tell you which ones. Why is it correct to say that I'm bringing *suitcases* on a trip, in the plural, but not *luggages*?

Teachers trained in applied linguistics can identify these remaining errors, explain them, and give you instructional material to work on correction, but these last barriers to complete fluency can be extremely difficult to overcome. Although many of these errors have little effect on the meaning of a sentence that is otherwise clear, they stand out as "foreign" errors because they differ from the ones native speakers of English often make. Exaggerated concerns about error can then lead you to be overly cautious and self-conscious about using complex sentences and fully expressing what you need to say.

In the end, of course, the dissertations, research articles, or publication manuscripts you submit should conform to "standard English," but concerns about minor errors of these types shouldn't interfere with the more important work of fully explaining and substantiating your research in earlier drafts. Correcting and polishing these drafts can occur most efficiently at the end of the process when you've completed other changes. At this stage, if my students can't spot and correct these lingering errors on their own, I often recommend that they should hire a good proofreader, if they can afford one. For the purpose of meeting degree requirements, graduate students sometimes view this professional help as cheating, as it might be in undergraduate courses, but graduate schools and writing centers often maintain lists of professional editors available for this purpose. If the drafts you give them represent the communication of your own knowledge and ideas, if they are simply correcting and polishing these drafts, and if you acknowledge their assistance in the final version, the help they provide isn't substantially different from the roles of copyeditors for publications, on whom all of us rely.

Patterns of error and related problems in the work of international students are relatively easy for experienced teachers to identify, explain, and correct. Problems resulting from cultural differences can be more subtle but also more important. Although fields of scholarship and forms of academic writing have become increasingly globalized, educational systems and values still differ in ways that are influenced by their surrounding cultures.

A central premise of this book is *all* graduate students must adapt to unfamiliar academic environments, because the systems and values of specialized graduate programs differ from those of undergraduate education, even in the same universities. If you are studying abroad, however, this transition might be particularly disorienting. In a collection of essays edited by Christine Casanave and Xiaoming Li (2008), *Learning the Literacy Practices of Graduate School*, current and former graduate students and faculty advisors describe the diverse challenges of learning the largely implicit rules for fitting into academic communities as apprentice scholars and writers, both for foreign students and "domestic" ones who often conceal their struggles. These essays also offer valuable advice for negotiating these complex problems of assimilation.

If you were previously educated in another culture and academic system, my accounts of the roles and identities you need to assume in doctoral programs—what you need to fit *into*—will apply to you, but my accounts of what it means to be a student and student writer, based primarily on American systems, may not. The student identities, habits of learning, and ways of writing that graduate students bring to advanced studies differ substantially in ways that affect the process of transition and adjustment. Some of the rules and conventions you need to learn in a foreign system (such as expectations for class attendance and participation) are explicit, but most are not, and you have to learn them through observation or trial and error. When I was a visiting graduate student in an Indian university, for example, in a program ostensibly based on American models, I was befuddled at the end of a department lecture by a visiting archaeologist. After members of the faculty, all sitting at the front, had asked questions in order of their rank, the room fell silent and everyone looked at me. Although I knew nothing about the subject of the talk, I realized I was supposed to ask a question next, and after I made up something to ask, Indian graduate students sitting toward the back asked a few questions in their orders of perceived status. I then realized I was sitting in the wrong place. As the audience filed out of the room, speaker and senior faculty first, graduate students sitting in front of me waited for me to leave before them. I was embarrassed and, as an anthropologist, felt that I should have figured out these rules much faster than I did.

These unfamiliar rules I was learning concerned representations of academic status and authority, and related values can be crucial to a graduate student's performance. *Who is entitled to speak with authority in academic discourse, and who is not? Who is entitled to criticize established authorities or make broad theoretical claims? What constitutes a significant research question, claim, or argument in a particular journal or forum? What constitutes an original or "novel" claim, and to what extent do authors own it? When are you obliged to acknowledge the ideas and language of others? How do you do this in writing, and when are you committing "plagiarism"?* These and other questions are fundamental to academic writing, including dissertation work, but the answers can vary from one academic environment to another, often in ways that are difficult to fathom and follow.

In communities of scholars, graduate students occupy transitional positions that can be especially hard to negotiate for those of you who were raised in educational systems where students are taught deference to higher authorities. In the United States, within reference frames that acknowledge the work of other scholars, doctoral candidates are usually expected to come up with "original" ideas and positions they put forth as their own, including ones that might challenge established authorities in their fields. This graduate student from India, pursuing a PhD in the United States, explained how the academic culture of his home country affected his writing:

> Part of my problem of not enjoying writing was also because of the hierarchy and the social distance that existed between the teachers and students. The social relations between the teachers and students could be better characterized as that of masters and servants. We hardly dared speak before our teachers. So I believe that this hierarchical culture also averted me from enjoying my writing process.

This is one reason for which I advised you to think of introductions and literature reviews as referenced arguments for the significance of *your* research or as symposia in which invited speakers introduce your keynote address. I've known several brilliant international graduate students whose work was considered marginal in their programs because they were reluctant to make these assertions, attributed their own ideas to others, and produced dissertations that were primarily literature reviews. Writers who don't clearly distinguish their own positions or rely too heavily on summary or paraphrase of authoritative sources can also drift into plagiarism, not because they are trying to deceive readers but because the boundaries between their ideas and those of other writers are blurred. In "Learning to Write a Thesis with an Argumentative Edge," one of the essays in *Learning the Literacy Practices of Graduate School*, Xiaoming Li (2008) describes the cultural challenges he faced in taking assertive positions and making knowledge claims, "edging into the risky world of the unclaimed" (p. 48).

Due to your transitional status as PhD candidates, however, figuring out what you are authorized to say can be tricky, and I'm not suggesting that professional status is irrelevant. Because the central argument in one candidate's dissertation directly challenged the theoretical position of the most prominent scholar in his field, his advisor refused to support the project on the grounds that it was too ambitious and professionally dangerous. This was a sensible, responsible warning, but the candidate wasn't willing to abandon a position he believed in and considered valid. To resolve the issue, he took the courageous step of contacting the scholar directly to explain his position, with a sample draft of his criticism. When he received a reply that his argument was interesting, with encouragement to pursue the project, his advisor gave his approval as well, and he completed his PhD successfully. This example illustrates the important role of advisors in helping you to determine the kinds of claims or arguments you are sufficiently authorized to make in your fields as PhD candidates.

Cultural variations can affect writing even at subtle levels of sentence structure and style. A doctoral student from Japan once asked me for help with essays that his professor, in a course on the philosophy of law, had sharply criticized. The problem had nothing to do with this student's level of fluency in English. He could explain extremely complex, abstract concepts without error, yet his professor found his essays unclear and indirect and often singled out his use of the passive voice. When I revised some of these passive constructions in the active voice, in a paper on the narrative roles of judges in maintaining and revising legal traditions, he didn't like the results because they didn't represent what he could comfortably say. The problem, he explained, was that he didn't want to attribute agency, "like pointing a finger," so directly to a figure of such authority as a judge, even in an essay that was *about* that figure's role as an active agent. In the end, he fully understood what his professor wanted him to do, but he wasn't willing to do it and accepted a lower grade.

The perceived value or significance of research findings can also vary from one academic culture to another, even in fields of extensive international collaboration. The ways in which you frame the significance of your work can heavily influence its reception. I consulted for several months with a scientist from China who had published extensively in his home country but had failed to get articles on the same research accepted in American journals. He initially believed that weaknesses in his English were responsible for rejections, but when we corrected and clarified a manuscript for resubmission, it was rejected as well. Further analysis of peer reviews revealed criticism that his articles inadequately explained the mechanism involved in his research on the growth of particular plant species in a particular context. In the terms I've used, for these reviewers his articles were conceptually unbalanced: too heavily weighted toward narrow research questions about specific problems and data in "The World" and too light on disciplinary theory and significance.

Why was this a "cultural" problem? Because the journals in which he had published in China favored scientific articles on applications: solutions to specific real-world problems. The American journals in which he was now trying to publish favored articles on "basic science": research that changes or refines our understanding of more fundamental principles or mechanisms underlying broader ranges of phenomena. Polishing the style of these manuscripts and proofreading for "ESL" errors would not solve this conceptual problem. Successful revision required more extensive changes: revision of the research question with a focus on the growth mechanism involved; construction of a broader reference frame concerning the significance of this question; and related revisions of the discussion/conclusion, with emphasis on the theoretical problem and a broader range of potential applications. Methods and results were less extensively changed, but the specific application they concerned, previously the central focus of an article, became a case study of a larger theoretical and methodological problem.

How can you successfully adapt to these cultural patterns, values, and expectations in an unfamiliar environment? I recommend that you think of yourselves not just as foreign students, trying to follow rules and avoid mistakes, but as ethnographers who are actively studying the contexts in which you find yourselves.

Pay close attention to what others are doing, talk to them, and associate with people from a wide range of backgrounds. Foreign travelers of all kinds tend to get trapped in narrow enclaves of people like themselves, who most easily understand them and speak their languages. Because international students often follow this pattern, teachers and advisors commonly urge them to break out of their comfort zones and broaden their social networks. These social relations will improve your fluency in a foreign language, but they will also deepen your understanding of ways of thinking and learning that might otherwise remain bewildering.

For purposes of research design and writing, deliberately study the structures of research articles, books, or finished dissertations in your field. Identify the central research questions in these texts. What makes them significant, and how do the writers frame this significance in introductions and literature reviews? Read review articles in journals closest to your research fields and pay close attention to their critical assessments of strengths and weaknesses. Note that the Chinese scholar mentioned above didn't recognize the underlying implications of his article rejections until he analyzed peer reviews with a mind open to the possibility that his assumptions about the value and significance of his research were incorrect. What are these expert readers looking for? What kinds of research do they appreciate?

When you are reading this professional literature, also listen to the voices authors use, as ones you might adopt or emulate in your own writing. To some extent, of course, these individual tones and styles will vary, but only within a certain range. In good scholarly writing, as a rule, the author's voice is calm and detached, somewhat dispassionate, but also engaged: deeply interested in the subject and confident about one's own authority. Good academic writing, especially in American scholarship, is both direct and directive. Clarity relies heavily on direct subject-verb-object constructions in the active voice, as my Japanese student discovered, and the author explicitly guides the reader from beginning to end with marked transitions and directional cues that indicate turning points, topic shifts, and sequences. In this tone of reasoned discourse, references to the work of other scholars may be critical, but critical assessments are typically restrained and rationalized as intellectual disagreements or the observation of logical flaws, not as emotional conflicts or attacks. Appreciation of brilliant work, in turn, is rarely deferential or submissive. The tone, instead, is normally that of collegial exchange among scholars who share common interests, may agree or disagree, but are trying to solve the same problems and reach common understandings. To adopt a voice for your own writing, you can imagine that you are entering a conversation with these scholars, adding your own voice appropriate for the gathering, and making your own contributions to its substance.

This attentive listening to voices, picking up an intuitive sense for their tones and inflections, is the way we become fully fluent in any language, and in academic work as elsewhere this learning occurs most effectively if you are actually talking with these natives of your disciplines—in your programs and campuses or at conferences where they gather—like a good ethnographer.

References

Belcher, W. L. (2009). *Writing your journal article in twelve weeks: A guide to academic publishing success*. Thousand Oaks, CA: Sage Publications.

Casanave, C. P. & Li, X. (eds.). (2008). *Learning the literacy practices of graduate school: Insiders' reflections on academic enculturation*. Ann Arbor, MI: University of Michigan Press.

Li, X. (2008). Learning to write a thesis with an argumentative edge. In C. P. Casanave & X. Li (eds.), *Learning the literacy practices of graduate school: Insiders' reflections on academic enculturation* (pp. 46–57). Ann Arbor, MI: University of Michigan Press.

Sowell, R. (2008). PhD completion and attrition: Analysis of baseline data. [Research Report] Retrieved from Council of Graduate Schools website: www.phdcompletion.org/resources/cgsnsf2008_sowell.pdf.

Swales, J. M. & Feak, C. (2012). *Academic writing for graduate students: Essential tasks and skills.* (3rd ed.) Ann Arbor, MI: University of Michigan Press.

8 Looking Ahead

Throughout this book, I've described the condition of *being* a doctoral candidate as an ongoing, transitional process of *becoming* a scholar: learning to produce knowledge of current significance in specialized research communities and preparing to become members of these communities. From this perspective, PhD candidates write dissertations in preparation for writing and publishing similar work as research specialists and faculty members in higher education. I appear to assume, in other words, that when you complete PhDs, all or most of you will follow the trajectories of your advisors and pursue academic careers. Heading in this direction, on the strength of your dissertation research and other credentials, you should apply for professorial positions as scholars and teachers, preferably at other research universities. This is supposed to be your primary motivation for completing a PhD, and it's what most doctoral programs train you to do.

Thus far, I've maintained these traditional assumptions because they continue to govern systems of doctoral education and faculty expectations of PhD candidates. Regardless of your actual career goals and options, in that world of the imagination in which writing occurs and dissertations are completed, you are obliged to imagine yourselves as scholars, communicating with other scholars in a specialized field of inquiry. For the purpose of completing your PhDs, this is the voice and persona you must adopt, as convincingly as possible.

With reference to the writing process, however, I've also argued that you should be *disillusioned* about the ways in which convincing, accomplished works of scholarship actually come about. Here I'll argue that you should be equally disillusioned about the ways in which research universities and doctoral programs idealize the goals, values, and outcomes of this endeavor. The fact that you are obliged to *imagine* that you are a scholar while completing your dissertation shouldn't limit your awareness of the actual values of a PhD, the trajectories you can actually follow, your own interests, or the real meanings of accomplishment and success. Such constructive disillusionment (or enlightenment) differs from cynicism or discouragement, but it begins, nonetheless, with awareness of some sobering realities.

When we consider current academic job markets and the actual career paths of PhDs, idealized assumptions about the goals of doctoral programs and the futures of their graduates seem archaic and naive. Although job markets vary considerably across disciplines, American doctoral programs now produce several times as many PhDs as markets for tenure-track faculty can absorb. Because this imbalance between supply and demand has worsened for more than 30 years, new applicants for faculty positions must compete with compounding numbers of those who weren't hired in previous years, and postings often draw hundreds of applications. Most estimates of the proportion of recent PhDs who will eventually hold professorial positions in the United States fall under 15 percent, and the majority of the candidates hired for these positions received PhDs from a narrow field of top-ranked research universities. Prospects in the UK, most of Europe, Japan, and many other countries are even worse. In a book titled *The Graduate School Mess: What Caused It and How We Can Fix It*, Leonard Casutto (2015) offers this gloomy assessment of conditions:

> Thousands of professors are currently in the business of preparing thousands of graduate students for jobs that don't exist—or more precisely, those graduate students are being taught to want academic jobs that only a few will get, and in the process, they are learning to foreclose the prospects that actually exist for them.
>
> (p. 2)

Actually becoming a college professor, furthermore, doesn't necessarily mean that you will follow the narrow trajectories established in your doctoral studies. Because PhD granting universities supply the faculties of more than 4000 colleges and universities in the United States and in other countries, PhDs trained primarily as research specialists must adapt to a great variety of academic environments. In many of these faculty positions, heavy teaching and loads, advising, administrative responsibilities, and sparse facilities severely limit the time and resources available for continuing research and publication. Even for professors at research universities, as I've previously observed, the role of a research specialist cultivated in doctoral work must compete for time and attention with many other responsibilities.

What will the rest of you do? Roughly half of all PhDs remain in some sector of higher education, at least temporarily. The oversupply of PhDs has accompanied the expansion of postdoctoral fellowships, primarily in the sciences but more recently in the social sciences and humanities as well. Many new PhDs view these temporary positions as springboards for getting professorial jobs, but Leah Cannon (2016) points out that while professorial faculties haven't substantially increased since the 1980s, postdocs have, from roughly 20,000 to 60,000 in the United States. Rising numbers of temporary "visiting" assistant professorships and lecturer positions, more likely to involve teaching responsibilities, serve similar institutional purposes of supporting research and teaching without expanding professorial faculties. Many other PhDs who remain in higher education take campus jobs, now popularly termed "alt-ac," less directly related to their graduate work, in administration, fund-raising, libraries, technological support, and other campus offices or facilities. Graduate programs yield an abundance of smart people with useful skills, and the jobs they find as alternatives to faculty positions often become satisfying careers.

The most reprehensible use of their talents in higher education, however, is the recent proliferation of low-wage adjunct positions, often part-time, with short-term contracts and few benefits. Colleges and universities of all types have become increasingly dependent on the supplies of highly skilled, unemployed PhDs or ABDs that research universities generate, to accommodate rising undergraduate enrollments without hiring more expensive professorial faculty. Schools now rely on staffs of adjuncts so heavily that tenured and tenure-track faculty deliver less than 25 percent of undergraduate instruction nationwide.

In some branches of the sciences and engineering, applied mathematics, computer science, and a variety of other fields, PhDs often find better opportunities to continue their research elsewhere, in research and development departments of corporations, government agencies, or NGOs. Remaining PhDs disperse into a wide range of non-academic careers in small businesses and corporations, publishing and journalism, government and social services, foundations, international development organizations, museums, and health care systems, among many others. Some of these careers require further training in specialized skills, such as information technologies, and I've known several PhDs who returned to the university to complete professional degrees in fields such as computer science, management, or law. Outside the narrowing walls of that traditional, idealized academic pipeline, meant to deliver fresh PhDs to waiting professorships, alternative career paths head off in hundreds of directions. Finding these paths, however, can be difficult, costly, and disheartening for the individuals who face the necessity of doing so at the end of doctoral programs that trained them for academic careers.

Although critics of graduate education have been loudly complaining about these trends for several years, research universities and their doctoral programs appear to maintain a state of denial. In theory, they could easily solve the problem of oversupply by admitting fewer graduate students, and some programs have. Why, then, do most doctoral programs continue to admit several times as many graduate students as their academic professions can employ?

The short answer is that research universities have grown dependent on this large supply of cost-efficient and highly skilled labor, both from current graduate students and from former ones employed as postdocs, research assistants, or adjunct faculty. While undergraduate enrollments have expanded, public funding for higher education has diminished, and administrative positions and salaries have increased. To keep these complex institutions functioning under these conditions, graduate students perform a variety of essential roles that universities are reluctant to acknowledge. As research assistants with specialized knowledge and skills, they help to maintain faculty research, often in expensive facilities and elaborate, labor-intensive projects. As teaching assistants, they lead sections of lecture, laboratory, writing, and foreign language courses, meet with students in office hours, and help with course preparation, audio-visual systems, examinations, and grading. To support their studies, graduate students provide skilled labor in many other campus facilities and offices, including libraries and tech support services. In his critique of this system, *How the University Works*, Marc Bousquet (2008) suggests that traditional conceptions of academic "job markets" and "labor" conceal the changing realities of supply and demand in higher education. To understand what's really going on and to reform it equitably, Bousquet argues, we must scrap the notion that "going on the job market" only refers to the hunt for professorships or that the essential work graduate students do isn't really "labor." If all of you walked off the job, most of the university would shut down. Hiring lots of additional professors would have the double benefit of meeting some of these needs and improving job markets for PhDs, but under current economic conditions, most colleges and universities can't afford this option.

In the *How We Can Fix It* portions of his book, therefore, Casutto (2015) doesn't advocate drastic reductions of doctoral admissions or massive professorial hiring as realistic cures for this degenerative condition. Instead, he argues that doctoral programs need to face reality and train PhD candidates for a broader range of career options. This change would include clear recognition that many of you don't *want* to follow in your advisors' footsteps and become professors at research universities. Some of you want primarily to teach undergraduates, without heavy burdens of continuing research and publication. Some of you want primarily to continue research, without having to teach. Many of you have begun to doubt that the complicated, high-pressured life of a college professor suits you and are already considering alternative career options. From this perspective, the main problem is that doctoral programs fail to acknowledge and support this broad range of interests, aspirations, and options for PhDs. As a consequence, individuals who don't conform to the narrow, replicative mold of a protégé have to conceal their real motivations and feel like frauds or failures.

Casutto and many other critics of graduate education therefore recommend changes in doctoral admissions criteria, dissertation forms, curricula, professional development programs, career counseling, and job placement systems that correspond with the realities of PhD candidates' career goals and options. Central administrations and graduate schools at some universities have begun to make these changes, but individual doctoral programs, by and large, have not. Until they do, those of you who are currently enrolled in doctoral programs have to face these realities largely on your own, using whatever resources are available, and think about your futures with clear-headed skepticism and strategy.

For many of you, of course, the current gold standard of a tenure-track professorship in your field is both a strong personal commitment and a reasonable career goal. Job markets for assistant professors remain fairly strong in some disciplines, and some of you will get these jobs. Beyond the completion of a good dissertation, however, you need to work on building a considerably larger set of credentials as a scholar and teacher. This should include publications, conference presentations, and other professional activities, along with as much teaching experience as you can get. Research and publication remain essential criteria for hiring, even in undergraduate schools, and faculty advisors often view teaching assistantships just as ways to support your specialized research. In real job markets, however, teaching experience and training are much more important than many graduate students realize, and they're often shocked and unprepared when they have to submit teaching philosophy statements and course plans with their application materials. Several job candidates have told me they were disarmed when interviewers asked, "What makes you think you can teach our students?"

To meet these expectations, you can't afford to wait until you've finished your dissertation. As early as possible, look at the résumés of candidates for assistant professorships in your departments and think about what you need to do to build comparable credentials. Take advantage of professional development workshops and teacher training programs on your campuses, and look for opportunities to teach in a variety of courses. Keep a teaching portfolio, including course plans and student evaluations, and collect syllabi from other courses, so you will have material and ideas to use when you need them. Trying to assemble all of these credentials at the last minute is stressful and ineffective. Above all, don't underestimate the future value of professional activities that your advisors might consider marginal. A number of PhD candidates who were designing and teaching seminars in our interdisciplinary writing programs, and hoped to pursue careers primarily as teachers, told me that their advisors had warned them against "getting too interested in teaching" at the expense of their research. But several of them got job offers in other schools with similar writing programs partly because the departments needed faculty who could teach writing-intensive courses.

This advice is especially important for those of you who are primarily interested in teaching undergraduates and will look for positions in liberal arts colleges, community colleges, and other schools that are primarily undergraduate institutions. On the whole, research universities do a miserable job of preparing PhDs for these positions, and developing the necessary experience and skills requires a lot of initiative on your part. One reason is that teaching responsibilities in other schools are usually much broader than your fields of specialization, and academic departments are often much smaller. Those of you trained as research specialists in one branch of cognitive psychology, for example, might be expected to teach an introductory survey course in psychology or cognitive science, a course on social psychology, or one on intersections with neurobiology. Having specialized in a period of American literature, you might have to teach English literature or a freshman writing course. Broad, interdisciplinary interests and teaching experiences that seem marginal in your doctoral programs often turn out to be valuable assets in real job markets. The recently updated guide, *The Academic Job Search Handbook* by Miller, Furlong, and Lurie (2016) offers useful advice for developing job application strategies.

But what if you don't want a professorial position or aren't likely to get one in current job markets? If doctoral programs are training the majority of their PhDs for jobs they aren't likely to get or don't really want, as Casutto and others argue, what's the point of getting this degree?

Why Should You Continue?

Regardless of your career goals and prospects, there are some good reasons for finishing what you've started, especially in the dissertation stage. A large proportion of the graduate students who drop out of PhD programs do so in the first year or two, when they realize that they aren't motivated to continue, can't afford to do so, develop other interests and career goals that are more attractive, or get indications from faculty that they aren't very promising. These are usually good reasons to stop. In the dissertation stage, however, the costs of not finishing a PhD are higher. At that point, you have a lot more time and other costs invested, and there aren't many people who can just walk away from an unfinished dissertation project without feeling that they've wasted those investments and failed to finish something, along with other effects that Barbara Lovitts (2001) documented in *Leaving the Ivory Tower*. An unfinished dissertation can become psychological baggage that ABDs carry into other endeavors for years.

The best reason to complete a PhD, however, is that it remains a valuable credential and asset for a wide range of careers beyond those in higher education. Along with the knowledge and skills you've developed, having a PhD means you have the discipline, focus, and intellect to complete a rigorous program, and many employers hire PhDs for that reason. Once you step outside that narrow corridor that leads to a professorship and shake off the fog of believing that this is what you should do, you'll see that PhDs in your field lead people into dozens of careers, including many that can be more satisfying and lucrative than those in higher education. From this broader perspective, the main problem isn't just that doctoral programs don't acknowledge these options; it's that doctoral candidates don't acknowledge them either, don't value them, or don't consider them early enough. PhD programs induce a kind of tunnel vision that prevents candidates from asking themselves, *What am I going to do if I don't get an academic job or decide I don't want one?*

When you've acknowledged this possibility, the next question you should ask is, *What should I be doing now to prepare myself?* For this purpose, investigating alternative careers, using available career counseling, and developing a broader range of interests, skills, and contacts aren't distractions you should avoid or admissions of failure. They're sensible strategies for taking charge of your future. A few recent books on career options for PhDs, such as Kelsky (2015) and Sinche (2016), may help to broaden your horizons.

In the process, of course, you also need to complete your dissertation and related academic projects, and for that purpose all of the advice I've offered still applies, regardless of your eventual career paths. Whether you actually pursue an academic career and want to do so or not, you are completing training to pursue that career path, and a dissertation is an academic project: a contribution to knowledge in a particular field and the final requirement for a PhD. A research university may be a realm of illusions, disconnected in many ways from what students at all levels describe as "the real world," but this is the realm you currently inhabit and must navigate. The persona of a scholar that you must adopt for this purpose isn't the whole of your identity and may not represent the kind of person or professional you will become, but it's nonetheless the persona you must assume as a writer.

If you don't expect to pursue an academic career, does this mean you should conceal your real interests and plans? Unfortunately, sometimes it does. There are certainly faculty advisors who support alternative career plans, collaborate with industries or NGOs, and help PhDs to land jobs outside higher education. But there are also reasons for which candidates have spoken in hushed voices or closed my office door when they told me what they *really* hoped to do after they finished their PhDs, as though they were under surveillance from their advisors. On the whole, graduate students who seem most committed to specialized research and most likely to become college professors get the most attention and support in their programs. It's often wise to pretend that this is what you want to do, even if you really plan to become a journalist or a career counselor, work for a development organization, start a business, work for a charitable foundation, join a social reform movement, or teach in a high school—a few of the many careers that my own students have entered when they completed their PhD programs.

For all of you, regardless of your career goals and prospects, the underlying principle to keep in mind is that *the values and priorities of your doctoral programs differ from those of the real job markets and careers you will enter and, as a consequence, don't accurately represent your interests*. What I've called "constructive disillusionment" doesn't mean you should necessarily reject these institutional values or actively resist them while completing your PhDs. It just means that you should be aware of the differences, identify what your interests really are, and use the resources of a doctoral education to your own advantage, toward the end of leading a satisfying life.

With this end in mind, I'll conclude with a little parable, from the course I taught for entering graduate students in chemistry. One of them, Phil, confessed that he was worried by what he had learned about his program thus far. Having attended a small liberal arts college where he worked closely with his professors and maintained interests in a variety of subjects, he hoped most of all to pursue a teaching career, while continuing research, and become an educator. In this doctoral program, however, he felt that he was on the edge of a narrowing "pit" he was supposed to descend into, and when he reached the bottom and received his PhD, he was supposed to become a particular kind of inorganic chemist, inhabiting that narrow space with a few other inorganic chemists, in communication with those in comparable little pits at other universities. To explain what he meant, on the blackboard he drew these pits of inorganic, organic, or physical chemistry surrounded by those in other fields of the sciences, social sciences, and humanities. The pits of specialized research descended from the broad plain above where nomadic undergraduates roamed across the wider world of the university, to which bleary-eyed professors and graduate teaching assistants crawled out of their denizens for an hour or so to instruct them. This wasn't the kind of academic fate Phil wanted, and he was already trying to figure out how to avoid it.

Most of the other entering graduate students in the class thought this was a strange premonition to worry about at the beginning of their doctoral studies, when some of them were still looking for housing and trying to find their way across campus. But Phil's concerns echoed those of the Carnegie Foundation's (Boyer Commission, 1998) critique of research universities around the same time, in a report that described these institutions as fragmented "archipelagos of intellectual pursuit rather than connected and integrated communities." The Boyer Commission report idealistically encouraged research universities to reinvent themselves as "intellectual ecosystems" in which "The shared goals of investigation and discovery should bind together the disparate elements to create a sense of wholeness" (p. 9). This was the vision of an academic career that Phil hoped for, but it wasn't likely to materialize by the time he finished his PhD.

In another class for advanced PhD candidates from various fields, I explained Phil's concerns, drew a version of his pitted, layered view of the university on the board, and discovered a more constructive way of thinking about the problem. When I asked for comments, most of the students looked doleful and nodded their heads in resignation. This, it seemed, was their fate. But one of them looked angry and objected. "That's so negative and unnecessary!" she said. "Just turn your picture upside down and you have *peaks*. That's what the professors I admire are on, like my advisor. They move up and broaden their perspectives, and from the top they can see what's going on around them, what other specialists are doing, and what students are doing. That should be your goal as a graduate student."

And that, in fact, was what Phil did as well. In following years, while becoming a research specialist, he also devoted himself to teaching, looked for interesting TA assignments, developed innovative methods, and won a campus-wide teaching award. With these and other credentials, he did get a tenure-track job at a primarily undergraduate college that also had graduate programs. There, he won further teaching awards, engaged in curricular reform, and continued research and publication. If he hadn't pursued this career, however, I'm pretty certain that he would have found another rewarding use for his skills and commitments.

If you think of the research university as a rich compendium of resources you are fully entitled to use for your own purposes as PhD candidates, you'll find that there aren't many real barriers to what you can explore, learn, and become in this environment. If you think of it in this way, in your own interests, you can also flip Phil's drawing and ascend peaks of specialization, with expanding awareness of alternatives.

References

Bousquet, M. (2008). *How the university works: Higher education and the low-wage nation*. New York, NY: New York University Press.

Boyer Commission (1998). *Reinventing undergraduate education: A blueprint for America's research universities*. Princeton, NJ: Carnegie Foundation for the Advancement of Teaching.

Cannon, L. (2016, September 15). How many PhD graduates become professors? [Web log post] Retrieved from http://lifesciencenetwork11.connectedcommunity.org.

Casutto, L. (2015). *The graduate school mess: What caused it and how we can fix it*. Cambridge, MA: Harvard University Press.

Kelsky, K. (2015). *The professor is in: The essential guide to turning your PhD into a job*. New York, NY: Three Rivers Press.

Lovitts, B. E. (2001). *Leaving the Ivory Tower: The causes and consequences of departure from doctoral study*. Latham, MD: Rowman & Littlefield.

Miller, J., Furlong, J. S. & Lurie, R. (2016). *The academic job search handbook* (5th ed.). Philadelphia, PA: University of Pennsylvania Press.

Sinche, M. V. (2016). *Next gen PhD: A guide to career paths in science*. Cambridge, MA: Harvard University Press.

Index

Note: References in *italics* are to figures.